PENGUIN
GANG LEADER

Sudhir Venkatesh spent a decade living with the Black Kings gang in Chicago's South Side. His research later became famous in *Freakonomics* ('Why do drug dealers still live with their Moms?'). He is now Professor of Sociology and African-American Studies at Columbia University.

GANG LEADER FOR A DAY

A Rogue Sociologist
Crosses the Line

SUDHIR VENKATESH

PENGUIN BOOKS

PENGUIN BOOKS

Published by the Penguin Group
Penguin Books Ltd, 80 Strand, London WC2R 0RL, England
Penguin Group (USA) Inc., 375 Hudson Street, New York, New York 10014, USA
Penguin Group (Canada), 90 Eglinton Avenue East, Suite 700, Toronto, Ontario, Canada M4P 2Y3
(a division of Pearson Penguin Canada Inc.)
Penguin Ireland, 25 St Stephen's Green, Dublin 2, Ireland
(a division of Penguin Books Ltd)
Penguin Group (Australia), 250 Camberwell Road,
Camberwell, Victoria 3124, Australia (a division of Pearson Australia Group Pty Ltd)
Penguin Books India Pvt Ltd, 11 Community Centre,
Panchsheel Park, New Delhi – 110 017, India
Penguin Group (NZ), 67 Apollo Drive, Rosedale, North Shore 0632, New Zealand
(a division of Pearson New Zealand Ltd)
Penguin Books (South Africa) (Pty) Ltd, 24 Sturdee Avenue, Rosebank,
Johannesburg 2196, South Africa

Penguin Books Ltd, Registered Offices: 80 Strand, London WC2R 0RL, England

www.penguin.com

First published in the United States of America by The Penguin Press, a member of Penguin
Group (USA) Inc. 2008
First published in Great Britain by Allen Lane 2008
Published in Penguin Books 2009

009

Printed in England by Clays Ltd, St Ives plc

978-0-141-03091-3

www.greenpenguin.co.uk

MIX
Paper from
responsible sources
FSC   FSC® C018179

Penguin Books is committed to a sustainable
future for our business, our readers and our planet.
This book is made from Forest Stewardship
Council™ certified paper.

To Autry Harrison

CONTENTS

FOREWORD

Stephen J. Dubner

I believe that Sudhir Venkatesh was born with two abnormalities: an overdeveloped curiosity and an underdeveloped sense of fear.

How else to explain him? Like thousands upon thousands of people, he entered graduate school one fall and was dispatched by his professors to do some research. This research happened to take him to the Robert Taylor Homes in Chicago, one of the worst ghettos in America. But blessed with that outlandish curiosity and unfettered by the sort of commonsensical fear that most of us would experience upon being held hostage by an armed crack gang, as Venkatesh was early on in his research, he kept coming back for more.

I met Venkatesh a few years ago when I interviewed him for *Freakonomics,* a book I wrote with the economist Steve Levitt. Venkatesh and Levitt had collaborated on several academic papers about the economics of crack cocaine. Those papers were interesting, to be sure, but Venkatesh himself presented a whole new level of fascination. He is soft-spoken and laconic; he doesn't volunteer much information. But every time you ask him a question, it is like tugging a thread on an old tapestry: the whole thing unspools and falls at your feet. Story after story, marked by lapidary detail and hard-won insight: the rogue cop who terrorized the neighborhood, the jerry-built network through which poor families hustled to survive, the time Venkatesh himself became gang leader for a day.

Although we wrote about Venkatesh in *Freakonomics* (it was many readers' favorite part), there wasn't room for any of these stories. Thankfully, he has now written an extraordinary book that details all his adventures and misadventures. The stories he tells are far stranger than fiction, and they are also more forceful, heartbreaking, and hilarious. Along the way he paints a unique portrait of the kind of neighborhood that is badly misrepresented when it is represented at all. Journalists like me might hang out in such neighborhoods for a week or a month or even a year. Most social scientists and do-gooders tend to do their work at arm's length. But Venkatesh practically lived in this neighborhood for the better part of a decade. He brought the perspective of an outsider and came away with an insider's access. A lot of writing about the poor tends to reduce living, breathing, joking, struggling, sensual, moral human beings to dupes who are shoved about by invisible forces. This book does the opposite. It shows, day by day and dollar by dollar, how the crack dealers, tenant leaders, prostitutes, parents, hustlers, cops, and Venkatesh himself tried to construct a good life out of substandard materials.

As much as I have come to like Venkatesh, and admire him, I probably would not want to be a member of his family: I would worry too much about his fearlessness. I probably wouldn't want to be one of his research subjects either, for his curiosity must be exhausting. But I am very, very happy to have been one of the first readers of Venkatesh's book, for it is as extraordinary as he is.

PREFACE

I woke up at about 7:30 A.M. in a crack den, Apartment 1603 in Building Number 2301 of the Robert Taylor Homes. Apartment 1603 was called the "Roof," since everyone knew that you could get very, very high there, even higher than if you climbed all the way to the building's actual rooftop.

As I opened my eyes, I saw two dozen people sprawled about, most of them men, asleep on couches and the floor. No one had lived in the apartment for a while. The walls were peeling, and roaches skittered across the linoleum floor. The activities of the previous night—smoking crack, drinking, having sex, vomiting—had peaked at about 2:00 A.M. By then the unconscious people outnumbered the conscious ones—and among the conscious ones, few still had the cash to buy another hit of crack cocaine. That's when the Black Kings saw diminishing prospects for sales and closed up shop for the night.

I fell asleep, too, on the floor. I hadn't come for the crack; I was here on a different mission. I was a graduate student at the University of Chicago, and for my research I had taken to hanging out with the Black Kings, the local crack-selling gang.

It was the sun that woke me, shining through the Roof's doorway. (The door itself had disappeared long ago.) I climbed over the other stragglers and walked down to the tenth floor, where the Patton family lived. During the course of my research, I had gotten to know the Pattons—a law-abiding family, it should be said—and they treated me kindly, almost like a son. I said good morning to Mama Patton, who was cooking breakfast for her husband, Pops, a seventy-year-old retired factory worker. I washed my face, grabbed a slice of cornbread, and headed outside into a breezy, brisk March morning.

Just another day in the ghetto.

Just another day as an outsider looking at life from the inside. That's what this book is about.

GANG LEADER FOR A DAY

ONE

How Does It Feel to Be Black and Poor?

During my first weeks at the University of Chicago, in the fall of 1989, I had to attend a variety of orientation sessions. In each one, after the particulars of the session had been dispensed with, we were warned not to walk outside the areas that were actively patrolled by the university's police force. We were handed detailed maps that outlined where the small enclave of Hyde Park began and ended: this was the safe area. Even the lovely parks across the border were off-limits, we were told, unless you were traveling with a large group or attending a formal event.

It turned out that the ivory tower was also an ivory fortress. I lived on the southwestern edge of Hyde Park, where the university housed a lot of its graduate students. I had a studio apartment in a ten-story building just off Cottage Grove Avenue, a historic boundary between Hyde Park and Woodlawn, a poor black neighborhood. The contrast would be familiar to anyone who has spent time around an urban university in the United States. On one side of the divide lay a beautifully manicured Gothic campus, with privileged students, most of them white, walking to class and playing sports. On the other side were down-and-out African Americans offering cheap labor and services (changing oil, washing windows, selling drugs) or panhandling on street corners.

I didn't have many friends, so in my spare time I started taking long walks, getting to know the city. For a budding sociologist, the streets of Chicago were a feast. I was intrigued by the different ethnic neighborhoods, the palpable sense of culture and tradition. I liked that there was one part of the city, Rogers Park, where Indians, Pakistanis, and Bangladeshis congregated. Unlike the lily-white suburbs of Southern California where I'd grown up, the son of immigrants from South Asia, here Indians seemed to have a place in the ethnic landscape along with everyone else.

I was particularly interested in the poor black neighborhoods surrounding the university. These were neighborhoods where nearly half the population didn't work, where crime and gang activity were said to be entrenched, where the welfare rolls were swollen. In the late 1980s, these isolated parts of the inner cities gripped the nation's attention. I went for many walks there and started playing basketball in the parks, but I didn't see any crime, and I didn't feel particularly threatened. I wondered why the university kept warning students to keep out.

As it happened, I attracted a good bit of curiosity from the locals. Perhaps it was because these parks didn't attract many nonblack visitors, or perhaps it was because in those days I dressed like a Deadhead. I got asked a lot of questions about India—most of which I couldn't answer, since I'd moved to the States as a child. Sometimes I'd come upon a picnic, and people would offer me some of their soul food. They were puzzled when I turned them down on the grounds that I was a vegetarian.

But as alien as I was to these folks, they were just as alien to me.

As part of my heavy course load at the U of C, I began attending seminars where professors parsed the classic sociological questions: How do an individual's preferences develop? Can we predict human behavior? What are the long-term consequences, for instance, of education on future generations?

The standard mode of answering these questions was to conduct widespread surveys and then use complex mathematical methods to analyze the survey data. This would produce statistical snapshots meant to predict why a given person might, say, fail to land a job, or end up in prison, or have a child out of wedlock. It was thought that the key to formulating good policy was to first formulate a good scientific study.

I liked the questions these researchers were asking, but compared with the vibrant life that I saw on the streets of Chicago, the discussion in these seminars seemed cold and distant, abstract and lifeless. I found it particularly curious that most of these researchers didn't seem interested in meeting the people they wrote about. It wasn't necessarily out of any animosity—nearly all of them were well intentioned—but because the act of actually talking to research subjects was seen as messy, unscientific, and a potential source of bias.

Mine was not a new problem. Indeed, the field of sociology had long been divided into two camps: those who use quantitative and statistical techniques and those who study life by direct observation, often living among a group of people.

This second group, usually called ethnographers, use their firsthand approach to answer a particular sort of question: How do people survive in marginal communities? for instance, or What makes a government policy work well for some families and not for others?

The quantitative sociologists, meanwhile, often criticized the ethnographers' approach. They argued that it isn't nearly scientific enough and that the answers may be relevant only to the particular group under observation. In other words, to reach any important and generalizable conclusion, you need to rely on the statistical analyses of large data sets like the U.S. Census or other massive surveys.

My frustration with the more scientific branch of sociology hadn't really coalesced yet. But I knew that I wanted to do something other than sit in a classroom all day and talk mathematics.

So I did what any sensible student who was interested in race and poverty would do: I walked down the hallway and knocked on the door of William Julius Wilson, the most eminent living scholar on the subject and the most prominent African American in the field of sociology. He had been teaching at the U of C for nearly twenty years and had published two books that reshaped how scholars and policy makers thought about urban poverty.

I caught Wilson just in time—he was about to go to Paris for a sabbatical. But he was also about to launch a new research project, he said, and I could participate if I liked.

Wilson was a quiet, pensive man, dressed in a dark blue suit. Although he had stopped smoking his trademark pipe long ago, he still looked like the kind of professor you see in movies. If you asked him a question, he'd often let several long moments of silence pass—he could be more than a little bit intimidating—before offering a thoughtful response.

Wilson explained that he was hoping to better understand how young blacks were affected by specific neighborhood factors: Did growing up as a poor kid in a housing project, for instance, lead to worse educational and job outcomes than if a similarly poor kid grew up outside the projects? What about the difference between growing up in a neighborhood that was surrounded by other poor areas and growing up poor but near an affluent neighborhood? Did the latter group take advantage of the schools, services, and employment opportunities in the richer neighborhoods?

Wilson's project was still in the planning stages. The first step was to construct a basic survey questionnaire, and he suggested I help his other graduate students in figuring out which questions to ask. This meant going back to earlier studies of black youth to see what topics and questions had been chosen by earlier sociologists. Wilson gave me a box of old questionnaires. I should experiment, he said, by borrowing some of their questions and developing new ones as needed. Sociologists liked to use survey questions that their peers had already used, I learned, in order to produce comparable results. This was a key part of the scientific method in sociology.

I thanked Wilson and went to the library to begin looking over the questionnaires he'd given me. I quickly realized I had no idea how to interview anyone.

Washington Park, situated just across Cottage Grove Avenue from the U of C, is one of Chicago's stateliest parks. Designed in the 1870s by Frederick Law Olmsted and Calvert Vaux, it has a beautiful swimming pool, indoor and outdoor basketball courts, dazzling flower gardens, and long, winding paths that crisscross its nearly four hundred acres. I liked to go running on the clay track that encircled the park, a track that decades earlier had hosted horse and auto races. Until the 1940s the surrounding neighborhood was mainly Irish, but when black families started buying homes nearby, most of the white families moved away. I was always surprised that the university actively dissuaded its students from spending time in Washington Park. I failed to see the danger, at least in the daylight.

After my run I sometimes stopped by the broad, marshy lagoon in the middle of the park. The same group of old black men, usually a half dozen or so, congregated there every day—playing cards, drinking beer, fishing for bass and perch in the lagoon. I sat and listened to them for hours. To this point I had had little exposure to African-American culture at all, and no experience whatsoever in an urban ghetto. I had moved to Chicago just a year earlier from California, where I'd attended a predominantly white college situated on the beach, UC San Diego.

I had been reading several histories of Chicago's black community, and I sometimes asked these men about the events and people of which I'd read. The stories they told were considerably more animated than the history in the books. They knew the intricacies of machine politics—whom you had to befriend, for instance, to get a job or a building permit. They talked about the Black Panther Party of their youth and how it was radically different from today's gangs. "The Panthers had breakfast programs for kids, but these gangs just shoot 'em and feed 'em drugs," one man lamented. I already knew a bit about how the Panthers operated in Chicago during the civil-rights era. What little I knew about modern gangs, however, came from the movies and newspapers—and, of course, the constant cautions issued by the U of C about steering clear of certain neighborhoods.

I was particularly intrigued by the old men's views on race, which boiled down to this: Whites and blacks would never be able to talk openly, let alone live together. The most talkative among them was Leonard Combs, a.k.a. Old Time. "Never trust a white man," he told me one day, "and don't think black folk are any better."

Old Time came to Washington Park every day with his fishing

gear, lunch, and beer. He wore a tired beige fishing hat, and he had lost so many teeth that his gums smacked together when he spoke. But he loved to talk, especially about Chicago.

"We live in a city within a city," he said. "They have theirs and we have ours. And if you can understand that it will never change, you'll start understanding how this city works."

"You mean whites and blacks will never get along?" I asked.

A man named Charlie Butler jumped in. "You got two kinds of whites in this city," he said, "and two kinds of blacks. You got whites who'll beat you if you come into their neighborhood. They live around Bridgeport and on the Southwest Side. Then you got another group that just won't invite you in. They'll call the police if you come in their neighborhood—like where *you* live, in Hyde Park. And the police *will* beat you up."

Charlie was a retired factory worker, a beefy man with tattooed, well-developed arms, a college football star from long ago. Charlie sometimes came to Hyde Park for breakfast or lunch at one of the diners where other blacks hung out, but he never stayed past sundown and he never walked on residential streets, he said, since the police would follow him.

"What about blacks?" I asked.

"You got blacks who are beating their heads trying to figure out a way to live where *you* live!" Charlie continued. "Don't ask me why. And then you got a whole lot of black folk who realize it ain't no use. Like us. We just spend our time trying to get by, and we live around here, where it ain't so pretty, but at least you won't get your ass beat. At least not by the police."

"That's how it's been since black folk came to the city," Old Time said, "and it's not going to change."

"You mean you don't have *any* white friends?" I asked.

"You have any *black* friends?" Old Time countered with a sly grin. I didn't need to answer. "And you may want to ask your professors if *they* have any," he said, clearly pleased with his rebuke.

From these conversations I started to gain a bit of perspective on what it was like to be black in Chicago. The overriding sentiment was that given how the city operated, there was little chance for any significant social progress.

This kind of fatalism was foreign to me. When you grew up in affluent Southern California, even for someone as politically disengaged as I, there was a core faith in the workings of American institutions and a sustaining belief that people can find a way to resolve their differences, even racial ones. I was now beginning to see the limits of my narrow experience. Nearly every conversation with Old Time and his friends wound up at the intersection of politics and race. I couldn't follow all the nuances of their arguments, especially when it came to local politics, but even I could see the huge gap between how they perceived the world and how sociologists presented the life of urban poor people.

One day I asked Old Time and his friends if they'd be willing to let me interview them for Professor Wilson's survey. They agreed, and I tried for a few days. But I felt I wasn't getting anywhere. Most of the conversations ended up meandering along, a string of interruptions and half-finished thoughts.

Charlie could see I was dejected. "Before you give up," he said, "you should probably speak to the people who you really want to talk to—*young* men, not us. That's the only way you're going to get what you need."

So I set out looking for young black men. At the U of C library, I checked the census records to find a tract with poor black families with people between the ages of sixteen and twenty-four.

The Lake Park projects looked good, at least on paper, and I randomly chose Building Number 4040, highlighting on my census printout the apartments where young people lived. Those were the doors I'd be knocking on. Old Time told me that I could go any day I wanted. "Most black folk in the projects don't work," he said, "so they don't have nowhere else to be." Still, I thought a weekend would be the best time to find a lot of people.

On a brisk Saturday afternoon in November, I went looking for 4040 South Lake Park, one of several high-rise projects in Oakland, a lakefront neighborhood about two miles north of the U of C. Oakland was one of the poorest communities in Chicago, with commensurately high rates of unemployment, welfare, and crime. Its population was overwhelmingly black, dating back to the early-twentieth-century southern migration. The neighborhood surrounding the Lake Park projects wasn't much of a neighborhood at all. There were few people on the streets, and on some blocks there were more vacant lots than buildings. Aside from a few liquor stores and broken-down bodegas, there wasn't much commerce. It struck me that most housing projects, even though they are built in cities, run counter to the very notion of urban living. Cities are attractive because of their balkanized variety: wandering the streets of a good city, you can see all sorts of highs and lows, commerce and recreation, a multitude of ethnicities and just as many expressions of public life. But housing projects, at least from the outside, seemed to be a study in joyless monotony, the buildings clustered tightly together but set apart from the rest of the city, as if they were toxic.

Up close, the buildings looked like tall checkerboards, their dull yellow-brick walls lined with rows of dreary windows. A few of the windows revealed the aftermath of an apartment fire, black smudges spreading upward in the shape of tombstones. Most of the buildings had only one entrance, and it was usually clogged with young people.

By now I was used to being observed carefully when I walked around a black neighborhood. Today was no different. As I approached one of the Lake Park projects, five or six young men stared me down. It should be said here that I probably deserved to be stared at. I was just a few months removed from a long stretch of time I'd spent following the Grateful Dead, and I was still under the spell of Jerry Garcia and his band of merrymakers. With my ponytail and tie-dyed shirt, I must have looked pretty out of place. I tended to speak in spiritually laden language, mostly about the power of road trips; the other grad students in my department saw me as a bit naïve and more than a little loopy. Looking back, I can't say they were wrong.

But I wasn't so naïve that I couldn't recognize what was going on in the lobby of the building that I now approached. Customers were arriving, black and white, by car and on foot, hurrying inside to buy their drugs and then hurrying back out. I wasn't sure if this building was Number 4040, and I couldn't find the number anywhere, so I just walked inside. The entryway smelled of alcohol, soot, and urine. Young men stood and crouched on plastic milk crates, a couple of them stomping their feet against the cold. I put my head down, took a breath, and walked past them quickly.

Their eyes felt heavy on me as I passed by. One huge young man, six foot six at least, chose not to move an inch as I passed. I brushed up against him and nearly lost my balance.

There was a long row of beaten-up metal mailboxes, many of them missing their doors. Water was dripping everywhere, puddling on the ground. Shouts and shrieks cascaded down from the higher floors, making the whole building feel like some kind of vibrating catacomb.

Once I got past the entryway, it was darker. I could make out the elevator, but I seemed to be losing any peripheral vision, and I couldn't find the button. I sensed that I was still being watched and that I ought to press the button fast, but I groped around in vain. Then I started looking for the stairwell, but I couldn't find that either. To my left was a large barrier of some kind, but I was too nervous to go around it. To my right was a corridor. I decided to go that way, figuring I'd come across a stairwell or at least a door to knock on. As I turned, a hand grabbed my shoulder.

"What's up, my man, you got some business in here?" He was in his twenties, about as tall and dark as I was. His voice was deep and forceful but matter-of-fact, as if he asked the same question regularly. He wore baggy jeans, a loose-fitting jacket, and a baseball cap. His earrings sparkled, as did the gold on his front teeth. A few other young men, dressed the same, stood behind him.

I told them that I was there to interview families.

"No one lives here," he said.

"I'm doing a study for the university," I said, "and I have to go to Apartments 610 and 703."

"Ain't nobody lived in those apartments for the longest," he said.

"Well, do you mind if I just run up there and knock on the door?"

"Yeah, we do mind," he said.

I tried again. "Maybe I'm in the wrong building. Is this 4040?"

He shook his head. "No one lives here. So you won't be talking to anybody."

I decided I'd better leave. I walked back through the lobby, bag and clipboard in hand. I crossed in front of the building, over an expansive patch of dead grass littered with soda cans and broken glass. I turned around and looked back at the building. A great many of the windows were lit. I wondered why my new friend had insisted that the building was uninhabited. Only later did I learn that gang members routinely rebuffed all sorts of visitors with this line: "No one by that name lives here." They would try to prevent social workers, schoolteachers, and maintenance personnel from coming inside and interrupting their drug trade.

The young men from the building were still watching me, but they didn't follow. As I came upon the next high-rise, I saw the faint markings on the pale yellow brick: Number 4040. At least now I was in the right place. The lobby here was empty, so I quickly skirted past another set of distressed mailboxes and passed through another dank lobby. The elevator was missing entirely—there was a big cavity where the door should have been—and the walls were thick with graffiti.

As I started to climb the stairs, the smell of urine was overpowering. On some floors the stairwells were dark; on others there was a muted glow. I walked up four flights, maybe five, trying to keep count, and then I came upon a landing where a group of young men, high-school age, were shooting dice for money.

"Nigger, what the fuck are you doing here?" one of them shouted. I tried to make out their faces, but in the fading light I could barely see a thing.

I tried to explain, again. "I'm a student at the university, doing a survey, and I'm looking for some families."

The young men rushed up to me, within inches of my face. Again someone asked what I was doing there. I told them the numbers of the apartments I was looking for. They told me that no one lived in the building.

Suddenly some more people showed up, a few of them older than the teenagers. One of them, a man about my age with an oversize baseball cap, grabbed my clipboard and asked what I was doing. I tried to explain, but he didn't seem interested. He kept adjusting his too-big hat as it fell over his face.

"Julio over here says he's a student," he told everyone. His tone indicated he didn't believe me. Then he turned back to me. "Who do you represent?"

"Represent?" I asked.

"C'mon, nigger!" one of the younger men shouted. "We know you're with somebody, just tell us who."

Another one, laughing, pulled something out of his waistband. At first I couldn't tell what it was, but then it caught a glint of light and I could see that it was a gun. He moved it around, pointing it at my head once in a while, and muttered something over and over— "I'll take him," he seemed to be saying.

Then he smiled. "You do *not* want to be fucking with the Kings," he said. "I'd just tell us what you know."

"Hold on, nigger," another one said. He was holding a knife with a six-inch blade. He began twirling it around in his fingers, the handle spinning in his palm, and the strangest thought came over me: *That's the exact same knife my friend Brian used to dig a hole for our tent in the Sierra Nevadas.* "Let's have some fun with this boy," he said. "C'mon, Julio, where you live? On the East Side, right? You don't look like the West Side Mexicans. You flip right or left? Five or six? You run with the Kings, right? You know we're going to find out, so you might as well tell us."

Kings or Sharks, flip right or left, five or six. It appeared that I was Julio, the Mexican gang member from the East Side. It wasn't clear yet if this was a good or a bad thing.

Two of the other young men started to search my bag. They pulled out the questionnaire sheets, pen and paper, a few sociology books, my keys. Someone else patted me down. The guy with the too-big hat who had taken my clipboard looked over the papers and then handed everything back to me. He told me to go ahead and ask a question.

By now I was sweating despite the cold. I leaned backward to try to get some light to fall on the questionnaire. The first question was one I had adapted from several other similar surveys; it was one of a set of questions that targeted young people's self-perceptions.

"How does it feel to be black and poor?" I read. Then I gave the multiple-choice answers: "Very bad, somewhat bad, neither bad nor good, somewhat good, very good."

The guy with the too-big hat began to laugh, which prompted the others to start giggling.

"Fuck you!" he told me. "You got to be fucking kidding me."

He turned away and muttered something that made everyone laugh uncontrollably. They went back to quarreling about who I was. They talked so fast that I couldn't easily follow. It seemed they were as confused as I was. I wasn't armed, I didn't have tattoos, I wasn't wearing anything that showed allegiance to another gang—I didn't wear a hat turned toward the left or right, for instance, I wasn't wearing blue or red, I didn't have a star insignia anywhere, either the five- or six-point variety.

Two of them started to debate my fate. "If he's here and he don't get back," said one, "you know they're going to come looking for him."

"Yeah, and I'm getting the first shot," said the other. "Last time I had to watch the crib. Fuck that. This time I'm getting in the car. I'm *shooting* some niggers."

"These Mexicans ain't afraid of shit. They kill each other in prison, over *nothing*. You better let me handle it, boy. You don't even *speak* Mexican."

"Man, I met a whole bunch of them in jail. I killed three just the other day."

As their claims escalated, so did their insults.

"Yeah, but your mama spoke Mexican when I was with her."

"Nigger, your *daddy* was a Mexican."

I sat down on a cold concrete step. I struggled to follow what they were talking about. A few of them seemed to think that I was an advance scout from a Mexican gang, conducting reconnaissance for a drive-by attack. From what I could glean, it seemed as if some black gangs were aligned with certain Mexican gangs but in other cases the black gangs and Mexican gangs were rivals.

They stopped talking when a small entourage entered the stairwell. At the front was a large man, powerfully built but with a boyish face. He also looked to be about my age, maybe a few years older, and he radiated calm. He had a toothpick or maybe a lollipop in his mouth, and it was obvious from his carriage that he was the boss. He checked out everyone who was on the scene, as if making a mental list of what each person was doing. His name was J.T., and while I couldn't have known it at this moment, he was about to become the most formidable person in my life, for a long time to come.

J.T. asked the crowd what was happening, but no one could give him a straight answer. Then he turned to me. "What are you doing here?"

He had a few glittery gold teeth, a sizable diamond earring, and deep, hollow eyes that fixed on mine without giving away anything. Once again, I started to go through my spiel: I was a student at the university, et cetera, et cetera.

"You speak Spanish?" he asked.

"No!" someone shouted out. "But he probably speaks Mexican!"

"Nigger, just shut the fuck up," J.T. said. Then someone mentioned my questionnaire, which seemed to catch his interest. He asked me to tell him about it.

I explained the project as best as I could. It was being overseen by a national poverty expert, I said, with the goal of understanding the lives of young black men in order to design better public policy.

My role, I said, was very basic: conducting surveys to generate data for the study. There was an eerie silence when I finished. Everyone stood waiting, watching J.T.

He took the questionnaire from my hand, barely glanced at it, then handed it back. Everything he did, every move he made, was deliberate and forceful.

I read him the same question that I had read the others. He didn't laugh, but he smiled. *How does it feel to be black and poor?*

"I'm not *black*," he answered, looking around at the others knowingly.

"Well, then, how does it feel to be *African American* and poor?" I tried to sound apologetic, worried that I had offended him.

"I'm not African American either. I'm a nigger."

Now I didn't know what to say. I certainly didn't feel comfortable asking him how it felt to be a *nigger*. He took back my questionnaire and looked it over more carefully. He turned the pages, reading the questions to himself. He appeared disappointed, though I sensed that his disappointment wasn't aimed at me.

"*Niggers* are the ones who live in this building," he said at last. "*African Americans* live in the suburbs. African Americans wear ties to work. Niggers can't find no work."

He looked at a few more pages of the questionnaire. "You ain't going to learn shit with this thing." He kept shaking his head and then glanced toward some of the older men standing about, checking to see if they shared his disbelief. Then he leaned in toward me and spoke quietly. "How'd you get to do this if you don't even know who we are, what we're about?" His tone wasn't accusatory as much as disappointed, and perhaps a bit bewildered.

I didn't know what to do. *Perhaps I should get up and leave?* But then *he* turned quickly and left, telling the young men who stayed behind to "watch him." Meaning me.

They seemed excited by how things had turned out. They had mostly stood still while J.T. was there, but now they grew animated. "Man, you shouldn't mess with him like that," one of them told me. "See, you should've just told him who you were. You might have been gone by now. He might have let you go."

"Yeah, you fucked up, nigger," another one said. "You really fucked this one up."

I leaned back on the cold step and wondered exactly what I had done to "fuck up." For the first time that day, I had a moment to ponder what had been happening. Random thoughts entered my mind, but, oddly, none of them concerned my personal safety: *What the hell is Bill Wilson going to do if he finds out about this? How am I supposed to know whether to address an interview subject as black, African American, or Negro? Did every Ph.D. student have to go through this? Can I go to the bathroom?* The sun had set, and it was getting colder. I pulled my jacket tighter and bent over, trying to keep out of the wintry draft.

Yo! Freeze, you want one?"

An older man walked in with a grocery bag full of beers and offered a bottle to one of the young men guarding me. He passed out beers to everyone there. Pretty soon they were all in a better mood. They even gave me a bottle.

By now it was well into the evening. No one seemed to have anywhere to go. The young men just sat in the stairwell telling one another all kinds of stories: about sexual conquests, the best way to smoke a marijuana cigarette, schoolteachers they'd like to have sex with, the rising cost of clothing, cops they wanted to kill, and where they would go when their high-rise building was torn down. This last fact surprised me. Nothing in our records at the university suggested that these projects were closing.

"You have to leave?" I asked. "What kind of neighborhood will you be going to?"

"Nigger, did someone tell you to talk?" one of them said.

"Yeah, Julio," said another, moving in closer. "You ain't got no business here."

I shut my mouth for a while, but some other men stopped by, and they were more talkative. I learned that the Chicago Housing Authority (CHA) was indeed tearing down the Lake Park projects in order to build condominiums and town houses. Some residents were staying on as squatters, and the gang was helping them by pirating electricity.

It was clear to me at this point that the young men I'd stumbled upon in this stairwell were junior members of a broad-based gang, the Black Kings, that sold crack cocaine. The older members explained that the gang was trying to forestall demolition but that it wasn't a pure act of charity: When this building was torn down, they would lose one of their best drug-selling locations.

Once in a while, I tried to interject a research question—What kinds of jobs did the people who lived here have? Why weren't the police in the building?—but they seemed less interested in answering me than in talking among themselves about sex, power, and money.

After a few hours, J.T. returned with a few other men, each of them carrying a grocery bag. More beer. It was late, and everyone seemed a little punchy. The air was stale, and some of the young men had been wondering when they might be able to leave. For the moment, however, the beer seemed to settle them down.

"Here," J.T. said, tossing me another bottle. Then he came closer. "You know you're not supposed to be here," he said quietly. He seemed to feel sorry for me and, at the same time, curious about my presence. Then he, too, began talking about the scheduled demolition of the Lake Park projects. He explained that he and his men had holed up in this building partly out of protest, joining the residents to challenge the housing authority's decision to kick them out.

Then he asked me where I was from.

"California," I said, surprised at the change in topic. "Born in India."

"Hmm. So you don't speak Spanish."

"Actually, I do."

"See! I told you this nigger was a Mexican," said one young gangster, jumping up with a beer in his hand. "We should've beat his ass back then, man! Sent him back to his people. You know they're coming around tonight, you know they *will* be here. We need to get ready—"

J.T. shot the young man a look, then turned back to me. "You're not from Chicago," he said. "You should really not be walking through the projects. People can get hurt."

J.T. started tossing questions at me. What other black neighborhoods, he asked, was I going to with my questionnaire? Why do researchers use multiple-choice surveys like the one I was using? Why don't they just *talk* with people? How much money can you make as a professor?

Then he asked what I hoped to gain by studying young black people. I ticked off a few of the pressing questions that sociologists were asking about urban poverty.

"I had a few sociology classes," he said. "In college. Hated that shit."

The last word I expected to exit this man's mouth was "college." But there it was. I didn't want to push my luck, so I thought I'd just keep listening and hope for a chance to ask about his background.

By now everyone seemed fairly drunk and, more alarmingly, excited at the prospect of a gang war with the Mexicans. Some of the older men started talking logistics—where to station the gang members for the fighting, which vacant apartments could be used as lookout spots, and so on.

J.T. dismissed their belief that something was going to happen that night. Once again he ordered two of the younger men to stay with me. Then he left. I returned to my seat, sipping a beer now and then. It looked like I would be spending the night with them, so I tried to accept my fate. I was grateful when they said I could go to the bathroom—which, as it turned out, was another stairwell a few floors up. Considering that water, and probably urine, were constantly dripping onto our own landing, I wondered why they didn't use a lower floor instead.

The young men stayed up in the stairwell all night, drinking and smoking. Some of them strayed out to the balcony once in a while to see if any cars had pulled up to the building. One of them threw an empty beer bottle to the ground six stories down. The sound of broken glass echoing through the stairwell gave me a fright, but no one else even flinched.

Every so often a few new people came in, always with more beer. They talked vaguely about gang issues and the types of weapons that different gangs had. I listened as attentively as I could but stopped asking questions. Occasionally someone asked me again about my background. They all at last seemed convinced that I was not in fact a Mexican gang member, although some of them remained concerned that I "spoke Mexican." A few of them dozed off inadvertently, sitting on the concrete floor, their heads leaning against the wall.

I spent most of the night sitting on the cold steps, trying to avoid the protruding shards of metal. I would have liked to sleep also, but I was too nervous.

Finally J.T. came back. The early-morning sun was making its way into the stairwell. He looked tired and preoccupied.

"Go back to where you came from," he told me, "and be more careful when you walk around the city." Then, as I began gathering up my bag and clipboard, he talked to me about the proper way to study people. "You shouldn't go around asking them silly-ass questions," he said. "With people like us, you should hang out, get to know what they do, how they do it. No one is going to answer questions like that. You need to understand how young people live on the streets."

I was astounded at what a thoughtful person J.T. appeared to be. It seemed as if he were somehow invested in my succeeding, or at least considered himself responsible for my safety. I got up and headed for the stairs. One of the older men reached out and offered me his hand. I was surprised. As I shook his hand, he nodded at me. I glanced back and noticed that everyone, including J.T., was watching.

What are you supposed to say after a night like this? I couldn't think of anything worthwhile, so I just turned and left.

As I walked back to my apartment in Hyde Park, everything seemed fundamentally different. Crossing from one neighborhood to the next, I speculated about gang boundaries. When I saw a group of people huddled on a corner, I wondered if they were protecting their turf. I had a lot of questions: Why would anyone join a gang? What were the benefits? Didn't they get bored hanging out in stairwells—and how could anyone possibly stand the smell of urine for that long? The surveys in my bag felt heavy and useless. I began to worry about my relationship with Professor Wilson. He certainly wouldn't approve of my experimental journey, done without his approval, and I wondered whether he would pull me off the project if he found out what I'd done. The voice of my father—a professor himself—entered my head. He had always given me advice about education. Throughout my college years, he stressed the need to listen to my teachers, and when I shipped off to Chicago, he told me that the key to success in graduate school would be to develop a good relationship with my advisers.

I took a shower and thought about the rest of my day. I had books to read, papers to write, some laundry to do. But none of that seemed very significant. I tried to sleep, but the rest was fitful. I couldn't get the previous night out of my head. I thought of calling someone, but whom? I wasn't close with any other members of Wilson's research team—and they, too, would probably be upset to find out what I'd done. I realized that if I truly wanted to understand the complicated lives of black youth in inner-city Chicago, I had only one good option: to accept J.T.'s counsel and hang out with people. So I headed back to the Lake Park projects to see if I could once again find J.T. and his gang.

I wasn't really scared as I walked north along Cottage Grove Avenue. A little nervous, certainly, but I was pretty sure that J.T. didn't see me as any kind of a threat. Worst-case scenario? Embarrassment. He and his gang would ask me to leave or they'd laugh at my desire to get to know them better.

It was maybe two o'clock in the afternoon when I arrived. This time I came bearing a six-pack of beer. There were about a dozen young men out front of Number 4040, standing around their cars.

Some of them began to point at me. A few others were playing handball by throwing a tennis ball against the building. As I drew close, all of them turned to watch me.

"You got to be kidding me," I heard someone say. Then I saw J.T., leaning back against a car, smiling and shaking his head.

"Beer?" I said, tossing him a bottle. "You said I should hang out with folks if I want to know what their life was like."

J.T. didn't answer. A few of the guys burst out laughing in disbelief. "He's crazy, I told you!" said one.

"Nigger thinks he's going to hang out with us!"

"I still think he's a Latin King."

Finally J.T. spoke up. "All right, the brother wants to hang out," he said, unfazed. "Let him hang out!"

J.T. grinned and opened up his bottle. Others came around and quickly grabbed the rest of the beers. Then, surprisingly, they all went back to their business. They didn't seem to be discussing anything very pressing, nor were they talking about any criminal activities. They mainly talked about what kind of rims to put on their cars. A few of them took care of the drug customers, handing vials of crack to the people who walked over from nearby buildings or drove up in run-down cars. In the distance I could see a few churchgoers on a Sunday stroll. A handful of gang members stood guard in front of Number 4040, and after a time some of the guys hanging out near the cars relieved them.

J.T. had a lot of questions for me: *You always use those surveys? Can you get a good job after you finish with this research? Why don't you study your own people?*

This last one would become one of his favorites. I felt a strange kind of intimacy with J.T., unlike the bond I'd felt even with good friends. It would have been hard to explain then and is just as hard now, but we had somehow connected in an instant, and deeply.

I tried to act nonchalant when J.T. asked me these questions, but inside I was overjoyed that he was curious about my work. I had a feeling that I was talking to someone about whom most people probably knew little. I didn't know exactly where our conversations might lead, but I sensed I was getting a unique perspective on life in a poor neighborhood. There were plenty of sociological studies on economically disenfranchised youth, but most relied on dry statistics of unemployment, crime, and family hardship. I had joined Bill Wilson's team in hopes of getting closer to the ground. My opportunity to do just that was standing right in front of me.

Every now and then, J.T. went inside the building to meet in private with someone who had driven up in a car.

I played a little handball and, showing off my hard-won suburban soccer skills, bounced the tennis ball off my head a few dozen times. Some of the older gang members were curious about my identity, my role at the university, and of course the reason I had returned. They all looked as tired as I was, and it felt as if we were all taking some welcome comic relief in one another's presence.

In general, I said very little. I asked no "meaningful" questions—mostly about their cars, why they were jacked up so high and whether they changed their own oil—and quickly saw that this strategy might actually work. I had learned the night before that they weren't very receptive to interview questions; they probably had plenty of that from cops, social workers, and the occasional journalist. So I just made small talk, trying to pass the time and act as if I'd been there before.

When J.T. returned from a trip into the building, everyone straightened up a bit.

"Okay!" he shouted. "They're ready, let's go over there." He ordered a few younger members into the building's lobby and motioned the others to get into their cars. He looked at me in a funny way. He smiled. I could tell that he was wondering what to say to me. I hoped he was going to invite me along to wherever they were going.

"You got balls," he said. "I'll give you that. We have to run. Why don't you meet me here next week. Early morning, all right?"

This offer took me by surprise. But I certainly wasn't going to turn him down. J.T. put out his hand, and I shook it. I tried again to think of something witty to say. "Yeah, sure," I said, "but you're buying next time."

He turned and hustled toward his car, a shiny purple Malibu Classic with gold rims. All of a sudden, there was no one left standing around but me.

TWO

First Days on Federal Street

I began spending time with J.T. We'd usually hang out for a little while with some of the more senior members of his gang, and then we'd go for a ride around the South Side.

Although it would take me a few years to learn about J.T.'s life in detail, he did tell me a good bit during our first few weeks together: He had grown up in this neighborhood, then gone to college on an athletic scholarship and found that he loved reading about history and politics. After college he took a job selling office supplies and industrial textiles at a midsize corporation in downtown Chicago. But he felt that his chances of success were limited because he was black; he got angry when he saw white people with lesser skills get promoted ahead of him. Within two years he left the mainstream to return to the projects and the gang life.

J.T. loved to talk about black Chicago as we drove around—the history of the neighborhood, the gangs, the underground economy. Like Old Time and the others who frequented Washington Park, J.T.

had his own personal version of history, replete with stories about great gang leaders and dramatic gang wars. He took me to his favorite restaurants, most of which had their own lively histories. One of them, Gladys's, was a soul-food restaurant where elected community and political leaders used to meet in private. Another marked the spot where two gangs once signed a legendary truce. J.T. always offered to pay for our meals and I, out of appreciation and a student's budget, always accepted.

J.T. once asked me what sociologists had to say about gangs and inner-city poverty. I told him that some sociologists believed in a "culture of poverty"—that is, poor blacks didn't work because they didn't value employment as highly as other ethnic groups did, and they transmitted this attitude across generations.

"So you want me to take pride in the job, and you're only paying me minimum wage?" J.T. countered. "It don't sound like you think much about the job yourself." His tone was more realistic than defensive. In fact, his rejoinder echoed the very criticisms that some sociologists applied to the "culture of poverty" view.

J.T. and I often passed time together at a diner. He might sit quietly, working through the details of his gang's operations, while I read for my sociology classes. Since he didn't want to generate tangible evidence of his enterprise, J.T. didn't write down very much, but he could keep innumerable details straight in his mind: the wages of each one of his two hundred members, the shifts each of them worked, recent spikes in supply or demand, and so on. Occasionally he drifted off, muttering calculations to himself. He didn't share many details with me, but he did sometimes give me a sort of quiz.

"Okay, I got something for you," he said one day over breakfast. "Let's say two guys are offering me a great deal on raw product." I knew enough to know that "raw product" meant powdered cocaine, which J.T.'s gang cooked up into crack. "One of them says if I pay twenty percent higher than the usual rate, he'll give me a ten percent discount a year from now, meaning that if the supply goes down, he'll sell to me before the other niggers he deals with. The other guy says he'll give me a ten percent discount now if I agree to buy from him at the regular price a year from now. What would you do?"

"This all depends on whether you think the supply will be affected a year from now, right?" I said.

"Right, so . . . ?"

"Well, I don't have any idea how this market works, so I'm not sure what to do."

"No, that's not how you need to think. You always take the sure bet in this game. *Nothing* can be predicted—not supply, not anything. The nigger who tells you he's going to have product a year from now is lying. He could be in jail or dead. So take your discount now."

As fascinating as I found such conversations, I rarely took notes in front of J.T., because I didn't want to make him cautious about what he said. Instead I waited until I got back to my apartment to write down as much as I could recall.

We often met a few times a week, but only when he wanted. He would phone me to arrange our meetings, sometimes just a few minutes in advance. J.T. didn't like to talk on the phone. In his soft voice, he'd tell me where and when to meet, and then he'd hang up. Once in a while, I didn't even have time to answer that I couldn't meet because I had a class—and then I'd cut class and meet him anyway. It was pretty thrilling to have a gang boss calling me up to go hang out with him. There were times I wanted to tell my professors the real reason I missed class now and then, but I never did.

Occasionally I hinted to J.T. that I would really, really like to learn more about gang life. But I was too meek to ask for any kind of formalized arrangement. Nor did he offer. Every time he dropped me off in front of my apartment building, he'd just stare out the window. I didn't know whether to say "Good-bye," "Hope to see you again," or "Call me sometime."

One morning, after I'd been hanging out with him for perhaps eight months, J.T. said we'd be visiting a different housing development, the Robert Taylor Homes. I had heard of Robert Taylor; *everybody* had heard of Robert Taylor. It was the largest public housing project in the United States, about ten times bigger than the Lake Park projects, with twenty-eight drab high-rise buildings stretched along a two-mile corridor. It lay a few miles away from the U of C, but since it ran alongside the Dan Ryan Expressway, one of Chicago's main arteries, pretty much everyone in the city drove past Robert Taylor at one time or another.

"I'm going to take you to meet somebody," J.T. said, "but I don't want you to open your mouth. Do you think you can do that?"

"Do I ever open my mouth?" I asked.

"No, but every so often you get a little excited, especially after you drink all that coffee. You open your mouth today, and that's it— we're through. Okay?"

Only once before had I heard such insistence in J.T.'s voice, and that was the night we first met in the stairwell of Building Number 4040 in the Lake Park projects. I finished my breakfast quickly, and then we jumped into his Malibu. The late-morning sky was overcast. J.T. was quiet except for asking me once in a while to see if any cops were following him. He had never asked this before. For the first time, I became fully conscious of just what I was doing: tagging along with the leader of a major crack-selling gang.

But I still hadn't admitted to myself that the man I sat next to was, at bottom, a criminal. I was too caught up in the thrill of observing the thug life firsthand. In the halcyon suburb where I grew up, people didn't even wash their cars on the street. In front of me here was a movie come to life.

There was something else, too, that helped me ignore the questionable morality of the situation. The University of Chicago scholars who helped invent the field of sociology, back when it first became a legitimate academic discipline, did so by venturing into the murkier corners of the city. They became famous through their up-close study of the hobo, the hustler, the socialite; they gained access to brothels and speakeasies and the smoky back rooms where politicians plied their art. Lately I'd been reading the works of these scholars. So even though I was hanging out with drug traffickers and thieves, at heart I felt like I was just being a good sociologist.

The street leading into the Robert Taylor Homes was lined with old, beat-up cars. A school crossing guard leaned on the hood of a car, her morning duty done, looking as if she'd been through a war. She waved knowingly at J.T. as we drove past. We pulled up in front of a high-rise, the lobby populated by a bunch of young men who seemed to stand at attention when they saw J.T.'s car. Unlike the Lake Park projects, which were nearly abandoned, Robert Taylor was thrumming with life. I could hear rap music blasting from a stereo. People stood around smoking cigarettes and, from the smell of it, marijuana. Every so often a parent and child passed through the loose crowd.

J.T. parked his Malibu and strode toward the building like a bad-ass cowboy swaggering into a bar. He stopped just short of the entrance, surveying the area and waiting as people came to greet him. As each young man made his way over, J.T. extended his hand graciously. Few words were spoken; most of the communication was in the form of subtle nods, signals familiar to everyone but me.

"When you gonna come and see me, baby?" one woman called out, and then another: "You gonna take me for a ride, sweetheart?" J.T. smiled and waved them off, playfully tapping their young children on the head as he passed. Two older women in bright blue jackets that read TENANT PATROL came up and hugged J.T., asked him why he didn't come around more often. J.T. was obviously well known in these parts, although I had no idea why.

Just then someone emerged from the lobby. He was obese, roughly J.T.'s age, and he was breathing heavily. His name was Curly, and—as if in mockery of my stereotypical preconceptions—he was a ringer for Rerun from *What's Happening!!* He and J.T. clasped hands, and then J.T. motioned for me to follow them.

"Your mama's house or mine?" Curly asked.

"Mama's pissed at me," J.T. said. "Let's go to your place."

I followed them up a few flights of stairs. We stepped inside an apartment furnished with couches and a few reclining chairs that faced a big TV. There was a Christian show playing. The walls were hung with family photos and a painting of Jesus Christ. Toys were strewn about the floor, and the kitchen counter was crowded with boxes of cereal and cookies. I could smell chicken and rice on the stove. Balls of yarn and knitting needles sat atop a drab glass table. The domestic scene surprised me a bit, for I had read so much about the poverty and danger in Robert Taylor, how children ran around without parents and how drugs had overtaken the community.

J.T. gestured for me to sit on the sofa, and then he and Curly sat down to talk. J.T. didn't introduce me, and before long I was forgotten entirely. Between their fast talk and the gangster vocabulary, I couldn't understand much of what they were saying, but I did manage to pick out some key words: "tax," "product," "monthly dues,"

"Cobras," "Kings," "police," "CHA security." They talked quickly and earnestly. After a while they began throwing numbers at each other in some kind of negotiation. A few times a young man arrived at the screen door and interrupted them, shouting "Five-Oh on Federal" or "Five-Oh in 26." Later J.T. would explain that that's how they communicated the whereabouts of the police: "Five-Oh" meant police, "26" was a building number in Robert Taylor, and "Federal" was a busy street flanking the projects. Cell phones hadn't yet arrived—the year was 1989—so gang members had to pass along such information manually.

I felt a sudden urge to go to the bathroom, but I didn't feel comfortable asking to use the one in the apartment. After some squirming I decided to stand up and walk around. As I made a move to get up, J.T. and Curly looked at me disapprovingly. I sat back down.

Their meeting had lasted at least two hours. "That's it," J.T. finally said. "I'm hungry. Let's pick it up tomorrow."

Curly smiled. "It'll be good to have you back," he said. "Ain't the same since you left."

Then J.T. glanced at me. "Oh, shit," he said to Curly. "I forgot about him. This is Sudhir. He's a cop."

The two of them began laughing. "You can go ahead and take a piss now," J.T. said, and they both laughed even harder. I began to sense that in exchange for access I was meant to serve as a source of entertainment for J.T.

On the car ride back to Hyde Park, J.T. told me what had just happened. He explained that he had grown up in the very Robert Taylor building we'd just visited. For the past couple of years, he'd been working out of the Lake Park projects because the Black Kings' citywide leaders had wanted to increase productivity there. But since the Lake Park projects were now slated for demolition, J.T. was returning to Robert Taylor, where he would be merging his own

Black Kings gang with the local BK faction, which was run by Curly. This merger was being executed at the behest of the gang's higher-ups. Curly had been installed as a temporary leader when J.T. was sent to turn around the Lake Park operation. Curly apparently wasn't a very good manager, which made the gang bosses' decision to bring J.T. back a simple one.

Robert Taylor and the other projects on State Street, J.T. told me, were "easy money," partly since thousands of customers lived nearby but also because of "the white folks who drive over to buy our shit." They came from Bridgeport, Armour Square, and other predominantly white ethnic neighborhoods on the far side of the Dan Ryan Expressway, buying mostly crack cocaine but also some heroin and marijuana. In his new assignment, J.T. told me, he hoped to earn "a hundred times" what he currently earned and buy a house for his mother, who still lived in Robert Taylor. He also said he hoped to buy an apartment for his girlfriend and their children. (In fact, he mentioned several such girlfriends, each of whom apparently needed an apartment.)

At the Lake Park projects, J.T.'s income had been dropping from a peak of about thirty thousand dollars a year. But he told me that now, in Robert Taylor, he stood to make as much as seventy-five thousand dollars or a hundred thousand if business was steady, which would put him nearly in the same league as some of the gang's higher-ups.

He made a few references to the gang's hierarchy and his effort to rise within it. There were a few dozen Black Kings officers above him, spread throughout Chicago, who earned their money by managing several gang factions like J.T.'s. These men were known as "lieutenants" and "captains." Above *them* was another level of gangsters who were known as the "board of directors." I had had no idea how much a street gang's structure mirrored the structure of just about any other business in America.

J.T. made it clear that if you rose high enough in the Black Kings dynasty, and lived long enough, you could make an awful lot of money. As he discussed his move up the ladder, I felt a knot in my stomach. Since meeting him I had entertained the notion that my dissertation research might revolve around his gang and its drug trafficking. I had spoken with him not only about his own gang "set" but about all the Black Kings sets in the city—how they collaborated or fought with one another over turf, how the crack-cocaine economy was fundamentally altering the nature of the urban street gang. Although there was a great deal of social-science literature on gangs, very few researchers had written about the actual business dealings of a gang, and even fewer had firsthand access to a gang's leadership. As we pulled up to my apartment, I realized that I had never formally asked J.T. about gaining access to his life and work. Now it seemed I might be getting shut out just as things were heating up.

"So when you do you think you'll be moving over to Robert Taylor?" I asked.

"Not sure," he said absentmindedly, staring out at the panhandlers who worked the gas station near my apartment.

"Well, I'm sure you'll be busy now—I mean, even busier than you've been. So listen, I just wanted to thank you—"

"Nigger, are we breaking up?" J.T. started laughing.

"No! I'm just trying to—"

"Listen, my man, I know you have to write a term paper—and what are you going to write it on? On me, right?" He giggled and stuck a cigar in his mouth.

It seemed that J.T. craved the attention. It seemed that I was more than just entertainment for him: I was someone who might take him seriously. I hadn't thought about the drawbacks of having my research dependent on the whims of one person. But now I turned giddy at the prospect of continuing our conversations. "That's right," I said. " 'The Life and Times of John Henry Torrance.' What do you think?"

"I like it, I like it." He paused. "Okay, get the fuck out, gotta run."

He offered his hand as I opened the car door. I shook it and nodded at him.

My short walk north to the Lake Park projects would now be replaced by a longer commute, usually by bus, to the Robert Taylor Homes. But as a result of his relocation, J.T. reported that he'd be out of touch for a few weeks. I decided to use that time to do some research on housing projects in general and the Robert Taylor Homes in particular.

I learned that the Chicago Housing Authority had built the project between 1958 and 1962, naming it after the agency's first African-American chairman. It was the size of a small city, with forty-four hundred apartments housing about thirty thousand people. Poor blacks had arrived in Chicago en masse from the South during the great migrations of the 1930s and 1940s, which left a pressing need for the city to accommodate them.

In the beginning, the project was greeted with considerable optimism, but it soon soured. Black activists were angry that Chicago politicians put the project squarely in the middle of an already crowded black ghetto, thereby sparing the city's white ethnic neighborhoods. Urban planners complained that the twenty-eight buildings occupied only 7 percent of the ninety-six-acre plot, leaving huge swaths of vacant land that isolated the project from the wider community. Architects declared the buildings unwelcoming and practically uninhabitable from the outset, even though the design was based upon celebrated French urban-planning principles.

And, most remarkably, law-enforcement officials deemed Robert Taylor too dangerous to patrol. The police were unwilling to provide protection until tenants curbed their criminality—and stopped hurling bottles or shooting guns out the windows whenever the police showed up.

In newspaper headlines, Robert Taylor was variously called "Congo Hilton," "Hellhole," and "Fatherless World"—and this was when it was still relatively new. By the end of the 1970s, it had gotten worse. As the more stable working families took advantage of civil-rights victories by moving into previously segregated areas of Chicago, the people left behind lived almost uniformly below the poverty line. A staggering 90 percent of the adults in Robert Taylor reported welfare—cash disbursements, food stamps, and Medicaid—as their sole form of support, and even into the 1990s that percentage would never get lower. There were just two social-service centers for nearly twenty thousand children. The buildings themselves began to fall apart, with at least a half dozen deaths caused by plunging elevators.

By the time I got to Chicago, at the tail end of the 1980s, Robert Taylor was habitually referred to as the hub of Chicago's "gang and drug problem." That was the phrase always invoked by the city's media, police, and academic researchers. They weren't wrong. The poorest parts of the city were controlled largely by street gangs like the Black Kings, which made their money not only dealing drugs but also by extortion, gambling, prostitution, selling stolen property, and countless other schemes. It was outlaw capitalism, and it ran hot, netting small fortunes for the bosses of the various gangs. In the newspapers, gang leaders were commonly reported as having multimillion-dollar fortunes. This may have been an exaggeration, but it was true that some police busts of the leaders' homes netted hundreds of thousands of dollars in cash.

For the rest of the community, the payout of this outlaw economy—drug addiction and public violence—was considerably less appealing. Combine this menace with decades of government neglect, and what you found in the Robert Taylor Homes were thousands of families struggling to survive. It was the epitome of an "underclass" urban neighborhood, with the poor living hard and virtually separate lives from the mainstream.

But there was surprisingly little reportage on the American inner city—and even less on how the gangs managed to control such a sprawling enterprise, or how a neighborhood like Robert Taylor managed to cope with these outlaw capitalists. Thanks to my chance meeting with J.T. and his willingness to let me tag along with him, I felt as if I stood on the threshold of this world in a way that might really change the public's—if not the academy's—understanding.

I wanted to bring J.T. to Bill Wilson's attention, but I didn't know how. I was already working on some of Wilson's projects, but these were large, survey-based studies that queried several thousand people at a time. Wilson's research team included sociologists, economists, psychologists, and a dozen graduate students glued to their computers, trying to find hidden patterns in the survey data that might reveal the causes of poverty. I didn't know anyone who was walking around talking to people, let alone gang members, in the ghetto. Even though I knew that my entrée into J.T.'s life was the stuff of sociology, as old as the field itself, it still felt like I was doing something unconventional, bordering on rogue behavior.

So while I devoted time to hanging out with J.T., I told Wilson and others only the barest details of my fieldwork. I figured that I'd eventually come up with a concrete research topic that involved J.T., at which point I could share with Wilson a well-worked-out set of ideas.

In late spring, several weeks after his meeting with Curly, J.T. finally summoned me to Robert Taylor. He had moved in with his mother in her apartment, a four-bedroom unit in the northern end of the complex. J.T. usually stayed in a different neighborhood, in one of the apartments he rented for various girlfriends. But now, he said, he needed to be in Robert Taylor full-time to get his gang firmly transplanted into its new territory. He told me to take the bus from Hyde Park down Fifty-fifth Street to State Street, where he'd have a few gang members meet me at the bus stop. It wasn't safe to walk around by myself.

Three of J.T.'s foot soldiers picked me up in a rusty Caprice. They were young and affectless and didn't have anything to say to me. As low-ranking members of the gang, they spent a lot of their time running errands for J.T. Once, when J.T. was a little drunk and getting excited about my writing his biography, he offered to assign me one of his gang members as a personal driver. I declined.

We drove up State Street, past a long stretch of Robert Taylor high-rises, and stopped at a small park in the middle of the complex. It was the sort of beautiful spring day, sunny, with a fresh lake breeze, that Chicagoans know will disappear once the brutal summer settles in. About fifty people of all ages were having a barbecue. There were colorful balloons printed with HAPPY BIRTHDAY CARLA tied to picnic tables. J.T. sat at one table, surrounded by families with lots of young children, playing and eating and making happy noise.

"Look who's here!" J.T. shouted. "The Professor. Welcome back."

His hands were sticky with barbecue sauce, so he just nodded, then introduced me to everyone at the table. I said hi to his girlfriend, whom I knew as Missie, and the young son they had together, Jamel.

"Is this the young man you've been telling me about?" said an older woman, putting her arm on my shoulder.

"Yes, Mama," J.T. said between bites, his voice as obedient as a young boy's.

"Well, Mr. Professor, I'm J.T.'s mother."

"They call her Ms. Mae," J.T. said.

"That's right," she said. "And you can call me that, too." She led me to another table and prepared a large plate of food for me. I told her I didn't eat meat, so she loaded me up with spaghetti, mac and cheese, greens, and cornbread.

We sat around for a few hours while the kids played. I spoke mostly to J.T.'s mother, and we forged a bond immediately. Sensing my interests, she began talking about the challenges of raising a family in public housing. She pointed to different people at the barbecue and filled in their stories. Carla, the birthday girl, was a one-year-old whose father and mother were both in jail for selling drugs. The adults in her building had decided to raise the child. This meant hiding her from the Department of Child and Family Services, which would have sent Carla into foster care. Different families took turns keeping Carla, shifting her to a new apartment whenever they caught wind that the social workers were snooping around. Ms. Mae talked about how teenage girls shouldn't have children so early, about the tragedy of kids getting caught up in violence, the value of an education, and her insistence that J.T. attend college.

J.T. came over to tell me about a big party the Black Kings were hosting later that afternoon. His gang had won a South Side basketball tournament, and everyone would be celebrating. He and I took a walk toward his building. Again I had so many questions: What did his mother think of the life he had chosen? How much did she even know? What did the typical Robert Taylor resident think about his organization?

Instead I asked a pretty tame one: "Why is everyone partying with you tonight? I thought you said it was a *gang* tournament."

"See, around here each building has an organization," he said.

"Organization," I knew, was one of the words that gang members sometimes used to refer to the gang; other words were "set" and "folks."

"And we don't just fight each other. We have basketball tournaments, softball tournaments, card games. Sometimes it's just people in the organization who play, but sometimes we find the best people in the building—like, we sometimes call Darryl, who used to play ball for Wisconsin, but he's not in the organization. So it's a building thing."

"So people in your building actually root for you?" I was puzzled as to how non–gang members viewed the Black Kings.

"Yeah! I know you think this sounds funny, but it's not like everyone hates us. You just have to see, it's a community thing."

He wasn't kidding. The party was held in a courtyard surrounded by three buildings, and several hundred people showed up to eat, drink beer, and party to the music of a DJ. All expenses were paid by the Black Kings.

I stayed close to J.T., sitting on the hood of his car, taking in all the activity. I watched young black men drive up in expensive sports cars, trailed by posses and girlfriends. They all greeted J.T. and congratulated him on winning the tournament.

J.T. explained that it was courtesy for leaders of some of the losing gangs to drop by. "The ones that are shooting at us won't come anywhere near us," he said, "but sometimes you got other organizations that you don't fight, that you just have a rivalry with." He told me that the various gangs' higher-ranking leaders tended to interact peacefully, since they often did business together—unlike the teenagers, or "shorties," he said. "They mostly just beat the shit out of each other in high school or at parties."

J.T. didn't introduce me to many people who stopped by, and I didn't feel comfortable leaving my spot. So I just sat and watched until the beers began making me drowsy. By dusk the party was dying down. That's when J.T. had one of his "shorties" drive me back to my apartment.

After about a month of commuting to his building, I managed to convince J.T. that I didn't need an escort to meet me at the bus stop. If the weather was okay, I'd even walk, which gave me a chance to see some of the neighborhoods that surrounded Robert Taylor. They were all poor, but even with their mixture of dilapidated homes and abandoned lots, not nearly as intimidating.

I always got nervous as I approached Robert Taylor, especially if J.T. wasn't there to meet me. But by now I was known to the gang members stationed out front. So instead of searching me—which they often did to strangers, even if it was an ambulance driver or a utility worker—they let me go up to Ms. Mae's apartment on the tenth floor. She'd fix me a plate of food, and then we would sit and talk.

I felt self-conscious that Ms. Mae had to entertain me while I waited for J.T. I also figured she couldn't really afford to feed another mouth. I once tried to give her a few dollars for my meal. "Young man, don't ever do that again," she scolded, pushing the bills back at me. "Let me tell you something about us. We may be poor, but when you come over here, don't pity us, don't pardon us, and don't hold us to a lower standard than you hold yourself up to."

Ms. Mae was a heavyset woman in her late fifties who, unless she was off to church, always wore an apron. She always seemed to be in the middle of housework. Today's apron was flowery, yellow and pink, with MS. MAE and GOD BLESS printed on it. She wore thick glasses and a warm, inviting look on her face. "You know, I came here with the clothes on my back," she said. "Arkansas. Mother said there was no life for me down there no more. She said, 'Go see your auntie in Chicago, get yourself a man and a job, and don't turn around.' And I didn't. I raised six children in Chicago. Never looked back."

I sat and ate as she spoke, trying to keep up with the stories she was telling as well as the food she kept heaping on my plate.

"We live in a *community,* understand? Not the *projects*—I hate that word. We live in a *community.* We need a helping hand now and then, but who doesn't? Everyone in this building helps as much as they can. We share our food, just like I'm doing with you. My son says you're writing about his life—well, you may want to write about this community, and how we help each other. And when I come over to *your* house, you'll share with me. You'll cook for me if I'm hungry. But when you're here, you're in my home and my community. And we'll take care of you."

I felt nervous as she spoke. Her warmth and her notion of community certainly challenged what I had read about Robert Taylor. Ms. Mae spoke to me as though she were teaching a child about life, not giving an academic researcher answers to scientific questions. Indeed, the time I was spending with families felt less and less like research. People who knew nothing about me nevertheless took me inside their world, talked to me with such openness, and offered me the food that they had probably budgeted for their own children.

No one back at the U of C had prepared me to feel such strong emotional connections to the people I studied. None of the ethnographic studies I'd read offered much guidance about the relation-ships a researcher formed during fieldwork and how to manage them. The books talked about the right way to ask a question or ad-dress a respondent during an interview, but little about managing re-lationships with the people you hung out with. In time I would meet the anthropologist Jean Comaroff, who taught me about the benefits and dangers of getting personally attached to sources, but that was still a few years away.

Nor was Ms. Mae's description of "community" something I was accustomed to from my own background. I don't think I could name more than a few people who lived on the nearby streets in the suburb where I grew up, and we certainly never borrowed from one another or planned activities together. Suddenly I envisioned Ms. Mae coming to my apartment someday for a visit and eating bland pasta and steamed vegetables, the only meal I could conceivably cook for her.

She and I kept speaking. I learned that Ms. Mae was the daugh-ter of sharecroppers, had spent two decades as a nanny and a domestic worker, and was forced to move into public housing when her hus-band, J.T.'s father, died of heart disease. He had been a quiet, easy-going man who worked for the city's transportation department. Moving into Robert Taylor, she said, was her last-ditch effort to keep the family intact.

Finally J.T. walked into the apartment. He took one look at me and laughed. "Is that *all* you do around here?" he said. "I'm begin-ning to think the only reason you come over here is to eat!"

His mother told him to hush and brought over some more sweet potato pie for me.

"C'mon, Mr. Professor, finish your food," J.T. said. "I need to sur-vey the building."

J.T. had by now firmly established his reign over a group of three buildings, one on State Street and two on Federal, each of which he liked to walk through at least once a week. "You have the CHA, the landlord, but then we also try to make sure that people are doing what they're told," he explained as we walked. "We can't have this place go crazy with niggers misbehaving. Because that's when police come around, and then customers stop coming around, and then we don't make our money. Simple as that."

As we entered the lobby of one of his buildings, 2315 Federal Street, he grabbed a few of his foot soldiers and told them to follow us. The August heat made the lobby's concrete walls sweat; they were cool to the touch but damp with humidity, just like all the people hanging around.

"I always start with the stairwells," J.T. said. There were three stairwells per building, two on the sides and one running up the middle, next to the elevator. "And I usually have my guys with me, just in case." He winked, as if I should know what "just in case" meant. I didn't, but I kept quiet. The foot soldiers, high-school kids with glittery, cheap necklaces and baggy tracksuits, walked quietly about five feet behind us.

We began climbing. It was only eleven on a weekday morning, but already the stairwells and landings were crowded with people drinking, smoking, hanging out. The stairwells were poorly lit and unventilated, and they smelled vile; there were puddles whose provenance I was happy to not know. The steps themselves were dangerous, many of the metal treads loose or missing. Who were all these people? Everybody we passed seemed to know J.T., and he had a word or a nod for each of them.

On the fifth floor, we came upon three older men, talking and laughing.

J.T. looked them over. "You all staying on the eleventh floor, right?" he asked.

"No," said one of them without looking up. "We moved to 1206."

"To 1206, huh? And who said you could do *that*?" None of them answered. "You need to settle up if you're in 1206, because you're *supposed* to stay in 1102, right?"

The men just cradled their beer cans, heads down, stung by the scolding.

J.T. called out to one of his foot soldiers, "Creepy, get these niggers over to T-Bone." T-Bone, I knew, was one of J.T.'s close friends and senior officers.

As we resumed our climbing, I asked J.T. what had just happened.

"Squatters," he said. "See, a lot of people who live around here don't have a lease. They just hang out in the stairs 'cause it's too cold outside, or they just need a safe place—maybe they're running from the police, or maybe they owe somebody money. We provide them protection. Sometimes they get out of hand, but most of them are pretty quiet. Anyway, they're here to stay."

"The gang protects the squatters?"

"Yeah, no one fucks with them if they're in here. I make sure of that. But we can't have two million of these niggers, so we have to keep track. They pay us."

As we continued our climb, we occasionally passed an older woman wearing a blue Tenant Patrol jacket. There were about a dozen of these women in each building, J.T. said. "They make sure that old folks are doing okay, and sometimes we help them." Somewhere around the thirteenth floor, J.T. stopped when he saw a Tenant Patrol woman bent over a man who was squirming on the floor.

"Morning, Ms. Easley," J.T. said. The man looked like he was just waking up, but I could also smell vomit, and he seemed to be in pain. He lay right outside the incinerator room, and the garbage smelled terrible.

"He's coming down," Ms. Easley told J.T. "He said someone sold him some bad stuff."

"Hmm-hmm," J.T. said disapprovingly. "They all say that when something goes bad. Always blaming it on us."

"Can one of your boys take him to the clinic?"

"Shit, he'll probably just be back tonight," J.T. said, "doing the same thing."

"Yeah, baby, but we can't have him sitting here."

J.T. waved over the remaining foot soldier, Barry, who was trailing us. "Get a few niggers to take this man down to Fiftieth." Barry started in on his task; "Fiftieth" referred to the Robert Taylor medical clinic, on Fiftieth Street.

"All right, Ms. Easley," J.T. said, "but if I see this nigger here tomorrow and he's saying the same shit, Creepy is going to beat his ass." J.T. laughed.

"Yes, yes, I know," she said. "And let me talk to you for a second." She and J.T. took a short walk, and I saw him pull out a few bills and hand them over. Ms. Easley walked back toward me, smiling, and set off down the stairwell. "Thank you for this, sweetheart," she called to J.T. "The kids are going to be very happy!"

I followed J.T. out to the "gallery," the corridor that ran along the exterior of the project buildings. Although you entered the apartments from the gallery, it was really an outdoor hallway, exposed to the elements, with chain-link fencing from floor to ceiling. It got its name, I had heard, because of its resemblance to a prison gallery, a metal enclosure meant to keep inmates in check. J.T. and I leaned up against the rail, looking out over the entire South Side and, beyond it, Lake Michigan.

Without my prodding, J.T. talked about what we had just seen. "Crackheads. Sometimes they mix shit—crack, heroin, alcohol, medicine—and they just can't see straight in the morning. Someone on the Tenant Patrol finds them and helps."

"Why don't you just call an ambulance?" I asked.

J.T. looked at me skeptically. "You kidding? Those folks almost never come out here when we call, or it takes them an hour."

"So you guys bring them to the hospital?"

"Well, I don't like my guys doing shit for them, but once in a while I guess I feel sorry for them. That's Creepy's decision, though. He's the one who runs the stairwell. It's up to him—usually. But this time I'm doing Ms. Easley a favor."

The stairwells, J.T. explained, were the one public area in the building where the gang allowed squatters to congregate. These areas inevitably became hangout zones for drug addicts and the homeless. J.T.'s foot soldiers, working in shifts, were responsible for making sure that no fights broke out there. "It ain't a pretty job," J.T. told me, laughing, "but that's how they learn to deal with niggers, learn to be tough on them."

The gang didn't charge the squatters much for staying in the building, and J.T. let the foot soldiers keep most of this squatter tax. That was one of the few ways foot soldiers could earn any money, since they held the lowest rank in the gang's hierarchy and weren't even eligible yet to sell drugs. From J.T.'s perspective, allowing his foot soldiers to police the stairwells served another important function: It let him see which junior members of his gang showed the potential for promotion. That's why he let guys like Creepy handle this kind of situation. "Creepy can take the man to the clinic, or he can just drag his ass out of the building and let him be," J.T. said. "That's on him. I try not to interfere, unless he fucks up and the police come around or Ms. Easley gets pissed."

I realized this was what J.T. had done the night I first stumbled upon his foot soldiers and was held overnight in the stairwell. He had wanted to see how they handled this stranger. Did they remain calm? Did they ask the right questions? Or did they get out of control and do something to attract the attention of tenants and the police?

"So what was going on with Ms. Easley?" I asked.

"You mean why did I give her money?" J.T. said. "That's what you want to know, right?"

I nodded, a little embarrassed that he could see through my line of indirect questioning.

"Tenant Patrol runs after-school parties for kids, and they buy school supplies. I give them money for that. It keeps them off our ass."

This was the first time J.T. had mentioned having to deal with tenants who might not like his gang's behavior. I asked what Ms. Easley might not like about his gang.

"I wouldn't say that she doesn't *like* us," he said. "She just wants to know that kids can walk around and not get hurt. And she just wants to keep things safe for the women. Lot of these crackheads are looking for sex, too, and they beat up women. It gets wild up in here at night. So we try to keep things calm. That's about it. We just help them, you know, keep the peace."

"So she lets you do what you want as long as you help her deal with people causing trouble? It's a give-and-take? There's nothing that you guys do that pisses her off?"

"We just keep the peace, that's all," he muttered, and walked away.

J.T. sometimes spoke vaguely like this, which I took as a sign to stop asking questions. At times he could be extraordinarily open about his life and his business; at other times he gave roundabout or evasive answers. It was something I'd learn to live with.

We kept climbing until we reached the top floor, the sixteenth. I followed J.T. down the hallway till we came to an apartment without a front door. J.T. told our foot soldier escort to stand guard outside. The young man nodded obediently.

Following J.T. inside, I was hit by a noxious odor of vomit, urine, and burned crack. It was so dark that I could barely see. There were several mattresses spread about, some with bodies on them, and piles of dirty clothing and fast-food wrappers. The holes in the walls were stuffed with rags to keep out the rats.

"Sudhir, come over here!" J.T. shouted. I followed a dim light that came from the rear of the apartment. "See this?" he said, pointing to a row of beat-up refrigerators. "This is where the squatters keep their food." Each fridge was draped with a heavy chain and padlock.

"Where do they get the fridges?" I asked.

"From the housing authority!" J.T. said, laughing. "The CHA managers sell fridges to the squatters for a few bucks instead of taking them back to get them fixed. *Everyone* is in on it. That's one thing you'll learn about the projects."

J.T. explained that this apartment was a "regular" squat, which meant that the people sleeping there paid the gang a rental fee and were therefore allowed to keep food and clothes inside. Ten people stayed in this apartment. A squatter known as C-Note, who had been in the community for more than two decades, was their leader. It was his duty to screen other squatters who wanted to take up quarters, help them find food and shelter, and make sure they obeyed all J.T.'s rules. "We let him run things inside," J.T. said, "as long as he pays us and does what we say."

There were other, less stable squats in the building, J.T. explained.

"We got a lot of apartments that are just basically for the hos and the crackheads. They get high and spend a few nights and then they leave. They're the ones that end up causing trouble around here. That's when the police come by, so we have to be tight with them."

Outside the squat I sat down on the gallery floor, finally able to take a clear breath. I felt overwhelmed by all the new information hitting me. I told J.T. I needed a rest. He smiled, seeming to understand, and told me he'd survey the other two buildings by himself. When I started to resist, worried I might not have this chance again, J.T. read my mind. "Don't worry, Mr. Professor. I do this every week."

"Yeah, you're right," I said. "I'm beat. I'll meet you back at your place. I've got to go write some of this down."

My heart froze after I realized what I'd just said. I had never actually told J.T. that I was keeping notes on all our conversations; I always waited until we split up before writing down what had transpired. Suddenly I feared he would think about everything we'd just witnessed and discussed, including all the illegal activities, and shut me down.

But he didn't even blink.

"Shorty, take Sudhir back to Mama's place," he told the young man who'd been standing guard outside the squat. "I'll be over there in an hour."

I quietly walked down the sixteen flights of stairs and over to Ms. Mae's building. The elevators in Robert Taylor worked inconsistently at best, so the only people who bothered to wait for them were old people and mothers with small children. The foot soldier accompanied me all the way to Ms. Mae's door, but we didn't talk; I tended never to talk to foot soldiers, since they never talked to me—which led me to think they'd probably been told not to.

I wound up sitting at the living room table in Ms. Mae's apartment, writing up my notes. In a short time the apartment had become the place I went whenever I needed a break or wanted to write up some field notes. J.T.'s family grew comfortable with my sitting quietly by myself or even napping on the couch if J.T. was busy.

Sometimes the apartment was peaceful and sometimes it was busy. At the moment J.T.'s cousin and her two children were staying there, as was one of J.T.'s sisters. But the living arrangements were very fluid. Like a lot of the more established households in the projects, Ms. Mae's apartment was a respite for a network of poor and needy relatives who might stay for a night, a month, or longer. Some of them weren't actually relatives at all but were "strays" who just needed a place to stay. It could be hard to sort out J.T.'s relatives from the strays. Several of his uncles, I learned, were high-ranking gang members. But I didn't even know how many siblings he had. I'd often hear him talk about "my sister" or "a brother of mine on the West Side," but I couldn't tell if these people were blood relatives or just friends of the family.

Still, they all seemed content to let me hang out at Ms. Mae's. And they all knew that J.T. didn't want me wandering through the neighborhood by myself. Sometimes Ms. Mae would wordlessly set down a plate of food for me as I wrote, her Christian radio station playing in the background. No one in the family, including J.T., ever asked to see my notes—although once in a while he'd stand over me and joke about whether I was describing him as "handsome." He loved the idea that I might be writing his biography. But in general everyone respected my privacy and let me do my work.

Eventually Ms. Mae even cleared out a space for me in the apartment to keep some clothes and books. Often, during a break from writing up my notes, I would start conversations with Ms. Mae and others in her apartment. They all seemed hesitant to answer specific questions—I'd already witnessed how tenants shied away from interviews with journalists or social workers—but they were more than willing to explain basic aspects of their lives and their community. Like Old Time and his friends in Washington Park, they talked openly about their family histories, Chicago politics, the behavior of the CHA and other city agencies, and life in the projects. As long as I didn't get too nosy—say, by asking about their income or who was living in an apartment illegally—they talked my head off. Just as important, I found I didn't have to hide my ignorance—which wasn't hard, since I was quite naïve about politics and race in urban America. My naïveté about these basic issues actually seemed to endear me to them.

In my brief exposure to J.T. and others in his building, I had already grown dismayed by the gap between their thoughtfulness and the denigrating portrayals of the poor I'd read in sociological studies. They were generally portrayed as hapless dupes with little awareness or foresight. The hospitality that Ms. Mae showed and the tenants' willingness to teach me not only surprised me but left me feeling extraordinarily grateful. I began to think I would never be able to repay their generosity. I took some solace in the hope that if I produced good, objective academic research, it could lead to social policy improvements, which might then better their living conditions. But I also wondered how I might pay them back in a more direct fashion. Given that I was taking out student loans to get by, my options were fairly limited.

Once J.T. saw how much I enjoyed accompanying him on his surveys of the buildings, he took me along regularly. But he often had other work to do, work he didn't invite me to see. And he wasn't ready yet to turn me loose in the buildings on my own, so I generally hung out around Ms. Mae's apartment. I felt a bit like a child, always in need of a baby-sitter, but I could hardly complain about the access I'd been granted into a world that was so radically different from anything I'd ever seen.

Ms. Mae introduced me to the many people who stopped by to visit. In their eyes I was just a student, a bit of an oddball to be sure; sometimes they jokingly called me "Mr. Professor," as they'd heard J.T. say. Several of J.T.'s aunts and cousins also lived in the building, and they warmed to me as well. They all seemed fairly close, sharing food and helping one another with errands or hanging out together on the gallery during the hot summer days.

Life on the gallery tended to be pretty lively. In the evenings families often set up a barbecue grill, pulling chairs or milk crates from their apartments to sit on. I probably could have made friends a lot more quickly if I hadn't been a vegetarian.

Little kids and teenage girls liked to tug my ponytail when I walked past. Others would chant "Gandhi" or "Julio" or "Ay-rab" in my direction. I was still enamored of the view of the city, and still nervous about the fencing that ran around the gallery.

Whenever a child ran toward the railing, I'd instinctively jump up and grab him. Once, a little boy's mother laughed at me. "Take it easy, Sudhir," she said. "Nothing's going to happen to them. It's not like the old days." In "the old days," I found out, some children did fall to their deaths off the Robert Taylor galleries, prompting the CHA to install a safety fence. But it was obvious that the first mistake had been building exterior hallways in windy, cold Chicago.

After dinner parents sent their kids inside the apartments and brought out tables and chairs, cards and poker chips, food and drink. They turned the galleries into dance floors and gambling dens; it could become carnivalesque.

I loved the nightlife on the galleries. And the tenants were generally in a good mood at night, willing to tell me about their lives if they weren't too high or too busy trying to make money. It was getting easier for me to determine when people were high. They'd stagger a bit, as if they were drunk, but their eyes sank back in their heads, giving them a look that was both dreamy and sinister.

It was hard to figure out the extent of crack use among the tenants. A lot of people pointed out that *other* people smoked crack— calling them "rock star" or "user" or "hype"—while insinuating that they themselves never did. Aside from a few older women, like J.T.'s mother, just about everyone was accused of smoking crack at one time or another.

After a while it became clear to me that crack use in the projects was much like the use of alcohol in the suburbs where I grew up: there was a small group of hard-core addicts and a much larger group of functional users who smoked a little crack a few days a week. Many of the crack users in Robert Taylor took care of their families and went about their business, but when they saved up ten or twenty dollars, they'd go ahead and get high. Over time I'd learn enough to estimate that 15 percent of the tenants were hardcore addicts while another 25 percent were casual users.

One of the first people I got to know on the gallery was named Clarisse. She was in her mid-thirties but looked considerably older. Beneath her worn and bruised skin, you could see a beautiful and thoughtful woman who nearly always had a smile ready. She worked as a prostitute in the building—"hustler" was the standard euphemism—and called herself "Clarisse the Mankiller," because, as she put it, "my love knocks 'em dead." Clarisse often hung around with J.T.'s family on their gallery. This surprised me, since I had heard J.T. and Ms. Mae openly disparage the prostitutes in their building.

"That's part of life around here," Ms. Mae had said, "but we keep away from them and I keep the kids away from them. We don't socialize together."

One quiet evening, as J.T.'s family was getting ready to barbecue, I was leaning against the gallery fence, looking out at the dusk, when Clarisse came up beside me. "You never tell me about the kind of women you like," she said, smiling, and opened a beer. By now I was used to Clarisse teasing me about my love life.

"I told you," I said, "my girlfriend is in California."

"Then you must get lonely! Maybe Clarisse can help."

I blushed and tried to change the subject. "How long have you been in the building, and how did you get to know J.T.?"

"They never told you!" Clarisse yelped. "I knew it! They just embarrassed, they don't like to admit I'm family."

"You're part of their family?"

"Man, I'm J.T.'s cousin. That's why I'm around. I live upstairs on the fifteenth floor with my man. And I work in the building, too. I'm the one in the family they don't like to talk about, because I'm open about what I do. I'm a *very* open person—I don't hide nothing from nobody. Ms. Mae knows that. Shit, *everyone* knows it. But, like I said, they don't always come clean about it."

"How can you live *and* work in the building?" I asked.

"You see these men?" Clarisse pointed at some of the tenants along the gallery, hanging out in front of their own apartments. "You should see how they treat women." I didn't understand what Clarisse meant; when she saw my face blank, she laughed. "Oh! We have a lot to talk about. Clarisse will educate you."

She then gestured toward a few women sitting on chairs. "See, all of them are hos. They all hustle. It's just that they do it quietly, like me. We have regulars, *and* we live here. We're not hypes who just come and go."

What's the difference, I asked her, between a "hype" and a "regular"?

"Regulars like me, we hustle to make our money, but we only go with guys we know. We don't do it full-time, but if we have to feed our kids, we may make a little money on the side. I got two kids I need to feed, and my man don't always help out. Then you got hypes that are just in it for the drugs. They don't live around here, but J.T. lets them work here, and they give him a cut. I don't hang around with them. They're the ones that cause trouble. Some of them have pimps, some of them work for the gang, but they're all in it for the drugs. Clarisse don't mess with drugs. And that's why a lot of people accept us—even if they say things behind our back. They know we're only trying to take care of our families, just like them."

"Are you working now?" I said.

"Baby, I'm always working if the price is right!" She laughed. "But J.T. probably don't want me working tonight, so I won't be hustling."

This confused me, since J.T. had specifically told me that his gang didn't run a prostitution racket. Most gangs didn't, he explained, since there wasn't much money to be made. Prostitutes were hard to manage and required a great deal of attention: They were constantly getting beat up and arrested, which meant long periods without income. They needed to be fed and clothed, and the ones who used drugs were notoriously unpredictable. They were also prone to stealing money.

"What do you mean?" I asked. "You mean J.T. controls you?"

"No, but he told me once that if I wanted to hang out with his family, I had to play by his rules: no hustling when there's a family thing going on. Like tonight. And he runs things around here, so I *have* to play by the rules."

Even though J.T.'s gang didn't actually control the prostitutes in his buildings, Clarisse explained that he did extract a monthly fee from both the hypes and the regulars. The regulars usually paid a flat fee (anywhere from fifteen to seventy-five dollars a month), and in return the gang would beat up any johns who abused the women. The hypes, meanwhile, turned over a cut of their income (ranging from 10 to 25 percent) to J.T.'s foot soldiers, who tried to keep track of how many tricks each woman turned. Clarisse said that J.T. was actually one of the nicer gang leaders on the South Side. He regularly lent money to women, helped them get medical care, even kept a few vacant apartments for them to use as brothels. So although J.T. didn't technically run a prostitution ring, he certainly controlled the flow of prostitution on his turf and profited from it.

The conversation with Clarisse that night made me realize that I was hardly the only person in the projects whose movements were dictated by J.T.

Whenever he took me on a survey of his buildings, I'd watch him deal with the various people who hung out in lobbies, stairwells, galleries, parking lots, and playgrounds. He warned a prostitute not to hustle out in the open. He told a man selling sneakers—they looked like counterfeit Nikes—to move away from the lobby where J.T.'s gang members were selling drugs. J.T. often forbade homeless men from hanging out in the playground, especially if they were drinking. And if he spotted a stranger on the premises, he'd have one of his senior officers interrogate that person to learn his business. J.T. hardly knew every single person out of the roughly five thousand in his domain, but he usually managed to figure out whether someone was a local, and if he couldn't figure it out, he had plenty of people to ask.

All of this was accomplished with little drama. "You folks need to move this activity somewhere else," he'd say matter-of-factly. Or,

"What did I tell you about hustling in the park when kids are playing?" Or, "You can't stay in this apartment unless you deal with Creepy first." I saw a few people resist, but none for any great length of time. Most of them seemed to respect his authority, or at least fear it.

In most of the sociological literature I'd read about gangs—they had been part of the urban fabric in the United States since at least the late nineteenth century—the gang almost always had heated relationships with parents, shopkeepers, social workers, and the police. It was portrayed as a nuisance at best, and more typically a major menace.

J.T.'s gang seemed different. It acted as the de facto administration of Robert Taylor: J.T. may have been a lawbreaker, but he was very much a lawmaker as well. He acted as if his organization truly did rule the neighborhood, and sometimes the takeover was complete. The Black Kings policed the buildings more aggressively than the Chicago police did. By controlling lobbies and parking lots, the BKs made it hard for tenants to move about freely. Roughly once a month, they held a weekend basketball tournament. This meant that the playgrounds and surrounding areas got thoroughly spruced up, with J.T. sponsoring a big neighborhood party—but it also meant that other tenants sometimes had to call off their own softball games or picnics at J.T.'s behest.

Over time J.T. became less reluctant to leave me alone in Robert Taylor. Occasionally he'd just go off on an errand and shout, "Hey, shorty, watch out for Sudhir. I'll be back." I generally didn't stray too far, but I did start up conversations with people outside the gang. That's how I first began to understand the complicated dynamic between the gang and the rest of the community.

One day, for instance, I ran into C-Note, the leader of the squatters, installing an air conditioner in Ms. Mae's apartment. C-Note was a combination handyman and hustler. For five or ten dollars, he'd fix a refrigerator or TV. For a few dollars more, he'd find an ingenious way to bring free electricity and gas into your home. When it came to home repair, there didn't seem much that C-Note couldn't, or wouldn't, do.

After he finished work at Ms. Mae's, I sat with C-Note on the gallery and had a beer. He told me that he had lived in the building for years and held various legitimate blue-collar jobs, but after being laid off several times he had lost his lease and become a squatter. He always found a little work and a place to sleep in J.T.'s building. He stayed out of people's way, he told me. He didn't make noise, didn't use drugs, and wasn't violent. He got his nickname, he explained, because "I got a hundred ways to make a hundred bucks."

I learned that a lot of tenants welcomed C-Note into their homes for dinner, let him play with their children, and gave him money for medicine or a ride to the hospital if he was hurt. But this began to change once J.T. moved his operations back into Robert Taylor. J.T. saw squatters as a source of income, not as charity cases. Nor was he pleased that C-Note was in the good graces of tenants, some of whom lobbied J.T. not to tax C-Note's earnings. Even J.T.'s mother was on C-Note's side in this matter.

But J.T. wasn't one to compromise when it came to money. He had to pay for the upkeep of a few cars as well as several girlfriends, each of whom needed her own apartment and spending allowance. J.T. also liked to go gambling in Las Vegas, and he took no small amount of pride in the fact that he owned dozens of pairs of expensive shoes and lots of pricey clothing. But instead of acting charitably toward someone like C-Note, J.T. was openly resentful of the idea that he was getting a free ride.

One hot Sunday morning, I was hanging out with C-Note and

some other squatters in the parking lot of J.T.'s building, across the street from a basketball court. The men had set up an outdoor auto-repair shop—changing tires, pounding out dents, performing minor engine repairs. Their prices were low, and they had lined up enough business to keep them going all day. Cars were parked at every angle in the lot. The men moved to and fro, hauling equipment, swapping tools, and chattering happily at the prospect of so much work. Another squatter had set up a nearby stand to sell soda and juice out of a cooler. I bought a drink and sat down to watch the underground economy in full bloom.

J.T. drove up, accompanied by four of his senior officers. Three more cars pulled up behind them, and I recognized several other gang leaders, J.T.'s counterparts who ran the other local Black Kings factions.

J.T. walked over to C-Note, who was peering into a car engine. J.T. didn't notice me—I was sitting by a white van, partially hidden from view—but I could see and hear him just fine.

"C-Note!" J.T. yelled. "What the fuck are you doing?"

"What the fuck does it look like I'm doing, young man?" C-Note barked right back without looking up from his work. C-Note wasn't usually quarrelsome, but he could be a hard-liner when it came to making his money.

"We have games running today," J.T. said. He meant the gang's monthly basketball tournament. "You need to get this shit out of here. Move the cars, get all this stuff off the court."

"Aw, shit, you should've told me." C-Note threw an oily cloth to the ground. "What the fuck can I do? You see that the work ain't finished."

J.T. laughed. He seemed surprised that someone would challenge him. "Nigger, are you kidding me?! I don't give a fuck about your work. Get these cars out of here." J.T. looked underneath the cars. "Oh, shit! And you got oil all over the place. You better clean that up, too."

C-Note started waving his hands about and shouting at J.T. "You're the only one who can make money, is that right? You own all this shit, you own all this land? Bullshit."

He pulled out a cigarette, lit it, and kept muttering, "Bullshit." The other squatters stopped working to see what would happen next. C-Note was drenched in sweat and angry, as if he might lose control.

J.T. looked down at his feet, then waved over his senior officers, who had been waiting by the car. A few of the other gang members also got out of their cars.

Once his henchmen were near, J.T. spoke again to C-Note: "I'm asking you one more time, nigger. You can either move this car or—"

"That's some bullshit, boy!" C-Note yelled. "I ain't going anywhere. I been here for two hours, and I told you I ain't finished working. So fuck you! Fuck you! Fuck you!" He turned to the other squatters. "This nigger do this every time," he said. "Every time. Fuck him."

C-Note was still chattering when J.T. grabbed him by the neck. In an instant two of J.T.'s officers also grabbed C-Note. The three of them dragged him toward a concrete wall that separated Robert Taylor from the tracks where a commuter train ran. C-Note kept shouting, but he didn't physically resist. The other squatters turned to watch. The gang leaders nonchalantly took some sodas from the cooler without paying.

"You can't do this to us!" C-Note shouted. "It ain't fair."

J.T. pushed C-Note up against the concrete wall. The two officers, their muscular arms plastered with tattoos, pinned him in.

"I told you, nigger," J.T. said, his face barely an inch away from C-Note's, "but you just don't listen, do you?" He sounded exasperated, but there was also a sinister tone to his voice I'd never heard before. "Why are you making this harder?"

He started slapping C-Note on the side of the head, grunting with each slap, C-Note's head flopping back and forth like a toy.

"Fuck you!" C-Note shouted. He tried to turn to look J.T. in the eye, but J.T. was so close that C-Note butted the side of J.T.'s head with his own. This only irked J.T. more. He cocked his arm and pounded C-Note in the ribs. C-Note held his gut, coughing violently, and then J.T.'s henchmen pushed him to the ground. They took turns kicking him, one in the back and the other in the stomach. When C-Note curled up, they kicked him in the legs. "You should've listened to the man, fool!" one of them shouted.

C-Note lay in a fetal position, struggling to catch his breath. J.T. rolled him over and punched him in the face one last time. "Dumb nigger!" he shouted, then walked back toward us, head down, flexing his hand as if he had hurt it on C-Note's skull.

J.T. reached into the squatter's cooler for a soda. That's when he finally noticed me standing there. He frowned when our eyes met. He quickly moved away, going toward the high-rise, but his look gave me a chill. He was clearly surprised to see me, and he seemed a little peeved.

I had been hanging around J.T. and his gang for several months by now, and I'd never seen J.T. engage in violence. I felt like his scribe, tailing a powerful leader who liked to joke with the tenants and, when he needed to be assertive, did so quietly. I was naïve, I suppose, but I had somehow persuaded myself that just because I hadn't seen any violence, it didn't exist. Now I *had* seen a different side of his power, a far less polished presentation.

In the weeks afterward, I began to contemplate the possibility that

I would see more beatings, perhaps even fatal incidents. I still felt exhilarated by my access to J.T.'s gang, but I was also starting to feel shame. My conviction that I was merely a sociological observer, detached and objective, was starting to feel false. Was I really supposed to just stand by while someone was getting beat up? I was ashamed of my desire to get so close to the violence, so close to a culture that I knew other scholars had not managed to see.

In reality I probably had little power to stop anyone from getting abused by the gang. And for the first time in my life, I was doing work that I truly loved; I was excited by my success. Back at the university, my research was starting to attract attention from my professors, and I certainly didn't want to let that go. I told Wilson about the young men I had met and their involvement with gangs. I kept things pretty abstract; I didn't tell him every detail about what I saw. He seemed impressed, and I didn't want to lose his support, so I figured that if I could forget about the shame, maybe it would simply go away.

As time passed, I pretty much stopped talking about my research to friends and family. I just wrote down my notes and tried not to draw attention to myself, except to tell my advisers a few stories now and then.

When I went home to California on vacations or holidays and saw my parents, I told them relatively little about my work in the projects. My mother, who worked as a hospital records clerk, was already worried about my living so far from home, so I didn't want to heighten her concern with stories of gang beatings. And I knew that my father would be upset if he learned that I hid things from my advisers. So I hid my fieldwork from him as well. Instead I just showed them my grades, which were good, and said the least I could get away with.

In retrospect the C-Note beating at least enabled me to view my relationship with J.T. more realistically. It made me appreciate just how deeply circumscribed my interactions with the Black Kings had been. What I had taken to be a fly-on-the-wall vantage point was in fact a highly edited view. It wasn't that I was seeing a false side of the gang, but there was plainly a great deal I didn't have access to. I knew that the gang made a lot of money in a lot of different ways— I had heard, for instance, that they extorted store owners—but I knew few details. All I saw was the flashy consumption: the jewelry, the cars, the parties.

And the gang obviously had an enormous impact on the wider community. It went well beyond telling residents they couldn't hang out in the lobby. The C-Note beating made that clear. But if I was really going to write my dissertation on gang activity, I'd have to learn an awful lot more about how the gang affected everyone else in the community. The problem was figuring the way out from under J.T.'s grip.

THREE

Someone to Watch Over Me

C-Note's friends took him to the hospital, where he received treatment for bruised ribs and cuts on his face. He spent the next couple of months recuperating in the apartment of a friend who lived nearby. Eventually he moved back into Robert Taylor. The building was as much his home as J.T.'s, and no one expected the beating to drive him away for good.

I wondered how J.T. would react the next time I saw him. Up to that point, he was always happy to have me follow him around, to have a personal biographer. "He's writing about my life," he'd boast to his friends. "If you-all could read, you'd learn something." He had no real sense of what I would actually be writing—because, in truth, I didn't know myself. Nor did I know if he'd be upset with me for having seen him beat up C-Note, or if perhaps he'd try to censor me.

I didn't return to Robert Taylor for a week, until J.T. called to invite me to a birthday party for his four-year-old daughter, Shuggie. She was one of two daughters that J.T. had with his girlfriend Joyce; the other girl, Bee-Bee, was two. J.T. and Joyce seemed pretty close. But then again J.T. also seemed close with Missie and their son, Jamel. As much as J.T. seemed to trust me and let me inside his world, he was fiercely protective of his private life. Except for benign occasions like a birthday party, he generally kept me away from his girlfriends and his children, and he often gave me blatantly contradictory information about his family life. I once tried asking why he was so evasive on that front, but he just shut me down with a hard look.

I was nervous as I rode the bus toward Robert Taylor, but my reunion with J.T. was anticlimactic. The party was so big, with dozens of friends and family members, that it was split between Ms. Mae's apartment and another apartment upstairs where J.T.'s cousin LaShona lived. Ms. Mae had cooked a ton of food, and there was a huge birthday cake. Everyone was having a good, loud time.

J.T. strode right over and shook my hand. "How you feel?" he asked—one of his standard greetings. He stared me down for a moment but said nothing more. Then he winked, handed me a beer, and walked away. I barely saw him the rest of the party. Ms. Mae introduced me to some of her friends—I was "Mr. Professor, J.T.'s friend," which conferred immediate legitimacy upon me. I stayed a few hours, played some games with the kids, and then took the bus home.

J.T. and I resumed our normal relationship. Even though I couldn't stop thinking about the C-Note beating, I kept my questions to myself. Until that incident I had seen gang members selling drugs, tenants taking drugs, and plenty of people engaged in small-time hustles to make money. While I was by no means comfortable watching a drug addict smoke crack, the C-Note affair gave me greater pause. He was an old man in poor health; he could hardly be expected to defend himself against men twice his size and half his age, men who also happened to carry guns.

What was I, an impartial observer—at least that's how I thought of myself—supposed to do upon seeing something like this? I actually considered calling the police that day. After all, C-Note had been assaulted. But I didn't do anything. I am ashamed to say that I didn't even confront J.T. about it until some six months later, and even then I did so tentatively.

The confrontation happened after I witnessed another incident with another squatter. One day I was standing outside the building's entryway with J.T. and a few other BKs. J.T. had just finished his weekly walk-through of his high-rise. He was having a quick meeting with some prostitutes who'd recently started working in the building, explaining the rules and taxes. The tenants, meanwhile, went about their business—hauling laundry, checking the mail, running errands.

A few of J.T.'s junior members came out to tell him that one of the squatters in the building, a man known as Brass, refused to pay the gang's squatting fee. They had brought Brass with them down to the lobby. I could see him through the entryway. He looked to be in his late forties, but it was hard to say. He had only a few teeth and seemed in pretty bad shape. I'd heard that Brass was a heroin addict with a reputation for beating up prostitutes. He was also known for moving around from building to building. He wasn't a regular squatter like C-Note, who was on familiar terms with all the tenants. Brass would anger the tenants in one building and then pack up and move along.

J.T. dispatched Price, one of his senior officers, to deal with Brass. Unlike C-Note, who offered only a little resistance, Brass decided to fight back. This was a big mistake. Price was generally not a patient man, and he seemed to enjoy administering a good beating. I could see Price punching Brass repeatedly in the face and stomach. J.T. didn't flinch. Everyone, in fact—gang members and tenants alike— just stood and watched.

Brass started to crawl toward us, making his way outside to the building's concrete entryway. Price looked exhausted from hitting Brass, and he took a break. That's when some rank-and-file gang members took over, kicking and beating Brass mercilessly. Brass resisted throughout. He kept yelling "Fuck you!" even as he was being beaten, until he seemed unconscious. A drool of blood spilled from his mouth.

Then he began flailing about on the ground in convulsion, his spindly arms flapping like wings. By now his body lay just a few feet from us. I groaned, and J.T. pulled me away. Still no one came to help Brass; it was as if we were all fishermen watching a fish die a slow death on the floor of a boat.

I leaned on J.T.'s car, quivering from the shock. He took hold of me firmly and tried to calm me down. "It's just the way it is around here," he whispered, a discernible tone of sympathy in his voice. "Sometimes you have to beat a nigger to teach him a lesson. Don't worry, you'll get used to it after a while."

I thought, *No, I don't want to get used to it.* If I did, what kind of person would that make me? I wanted to ask J.T. to stop the beating and take Brass to the hospital, but my ears were ringing, and I couldn't even focus on what he was telling me. My eyes were fixed on Brass, and I felt like throwing up.

Then J.T. grabbed me by the shoulders and turned me away so I couldn't watch. But out of the corner of my eye, I could see that a few tenants finally came over to help Brass, while the gang members just stood over him doing nothing. J.T. held me up, as if to comfort me. I tried instead to support my weight on his car.

That's when C-Note slipped into my thoughts.

"I understand that Brass didn't pay you the money he owed, but you guys beat up C-Note and he wasn't doing anything," I said impatiently. "I just don't get it."

"C-Note was challenging my authority," J.T. answered calmly. "I had told him months before he couldn't do his work out there, and he told me he understood. He went back on his word, and I had to do what I had to do."

I pushed a little harder. "Couldn't you just punish them with a tax?"

"Everyone wants to kill the leader, so you got to get them first." This was one of J.T.'s trademark sayings. "I had niggers watching me," he said. "I had to do what I had to do."

I recalled that on the day C-Note challenged him, J.T. had driven up to the building with a few Black Kings leaders from other neighborhoods. J.T. was constantly worried—practically to the point of paranoia, it seemed to me—that his own members and fellow leaders wanted to dethrone him and claim his territory. So he may have felt he couldn't afford to have his authority challenged in their presence, even by a senior citizen whose legs probably couldn't buy him one lap around a high-school track. Still, J.T.'s explanation seemed so alien to me that I felt I was watching a scene from *The Godfather*.

By now it was nearly a year since I'd started hanging out with J.T.'s gang. It was 1990, which was roughly the peak of the crack epidemic in Chicago and other big U.S. cities. Black and Latino gangs including the Kings, the Cobras, the Disciples, the Vice Lords, the

MCs (Mickey Cobras), and even the Stones, which had been temporarily dismantled a few years earlier, were capitalizing on a huge demand for crack and making a lot of money.

In the old days, a teenager with an appetite for trouble might have gotten involved in vandalism or shoplifting; now he was more likely to be involved in the drug trade. And the neighbor who might have yelled at that misbehaving teenager in the old days was less likely to do so, since that kid might well be carrying a gun.

Politicians, academics, and law-enforcement officials all offered policy solutions, to little avail. The liberal-minded deployed their traditional strategies—getting young people back into school and finding them entry-level jobs—but few gang members were willing to trade in their status and the prospect of big money for menial work. Conservatives attacked the crack epidemic by supporting mass arrests and hefty prison sentences. This certainly took some dealers off the streets, but there was always a surplus of willing and eager replacements.

The national mood had grown increasingly desperate—and punitive. Prosecutors won the right to treat gangs as organized criminal groups, which produced longer prison sentences. Judges gave the police permission to conduct warrantless searches and to round up suspected gang members who were hanging out in public spaces. In schools, mayors ruled out the wearing of bandannas and other clothing that might signal gang affiliation. With each day's newspaper bringing a fresh story about gang violence, these efforts met little political resistance, even if they weren't all that effective.

From J.T.'s perspective the real crisis was that all these measures conspired to make it harder to earn as much money as he would have liked.

Because crack was sold on street corners, with profits dependent on high volume and quick turnover, J.T. had to monitor a round-the-clock economic operation. He loved the challenge of running a business and making money. From all indications his transition to the Robert Taylor Homes was an unqualified success. This had won the attention of his superiors, a group of several dozen people in prison and on the streets known collectively as the Black Kings' board of directors. They had begun inviting J.T. to high-level meetings to discuss the big picture of their enterprise. Pleased with his managerial prowess and attention to detail, they rewarded J.T. with extra responsibilities. He had just been asked, for instance, to help the gang with its foray into Chicago politics.

"Even the gang needs friends with connections," J.T. told me. "And we're getting more successful, so we need more friends."

"I don't see why a gang wants to deal with politicians," I said. "I don't see what they get out of it. It seems they'd have a greater chance of getting caught if they started hanging out with politicos, no?"

He reminded me that his Black Kings gang was just one of about two hundred BK gangs around the city that were making money selling crack. With that much money, the citywide BK leadership needed to think about investing and laundering.

"Let's say, Sudhir, that you're making only a hundred bucks," he explained. "You probably don't have a lot of real headaches. You don't need to worry about niggers stealing it from you. You don't need to worry that when you go into a store, they'll ask you where you got the money. But let's say you got a thousand bucks. Well, you can't really carry it around, and you're a street nigger so you don't have a bank account. You need to keep it somewhere. So you start to have things to think about.

"Now let's say it's ten thousand. Okay, now you got niggers who are watching you buy a few things: a new TV, a new car. They say, 'Oh, Sudhir, he's got a new necklace. And he's a student. He don't work? So where'd he get the money? Maybe he has cash in his house.' So now you have more things to worry about.

"Now let's say it's a hundred thousand. You want to buy a car, but the car dealer has to report to the government when people pay for a car with thirty thousand dollars in cash. So what are you going to do? You may have to pay him a thousand bucks to keep his mouth shut. Then maybe you need to hire security, 'cause there's always some nigger that's going to take the chance and rob you. That's another few thousand, and you got to trust the security you hired, 'cause they know where you keep the money.

"Now let's say you got five hundred thousand or a million. Or more. That's what these niggers above me are worrying about. They need to find ways to clean the money. Maybe they hide it in a friend's business. Maybe they tell their sisters to open up bank accounts. Or they get their church to take a donation. They have to constantly be thinking about the money: keeping it safe, investing it, protecting themselves from other niggers."

"But I still don't understand why you need to deal with politicians."

"Well, see, an alderman can take the heat off of us," J.T. said with a smile. "An alderman can keep the police away. He can make sure residents don't get too pissed off at us. Let's say we need to meet in the park. The alderman makes sure the cops don't come. And the only thing they want from us is a donation—ten thousand dollars gets you an alderman for a year. Like I keep telling you, our organization is about helping our community, so we're trying to get involved in what's happening."

J.T.'s monologue surprised me on two fronts. Although I'd heard about corrupt aldermen in the old days—denying building permits to political enemies, for instance, or protecting a gang's gambling racket—I had a hard time believing that J.T. could buy off a politician as easily as he described. Even more surprising was J.T.'s claim about "helping our community." Was this a joke, I wondered, or did he really believe that selling drugs and bribing politicians would somehow help a down-and-out neighborhood pick itself up?

Besides the Black Kings' relationships with various aldermen, J.T. told me, the gang also worked with several community-based organizations, or CBOs. These groups, many of them created with federal funding during the 1960s, worked to bring jobs and housing to the neighborhood, tried to keep kids off the street with recreation programs, and, in places like the South Side, even enacted truces between warring gangs.

Toward the end of the 1980s, several CBOs tried instilling civic consciousness in the gangs themselves. They hired outreach workers (most of whom were former gangsters) to persuade young gang members to reject the thug life and choose a more productive path. These reformers held life-skills workshops that addressed such issues as "how to act when you go downtown" or "what to do when a lady yells at you for drinking beer in the park." They also preached the gospel of voting, arguing that a vote represented the first step toward reentry into the social mainstream. J.T. and some other gang leaders not only required their young members to attend these workshops but also made them participate in voter-registration drives. Their motives were by no means purely altruistic or educational: they knew that if their rank-and-file members had good relationships with local residents, the locals were less likely to call the police and disrupt the drug trade.

J.T.'s ambitions ran even higher. What he wanted, he told me, was to return the gang to its glory days of the 1960s, when South Side gangs worked together with residents to agitate for improvements in their neighborhoods. But he seemed to conveniently ignore a big difference: Gangs back then didn't traffic in drugs, extort money from businesses, and terrorize the neighborhood with violence. They were not innocent kids, to be sure. But their worst transgressions tended to be street fighting or intimidating passersby. Because J.T.'s gang *was* involved in drugs and extortion (and more), I was skeptical that he could enjoy much more support from the local residents than he currently had.

One cold November night, J.T. invited me to a meeting at a small storefront Baptist church. An ex-gangster named Lenny Duster would be teaching young people about the rights, responsibilities, and power of voting. The next election, while a full year away, would place in office a great many state legislators as well as city aldermen.

Lenny ran a small organization called Pride, which helped mediate gang wars. About a hundred young Black Kings attended the meeting, held in a small room at the rear of the church. They were quiet and respectful, although they had the look of teenagers who'd been told that attendance was mandatory.

Lenny was about six foot four, built lean and muscular. He was about forty years old, with streaks of blond hair, and he walked with a limp. "You-all need to see where the power is!" Lenny shouted to the assembly, striding about like a Caesar. "J.T. went to college, I earned a degree in prison. You-all are dropping out of school, and you're ignorant. You can't read, you can't think, you can't understand where the power comes from. It don't come from that gun you got—it comes from what's in your head. And it comes from the vote. You can change the world if you get the niggers that are coming down on you out of power. Think about it: No more police stopping you, no more abandoned buildings. You control your destiny!"

He talked to the young men about how to "work" responsibly. It was understood among gang members that "work" meant selling drugs—a tragic irony in that they referred to working in the legitimate economy as "getting a job," not "work."

"You-all are outside, so you need to respect who else is around you," he said. "If you're in a park working, leave the ladies alone. Don't be working around the children. That just gets the mamas mad. If you see kids playing, take a break and then get back to work. Remember, what you do says a lot about the Black Kings. You have to watch your image, take pride in yourself.

"You are not just foot soldiers in the Black Kings," he continued. "You are foot soldiers in the *community*. You will register to vote today, but then you must all go out and register the people in your buildings. And when elections come around, we'll tell you who to vote for and you'll tell them. That's an important duty you have when you belong to this organization."

For my classes at the U of C, I'd been reading about the history of the Chicago political machine, whose leaders—white and black alike—were famous for practicing the dark arts of ballot stuffing, bribery, and yes, predelivered voting blocs. Like his predecessors, Lenny did give these young men a partial understanding of the right to vote, and why it was important, but it seemed that the main point of the meetings was to tell them how to be cogs in a political machine. He held up a small placard with the names of candidates whom the gang was supporting for alderman and state legislator. There was no discussion of a platform, no list of vital issues. Just an insistence that the young men round up tenants in the projects and tell them how to vote.

When Lenny finished, J.T. told his young members they could leave. I sat for a while with J.T. and Lenny. Lenny looked drained. As he drank a Coke, he said he'd been speaking to at least four or five groups every day.

Lenny was careful to explain that his fees came from personal donations from gang members or their leaders. He wanted to distinguish these monies from the profits the gang made from selling drugs. In theory, I understood that Lenny was trying to convince me that he didn't accept drug money, but I found the distinction almost meaningless. Moreover, the gang leaders had a lot of incentive to pay Lenny to keep their gangs from fighting one another. After all, it was hard to conduct commerce in the midst of a gang war. Younger gang members, however, often wanted to stir things up, mostly to distinguish themselves as fighters. That's why some gang leaders even paid Lenny to discipline their own members. "*Disciplination* is an art form," Lenny said. "One thing I like is to hang a nigger upside down over the freeway as the cars come. Ain't never had a nigger misbehave after I try that one."

J.T. and Lenny talked in nostalgic terms about the gang's recent political engagement. Lenny proudly recalled his own days as a Black King back in the 1970s, describing how he helped get out the vote for "the Eye-talians and Jews" who ran his community. He then described, with equal pride, how the gangs "kicked the Eye-talian and Jewish mafia" out of his ward. Lenny even managed to spin the black takeover of the heroin trade as a boon to the community: it gave local black men jobs, albeit illegal ones, that had previously gone to white men. Lenny also boasted that black drug dealers never sold to children, whereas the previous dealers had exercised no such moral restraint. With all his bombast, he sounded like an older version of J.T.

I asked Lenny about his talk that night, how he could simultaneously preach the virtues of voting and the most responsible way to deal drugs. He said he favored a "nonjudgmental approach" with the gang members. "I tell them, 'Whatever you do, try to do it without pissing people off. Make everything a community thing.'"

About two weeks later, I got to witness this "community thing" in action. I followed four young Black Kings as they went door-to-door in J.T.'s building to register voters.

Shorty-Lee, a twenty-one-year-old gang member, was the head of the delegation. For about an hour, I trailed him on his route. Most of his knocks went unanswered. The few tenants who did sign their names looked as if they just wanted to make the gang members leave as quickly as possible.

At one apartment on the twelfth floor, a middle-aged woman answered the door. She was wearing an apron and wiping her wet hands on a dish towel; she looked surprised to see Shorty-Lee and the others. Door-to-door solicitation hadn't been practiced in the projects for a long time. "We're here to sign you up to vote," Shorty-Lee said.

"Young man, I *am* registered," the woman said calmly.

"No, we didn't say *register!*" Shorty-Lee shouted. "We said *sign up*. I don't care if you're registered."

"But that's what I'm saying." The woman eyed Shorty-Lee curiously. "I already signed up. I'm going to vote in the next primary."

Shorty-Lee was puzzled. He looked over to the three other BKs. They were toting spiral-bound notebooks in which they "signed up" potential voters. But it seemed that neither Lenny nor J.T. had told them that there was an actual registration form and that registrars had to be licensed.

"Look, you need to sign right here," Shorty-Lee said, grabbing one of the notebooks. He was clearly not expecting even this minor level of resistance. "And then we'll tell you who you're going to vote for when the time comes."

"Who I'm going to vote for!" The woman's voice grew sharp. She approached the screen door to take a better look. As she glanced at me, she waved—I recognized her from several parties at J.T.'s mother's apartment. Then she turned back to Shorty-Lee. "You can't tell me who to vote for," she said. "And I don't think that's legal anyway."

"Black Kings say who you need to vote for," Shorty-Lee countered, but he was growing tentative. He turned to his fellow gang members. "Ain't that right? Ain't that what we're supposed to do?" The others shrugged.

"Young man," the woman continued, "have *you* ever voted?"

Shorty-Lee looked at the others, who seemed quite interested in his answer. Then he looked at me. He seemed embarrassed. "No," he said. "I ain't voted yet. But I will."

"Did you know that you can't take anyone in the voting booth with you?" the woman asked him.

"Naw, that's a lie," Shorty-Lee said, puffing out his chest. "They told me that we'll all be voting together. Black Kings vote together. I told you that we'd be telling you who—"

"No, no, no—that's not what I mean," she interrupted. "I mean, first *you* vote. Then your friend votes, and then he votes—if he's old enough." She was staring now at the youngest boy in the group, a new gang member who looked about twelve years old.

"I'm old enough," the boy said, insulted.

"You have to be eighteen," the woman said with a gentle smile. "How old *are* you?"

"I'm Black Kings!" he cried out. "I can vote if I want to."

"Well, you'll probably have to wait," the woman said, by now exasperated. "And, boys, I got food cooking, so I can't talk to you right now. But if you come back, I can tell you all about voting. Okay? It's probably the most important thing you'll do with your life. Next to raising a family."

"Okay." Shorty-Lee shrugged, defeated.

The others also nodded. "Yes, ma'am," one of them muttered, and they walked off. I waved good-bye to the woman, who smiled as if she'd won the victory of a small-town schoolteacher: a promise that her children would learn.

I followed Shorty-Lee and the others down the gallery. None of them seemed to know what should happen next. Shorty-Lee looked pained, struggling to muster some leadership capacity and perhaps save face.

"You know you can't register people until five o'clock?" I said, wanting to break the silence. I was only a few years older than Shorty-Lee, but I found myself feeling strangely parental. "That's what J.T. told me."

J.T. hadn't told me to say this. But I felt so bad for Shorty-Lee that I wanted to give him an out. I figured I could talk to him later, when we were alone, and explain how registration actually worked.

Shorty-Lee gazed out silently through the gallery's chain-link fence.

"It's about two-thirty," I said. "That's probably why the woman said what she said. You should wait awhile before knocking some more. You'll get more people signed up if you wait. Why don't we go to Ms. Turner's and get some hamburgers? You can start again later."

"Yeah, that's cool," Shorty-Lee said, looking relieved. "I'm hungry, too!" He started barking out commands. "Blackie, you got to get back home, though. We'll get you some food. Kenny, hold my shit. Follow me. I'm getting a cheeseburger, if she still has any cheese left."

They ran off toward Ms. Turner's apartment, a makeshift store on the seventh floor where you could buy food, candy, soda, cigarettes, and condoms. I headed back to Ms. Mae's apartment, trying to think of how to tell J.T. about this "voter-registration drive" without laughing.

The door-to-door canvassing was thankfully just a small part of J.T.'s strategy to politicize the gang. I began attending dozens of rallies in high schools and social-service centers where politicians came to encourage young black men and women to get involved in politics. Newspaper reporters often attended these events. I'm sure they were interested in the gang's involvement, but their curiosity was also piqued by the participation of politicians like the Reverend Jesse Jackson, who urged young people to "give up the gun, pick up the ballot."

J.T. told me he never wanted to run for office, but he was certainly attracted to the new contacts he was gaining through the Black Kings' political initiatives. He talked endlessly about the preachers, politicians, and businesspeople he'd been meeting. J.T. knew that Chicago's gangs were politically active in the 1960s and 1970s, pushing for desegregation and housing reform. He told me more than a few times that he was modeling his behavior on those gang leaders'. When I asked for concrete examples of his collaboration with his new allies, he'd vaguely say that "we're working together for the community" or "we're just trying to make things right."

Perhaps, I thought, he didn't trust me yet, or perhaps there *wasn't* anything concrete to talk about. One of the few political activities I saw him directly manage was a series of educational meetings between Lenny Duster of Pride and various high-ranking Chicago gang leaders. Because the police rarely came around to Robert Taylor, it provided a relatively secure site for such meetings. This kept J.T. busy with providing security, keeping tenants out of the way, and otherwise ensuring a safe climate.

He firmly believed that the community would be stronger when the Black Kings entered the mainstream. "You need to talk about our political activities in your work," he told me. "It's part of who I am."

But he also admitted that the "legit" image was vital to the gang's underlying commercial mission: if law-abiding citizens viewed the gang as a politically productive enterprise, they might be less likely to complain about its drug sales. So J.T. continued to order his rank-and-file members to attend these political rallies, and he donated money to social organizations that called for gang members to turn their lives around. More than anything, I realized, J.T. was desperate to be recognized as something other than just a criminal.

I wasn't sure that I believed him. I had trouble seeing exactly how the Black Kings were a useful group to have around. But they did seem to have a few noncriminal ventures, and perhaps, I thought, I would see more down the line. By this point I had gotten a reputation around the U of C as "the Indian guy who hangs out with the gangs." In general this was a positive image, and I saw little reason to change things.

The more time J.T. spent with the citywide Black Kings leadership and their newfound political allies, the less time he had to escort me through the projects. This presented me with the opportunity I'd hoped for: getting to learn a bit more about the community for myself without J.T. watching over me.

Since I still wasn't very familiar with the neighborhood, I didn't stray too far from J.T.'s building. He had repeatedly told me that I wouldn't be safe walking around other parts of Robert Taylor. The longer I hung around the projects, he said, the more likely that I would be associated with his gang. So I would do well to keep to the gang's areas.

Strangely, while most people think of a gang as a threat, for me—an uninitiated person in the projects—the gang represented security. The courtyard in the middle of the three buildings that J.T. controlled was a closely guarded space. His gang members were everywhere: sitting in cars, leaning out of apartments, hanging around the playground and the parking lot. I didn't know most of them well enough to strike up a conversation, but I was familiar enough to receive the local sign for "friend"—a slight nod of the head, perhaps a raised eyebrow.

I wanted to learn more about the gang's influence on the greater community. C-Note and Clarisse had both suggested to me that the gang was simultaneously a nuisance, a source of fear, and an ally. But they were always a bit cagey.

"Oh, you know how J.T. is," Clarisse once said to me. "He's family, and you know what family is like."

"Them niggers are wearing me out, but I ain't gonna be the one to say nothing," C-Note told me, " 'cause they keep things safe around here."

They tended to look at me as if I knew exactly what they meant, which I didn't. But I was eager to figure it out.

I met the Johnson brothers, Kris and Michael, two Robert Taylor tenants known as expert car mechanics and consummate hustlers. They were both in their late thirties, skinny, with boyish faces, and they always had a positive outlook. Kris had been a promising baseball player until his career was ended by injury. Michael was a musician who'd never gained the level of success he sought. Now they both wanted good full-time jobs but couldn't find steady work. Their lives had been an odyssey of drug addiction, street hustling, jail time, and homelessness. For them, and other underemployed men like them, the projects were a refuge: a familiar home turf with at least a few slivers of opportunity.

These days the Johnson brothers repaired cars in various parking lots around the Robert Taylor Homes. Although J.T. was the ultimate authority in the neighborhood, Kris and Michael also had to strike a deal with C-Note, who was the nominal ruler of the local auto-repair trade. Sometimes C-Note did repair work himself. When he was too tired, he subcontracted it out to people like the Johnson brothers. In return he took a small cut of their profits and let the gang know that the Johnsons were operating with his blessing.

Kris and Michael had set up shop on Federal Street, in the corner of a parking lot littered with garbage and broken glass. About twenty yards down the street, next to an open fire hydrant, they were also running a car wash. The Johnson brothers always attracted a crowd.

"You want me to talk?" Kris asked me. "Then you need to find me some work, find me a customer!"

I was happy to oblige. Walking into the middle of Federal Street, I helped them flag down cars. Then Kris would approach the driver. "You need a wash?" he'd ask. Or, "Looks like your brakes are squeaking, ma'am. Why don't you step outside and let me take a look." Kris and Michael would charm the drivers until they broke down and agreed to have their cars looked at. If that failed, one brother would let the air out of the tires while the other brother occupied the driver. The more beer they drank, the more creative they became.

Toward the end of one hot summer day, T-Bone, one of J.T.'s senior officers, drove up to the car wash in a bright green Chevy Malibu. The Malibu seemed to be the thug's car of choice. Behind

T-Bone was a line of cars waiting for a wash, most of them classic gang vehicles—Malibus, Caprices, Lincoln Town Cars—all with shiny rims and bright paint jobs.

"Every week we need to wash their shit," Michael muttered. "What can you do?" The gang apparently taxed the brothers in the form of free car washes. He grabbed a bucket of soapy water and shouted for Kris to come help. But Kris, his head buried in the hood of a customer's car, shouted back that he was busy. So I offered to help.

When T-Bone saw me jog over with some clean rags, he nearly fell down laughing. "Oh, shit! Next thing he'll be moving in with them!" he said. "Hey, Sweetness, how much you paying the Professor?"

"Ain't paying nothing," answered Michael (a.k.a. Sweetness, apparently). "I'm giving him an education."

This made T-Bone laugh even harder. T-Bone and I got along pretty well, and unlike other members of the gang, he would routinely strike up a conversation with me. He was attending Kennedy-King College, a South Side community college, majoring in accounting. That's why J.T. had put him in charge of the gang's finances. T-Bone had two talkative, precocious children and the appearance of a nerd: he wore big, metal-framed glasses, always carried a notebook (which contained the gang's financial records, I would later learn), and constantly asked me about life at the U of C. "Hope it's harder than where I'm at," he'd say. "I'm getting A's, and I haven't had to pay nobody off yet!"

A commotion rose up from the parking lot where Kris was working: he had gotten into a fight with a customer. Even from afar I could see the veins popping on Kris's face. He kept trying to grab the other man's neck, and the other man kept pushing Kris backward. The other man kneed Kris in the stomach, sending him to the ground, and then Kris picked up a rock and hit his combatant in the head. Now both of them were on the ground, writhing and yelling.

Michael and T-Bone hurried over. "Nigger, not around here!" T-Bone said, laughing at the fairly pathetic display of fighting. "I told you about keeping this shit peaceful."

"It will be peaceful as long as he pays up," Kris said.

"Pays up?" the other man said. "He can finish, then I'll pay. Twenty bucks to fix my radiator? Fuck that! He got to do more than that for twenty."

"Nigger, I already washed the damn car," Kris said. He stood up, wincing. "You took this shit too far. I'm not doing nothing else for twenty bucks." Kris picked up a wrench and hit the man in the leg. The man groaned in pain, his face swollen with anger, and it looked as if he was going to go after Kris.

T-Bone grabbed Kris, even though he could barely keep himself from laughing. "Damn! What did I tell you? Lay that shit down. Now come over here."

T-Bone walked the two men over to the edge of the parking lot. They were both limping. Soon after, Kris started washing T-Bone's car while the other man sat on the ground, nursing his leg.

"I'll teach that nigger!" Kris said to himself loudly. "No one messes with me."

T-Bone walked over to Michael and me. "Nigger was right," he said, pointing to Kris. "He washed the man's car and fixed the radiator. And that costs twenty dollars. He don't need to do nothing else. I got the money for you. And five bucks extra for the hassle."

T-Bone handed Michael the money, slapped my face gently, winked, and hummed a song as he walked off. Michael didn't say anything.

That night, once it was too dark to work on cars, I sat with Michael and Kris by their beat-up white Subaru, and we drank some beers. Michael told me that T-Bone often settled customer disputes for them.

"Why would he do that?" I asked.

"Because we pay him to!" Michael said. "I mean, we don't have a choice."

Michael explained that he and Kris paid T-Bone 15 percent of their weekly revenue. Just as J.T.'s foot soldiers squeezed a little money from squatters and prostitutes, his higher-ranked officers supplemented their income with more substantial taxes. In return, the gang brought Kris and Michael customers and mediated any disputes. This occasionally included beating up a customer who became re-calcitrant or abusive. "That happens once a month," Kris said with satisfaction. "Best way to teach people not to fuck with us."

I asked Michael and Kris whether beating one customer might in fact deter other customers. The reply taught me a lot about the Black Kings.

"When *you* got a problem, I bet you call the police, right?" Michael said. "Well, we call the Kings. I call T-Bone because I don't have anyone else to call."

"But you *could* call the police," I said. "I don't understand why you can't call them if something goes wrong."

"If I'm out here hustling, or if you're in the building hustling, there's no police officer who's going to do what T-Bone does for us," Michael said. "Every hustler tries to have someone who offers them protection. I don't care if you're selling socks or selling your ass. You need someone to back you up."

"See, we were both Black Kings when we were younger," Kris said. "Most of the people you see, the older ones who live right here? They were Kings at one time. So it's complicated. I mean, if you own a business on Forty-seventh Street, you pay taxes and you get protection—from the police, from the aldermen—"

I interrupted Kris to ask why they'd need protection from the *aldermen*. He looked at me as if I was naïve—which I was—and explained that the aldermen's line workers, or "precinct captains," liked to tax any off-the-books entrepreneurial activity. "So instead we pay the gang, and the gang protects us."

"But it's more than that," Michael said. "I mean, you're stuck. These niggers make your life hell, but they're family. And you can't choose your family!" He started to laugh so hard that he nearly spilled his beer.

"Just imagine," Kris prodded me. "Let's say another gang came by and started shooting. Or let's say you got a bunch of niggers that get into the building and go and rob a bunch of people. Who's going to take care of that? Police? They never come around! So you got J.T. and the Kings. They'll get your stuff back if it was stolen. They'll protect you so that no niggers can come and shoot up the place."

Kris and Michael really seemed to believe, although with some reservations, that the gang was their extended family. Skeptical as I may have been, the gang plainly *was* looked upon as something other than a purely destructive force. I remembered what J.T. had told me a while back, a pronouncement that hadn't made much sense at the time: "The gang and the building," he had said, "are the same."

One hot afternoon, while hanging out in the lobby of J.T.'s building with some tenants and a few BKs, I saw another side of the relationship between the gang and the community. Outside the building a car was blasting rap music. A basketball game had just finished, and to combat the heat a few dozen people were drinking beer and enjoying the breeze off the lake.

I heard a woman shouting, maybe fifty yards away, in a small grove of oak trees. It was one of the few shady areas on the premises. The trees predated Robert Taylor and would likely be standing long after the projects were gone. The music was too loud for me to make out what the woman was saying, and so I—along with quite a few other people—hurried over.

Several men were physically restraining the woman, who looked to be in her forties. "Let go of me!" she screamed. "I'm going to kick his ass! Just let me at him. Let go!"

"No, baby," one of the men said, trying to calm her down. "You can't do it that way, you can't take care of it like that. Let us handle it."

"Hey, Price!" another man shouted. "Price, come over here."

Price had been a Black Kings member for many years and had a wide range of expertise. At present he was in charge of the gang's security, which matched up well with his love of fighting. He was tall and lanky, and he took his job very seriously. He strode over now to the screaming woman, trailed by a few Black Kings foot soldiers. I waved at Price, and he didn't seem to mind that I had put myself close to the action.

"What's going on?" he asked the men. "Why is Boo-Boo scream-ing like that?"

"She said the Ay-rab at the store fucked her baby," one man told him. "He gave her baby some disease."

Price spoke softly to her, trying to calm her down. I asked a young woman next to me what was going on. She said that Boo-Boo thought the proprietor of a nearby corner store had slept with her teenage daughter and given her a sexually transmitted disease. There were several such stores in the neighborhood, all of them run by Arab Americans. "She wants to beat the shit out of that Ay-rab," the woman told me. "She was just on her way over to the store to see that man."

By now about a hundred people had gathered around. We all

watched Price talking to Boo-Boo while one of the men locked Boo-Boo's arms behind her back. Suddenly he let her go, and Boo-Boo marched off toward the store, with Price beside her and a pack of tenants following behind. "Kick his ass, Boo-Boo!" someone hollered. There were other riled shouts: "Don't let them Ay-rabs do this to us!" and "Price, kill that boy!"

We arrived at a small, decrepit store known as Crustie's. The name wasn't posted anywhere, but the usual signs were: CIGARETTES SOLD HERE and FOOD STAMPS WELCOME and PLEASE DO NOT LOITER. By the time I arrived, Boo-Boo was already inside yelling, but it was hard to hear what she was saying. I moved closer to the entrance. Now I could see Boo-Boo taking boxes and cans of food off the shelves and throwing them, but I couldn't see her target. Price leaned against the refrigerator case, wearing a serious look. Then Boo-Boo reached for a big glass bottle, and Price grabbed her before she could throw it.

A few minutes later, a man ran outside. He looked to be Middle Eastern; he waved his arms and shouted in what I assumed was Arabic. He was in his early forties, clean-cut, with a short-sleeved, collared shirt. He broke through the crowd, pushing people aside. Some pushed back, but he managed to unlock his car and get inside.

But Boo-Boo followed him. She started throwing liquor bottles at the car. One burst on the hood, another missed entirely. The crowd started hooting, and some of the men grabbed her. We all watched as the car sped off, with Boo-Boo falling down in the middle of the street, still screaming, "You raped my baby girl! You raped her, you Ay-rab!"

Price walked slowly out of the store, accompanied by an older man I recognized as the store's manager. He also looked Middle Eastern and wore a striped dress shirt and khakis. He had a weary look about him, as if running a store in this neighborhood had taken a grave toll. He was talking quietly while Price stared straight ahead, nodding once in a while; the manager appeared to be pleading his case. Finally they shook hands, and Price moved aside, his foot soldiers trailing him.

Then the manager started to carry out cases of soda and beer, leaving them on the sidewalk. The crowd pounced. Most people grabbed just a few cans or bottles, but some were tough enough to wrest away a six-pack or two. The manager hauled out more and more cases, and these disappeared just as fast. He set them down with little emotion, although occasionally he'd glance at the crowd, as if he were feeding birds in a park, and wipe the sweat off his brow. When our eyes met, he just shook his head, shrugged, and walked back inside.

Price watched from a distance. I saw him speaking with Ms. Bailey, a woman in her late fifties who was the tenant president of the building where J.T. lived. I had met Ms. Bailey a few times already. She smiled now as I approached, then grabbed my hand and pulled me into a hug. She turned back to Price.

"We can't have people treat women like that, baby," she said to him. "You-all know that."

"I know, Ms. Bailey," Price said, exasperated. "Like I said, I'm taking care of it. But if *you* want to do it, go ahead!"

"I'll deal with it in my own way, but for now I want you to talk with him tomorrow, okay?"

"Okay, Ms. Bailey, we're on it," Price said matter-of-factly. "J.T. or I will take care of it."

Ms. Bailey started yelling at a few women who stood arguing with the store manager. "Everyone get your pop and get out of here," she said. "And you-all leave this man alone. He ain't the one you're looking for." She walked the manager inside and again told everyone to go home.

I caught up with Price and asked him to explain what had happened.

"That Ay-rab slept with Coco," he said with a smirk. "But he didn't give her no disease. That little girl got that herself—she's a whore. Sixteen and she's been around already."

"So what was all that about, then?" I asked. "Why the screaming, and what's up with the beer and soda?"

"Like I said, the man was sleeping with Coco, but he was giving her diapers and shit for Coco's baby." I had heard rumors that some store owners gave women free food and household items in exchange for sex. Some residents were very upset at the practice. In fact, I heard Ms. Mae regularly plead with J.T. to put a stop to this behavior. J.T.'s answer to his mother was nearly identical to what Price now told me: "You can't stop that shit. It's been happening like that for the longest time. It's just how people do things around here."

I asked Price what his role had been today. "I told Boo-Boo that I would go over to the store with her and let her yell at that man," he said. "She said she was going to cut off his dick, take a picture of it, and put it up everywhere. He freaked out. That's why he ran. Then I told his brother, the one who owns the store, that he had to do something, 'cause people would burn the store down if he didn't. He said he'd put all the soda and beer he had on the sidewalk if people would leave the store alone. I told him, 'Cool.' But I told him that I needed to speak with him tomorrow, because I don't want Boo-Boo killing his little brother, which she *will* do. So tomorrow we'll figure all this shit out so no one gets hurt."

I was just about to ask Price why he was responsible for mediating a dispute like this. But he preempted me. "That's what BKs are about," he said. "We just help keep the peace. We take care of our community."

This explanation didn't satisfy me, and I wanted to talk to J.T.

about it. But he was so busy these days that I barely saw him—and when I did, he was usually with other gang leaders, working on the political initiatives that the BKs were putting together.

And then, just before Labor Day, J.T.'s efforts to impress his superiors started to bear fruit. He told me that he was heading south for a few days. The highest-ranking BK leaders met downstate every few months, and J.T. had been invited to his first big meeting.

The Black Kings were a large regional gang, with factions as far north as Milwaukee, southward to St. Louis, east to Cleveland, and west to Iowa. I was surprised when J.T. first mentioned that the gang operated in Iowa. He told me that most Chicago gangs tried to recruit local dealers there, usually by hanging out at a high-school basketball or football game. But Iowa wasn't very profitable. Chicago gang leaders got frustrated at how "country" their Iowa counterparts were, even in places like Des Moines. They were undisciplined, they gave away too much product for free, they drank too much, and sometimes they plain forgot to go to work. But the Iowa market was large enough that most Chicago gangs, including the Black Kings, kept trying.

J.T. had made clear to me his ambition to move up in the gang's hierarchy, and this regional meeting was clearly a step in that direction.

In his absence, he told me, I could hang out as much as I wanted around his building. He said he'd let his foot soldiers know they should be expecting me, and he left me with his usual caution: "Don't walk too far from the building. I won't be able to help you."

After J.T. told me about his plans, I was both excited and nervous. I had hung around Robert Taylor without him, but usually only for a few hours at a stretch. Now I would have more time to walk around, and I hoped to meet more people who could tell me about the gang from their perspective. I knew I had to be careful with the line of questioning, but at last I'd been granted an opportunity to get out from under J.T.'s thumb and gain a wider view of the Black Kings.

I immediately ran into a problem. Because I'd been spending so much time with the Black Kings, a lot of the tenants wouldn't speak to me except for a quick hello or a bland comment about the weather. They plainly saw me as affiliated with the BKs, and just as plainly they didn't want to get involved with me.

Ms. Bailey, the building president, was one of the few tenants willing to talk. Her small, two-room office was located in J.T.'s building, where she lived as well. This was in the northern end of the Robert Taylor Homes, sometimes called "Robert Taylor A." A few miles away, at the southern end of the complex, was "Taylor B," where a different group of gangs and tenant leaders held the power. On most dimensions daily life was the same in Taylor A and Taylor B: they had similar rates of poverty and drug abuse, for instance, and similar levels of gang activity and crime.

But there was at least one big difference, Ms. Bailey told me, which was that Taylor B had a large Boys & Girls Club where hundreds of young people could shoot pool, play basketball, use the library, and participate in youth programs. Ms. Bailey was jealous that Taylor A had no such facility. Even though Taylor B was walking distance from Taylor A, gang boundaries made it hard to move freely even if you had nothing to do with a gang. It was usually teenagers who got hassled when they crossed over, but even adults could have trouble. They might get searched by a gang sentry when they tried to enter a high-rise that wasn't their own; they might also get robbed.

The best Ms. Bailey could offer the children in Taylor A were three run-down apartments that had been converted into playrooms.

These spaces were pathetic: water dripped from the ceilings, rats and roaches ran free, the bathrooms were rancid; all these playrooms had were a few well-worn board games, some stubby crayons, and an old TV set. Even so, whenever I visited, I saw that the children played with as much enthusiasm as if they were at Disney World.

One afternoon Ms. Bailey suggested that I visit the Boys & Girls Club in Taylor B. "Maybe with your connections you could help us raise money for a club like that in our area," she said.

I told her I'd be happy to help if I could. That Ms. Bailey saw me, a middle-class graduate student, as having "connections" said a lot about how alienated her community was from the powerful people in philanthropy and government who could actually make a difference.

Since Taylor B was controlled by the Disciples, a rival to J.T.'s Black Kings, Ms. Bailey personally walked me over to the Boys & Girls Club and introduced me to Autry Harrison, one of the club's directors.

Autry was about thirty years old, six foot two, and thin as a rail. He wore large, round glasses too big for his face and greeted me with a big smile and a handshake. "You got any skills, young man?" he asked brightly.

"I can read and write, but that's about it," I said.

Autry led me into the poolroom and yelled at a dozen little kids to come over. "This young man is going to read a book to you," he said, "and then I'd like you to talk about it with him." He whispered to me, "Many of their parents just can't read."

From that day forward, Autry was happy to have me at the club. I quickly got to know him well. He had grown up in Robert Taylor, served in the army, and, like a few caring souls of his generation, returned to his neighborhood to work with young people. Recently he'd gone back to school to study criminal justice at Chicago State

University and was working part-time there as a research assistant to a professor who was studying gangs. Autry was married, with a three-year-old daughter. Because of his obligations at the club and at home, he told me, he sometimes had to drop classes and even take a leave of absence from school.

In his youth Autry had made his fair share of bad choices: he'd been a pimp and a gang member, for instance, and he had engaged in criminal activity. He'd also suffered the effects of project living—he'd been beaten up, had his money stolen, watched friends get shot and die in a gang war.

Autry sometimes sat for hours, leaning back in a chair with his skinny arms propped behind his head, telling me the lessons he'd learned from his days as a pimp. These included "Never sleep with your ladies," "Always let them borrow money, because you got the power when they owe you shit," and "If you *do* sleep with them, always, always, always wear a condom, even when you're shaking their hand, because you just never know where they've been."

We got along well, and Autry became a great source of information for me on how project residents viewed the gang. The club, it turned out, wasn't a refuge only for children. Senior citizens played cards there, religious folks gathered for fellowship, and social workers and doctors provided free counseling and medical care. Just like many of the hustlers I'd been speaking to, Autry felt that the gang did help the community—giving away food, mediating conflicts, et cetera—but he also stressed that the community spent a lot of time "mopping up the gang's mistakes."

"What do you mean?" I asked.

"They kill, sometimes for the most stupid reasons," he said. "'You spoke to my girlfriend. . . .' 'You walked down the sidewalk in my territory. . . .' 'You looked at me funny— That's it, I'll kill you!'"

"So it's not always fights about drugs?"

"Are you kidding me?" He laughed. "See, the gang always says it's a business, and it is. But a fifteen-year-old around here is just like any fifteen-year-old. They want to be noticed. They don't get any attention at home, so they rebel. And at the club we're always mopping up their mistakes."

"How does that work?"

"Well, we settle shit when it gets out of hand. Like the other day—Barry knifed somebody from a different gang because the other boy was hanging out near his building. Just for hanging out! So I called my friend Officer Reggie, and we let the two fight it out."

"Fight it out? I thought you said you *settled* it."

"We did. That's how you settle shit sometimes. Let boys fight each other—no guns, no knives. Then you tell them, 'Okay, you-all see that you can fight without killing each other?' "

Autry told me that the club played a broad peacekeeping role in the community. He and other staff members worked with school authorities, social workers, and police officers to informally mediate all kinds of problems, rather than ushering young men and women into the criminal-justice system. The police regularly brought shoplifters, vandals, and car thieves to the club, where Autry and the others would negotiate the return of stolen property as well as, perhaps, some kind of restitution.

I never saw any of these mediations in person. Autry just told me about them after the fact. It didn't seem as if he were lying, but perhaps bragging a little. He told me that he even invited rival gang leaders to the club late at night to resolve their conflicts. My conversations with Autry were a bit like some of my conversations with J.T.: it was not always easy to independently verify their claims.

One busy morning Autry surprised me by asking if I wanted to come to a private meeting at the club later that day. He explained that a few neighborhood organizations were planning a midnight basketball league.

It would be open to all teenagers, but the real goal was to attract gang members. Local community leaders liked the idea of getting unruly teens to play basketball at the club instead of spending their nights on the street. For the young men, the price of admission was to sit through a motivational speech by a pastor or some other speaker before each game. In exchange, the teenagers would get free sneakers, T-shirts, and the chance to win a trophy.

Autry's work would soon command wide attention, when the Clinton administration used the Chicago midnight basketball league as a model for a nationwide movement. In reality there was only anecdotal evidence that the leagues reduced teenage violence, but in a climate where few programs were successful on any level, policy makers were eager to showcase an uplifting idea like midnight basketball.

When I showed up at the club that afternoon, Autry was sitting at a table bearing coffee and doughnuts, a handmade sign behind him on the wall: MIDNIGHT BASKETBALL MEETING IN CONFERENCE ROOM.

"Welcome, Sudhir," Autry said, beaming. "Everyone is inside." He mentioned the names of several tenant leaders, pastors, a Nation of Islam official, an ex–police officer. The basketball league was turning into a big deal for Autry. It represented his entrée into the elite group of community leaders, whom Autry very much wanted to join.

"You sure they won't mind if I sit in?" I asked.

"Not at all," Autry said, shuffling some papers. "And the niggers won't mind either."

"Who?" I asked.

"Man, we got them all!" He rubbed his hands together excitedly.

"We got *all* the leaders—Disciples, Black Kings, MCs, Stones. Everyone is coming!"

"You didn't tell me they'd be there," I said meekly.

Autry could tell I was concerned. "Don't worry. Just sit in the back and keep your mouth shut. I'll say you're with me. But help me with these first." He handed me three sets of flyers that needed to be passed out to everyone. One of them was titled "Rules for Buy-In," which specified the mandatory donation of each sponsoring "organization." Each gang was expected to contribute five thousand dollars and field four teams of ten players. The money would be used to pay for the referees, uniforms, and the cost of keeping the gym open at night.

"You're getting the gangs to pay for this?" I asked. "That doesn't bother you?"

"What would you rather that they do with their money?"

"Good point," I said. "But something doesn't feel right about it."

"I see." Autry put down the flyers and pulled a cigarette from his shirt pocket. "Two thousand niggers in this project making money by selling that poison, killing each other, killing everyone who buys it. We can't do *nothing* about it. And now we tell them that if they want to be selling that shit, they have to give back. They have to step up. And you look at *us* funny? It's them you should be asking these questions to."

"I would if I knew them," I said.

"Don't lie to me, nigger."

Autry knew I was on good terms with J.T., although I'd been cagey about the extent of our relationship. Many times he'd told me I needed to have the courage to ask J.T. more difficult questions about the gang, even if it would upset him. "At least you can ask *one* of these niggers the question," he said. "And he'll be here tonight." Autry let out a loud laugh and went outside to smoke his cigarette.

Shit. It would be the first time I'd seen J.T. in several weeks. I was usually careful to ask his permission before attending any event involving gangs, both to show respect and because I needed a patron. Otherwise, as he always told me, my personal safety couldn't be guaranteed.

I decided to wait outside the club to talk to J.T. when he arrived. Autry offered to wait with me. We stood on the sidewalk and watched the busy, noisy traffic along Federal Street. The club sat in the shadow of a project high-rise. You could hear people yelling from the sidewalk up to the open windows—there was no intercom system—and you could smell the smoke of marijuana and menthol cigarettes.

Before long, J.T. and the leaders of the other gangs began pulling up with their respective security entourages. The scene was straight out of a gangsta-rap video. Each vehicle—there were sports cars, fancy trucks, and one long, purple Lincoln Continental—was immaculate, rims sparkling from a fresh wash. They drove up in a line, as if in a funeral procession, parking across the street from the club. The first man out of each car was a bodyguard, even if the gang leader was the one who drove.

Autry crossed the street, as nonchalantly as his excitement allowed, to ensure them that the club was safe, neutral territory. They were all dressed similarly: new tracksuits, white sneakers, and plenty of gold on their wrists and around their necks. As they approached, each leader was trailed by one or two bodyguards, with another one or two staying behind with the cars. All the bodyguards wore sunglasses and baseball caps.

J.T. noticed me standing there and pushed his bodyguards aside. "You-all go in!" he shouted to the other gang leaders, "I'll see you in a bit." Then he turned to me. He shrugged his shoulders and glared, the universal signal for "What the fuck?"

Autry intervened before I could answer. "Hey, man," he said, "no worries, he's with me."

"He's with *you*?!" J.T. wasn't smiling. "You *know* him?"

"Yeah, big boss man, today he's with me." Autry smiled, his front teeth glistening as he leaned over and hugged J.T.

"Oh, so he's with you now," J.T. repeated, shaking his head. He pulled out a cigarette, and Autry lit it for him.

"Sorry," I said, "I haven't seen you in a while. Autry and I just met, and he said I could come to this meeting. I should've told you."

"Yeah, the brother didn't mean nothing," Autry said. "Not a big deal. No taping today, right, my brother?" Autry loved to walk into a room with me at the club and yell, "Sudhir is from the university, and he'll be taping everything you say today!"

"Not a big deal?" J.T. said, turning to Autry. "You're more ignorant than I thought you were. You pulled all these people together, and you're going to fuck it up like this."

"Whoa, my brother. Like I said, he's with me."

"And what if he comes by *my* building? Is he with you then? Huh? Is he with you then, nigger?"

"Fuck, no!" Autry laughed. "Then he's with *you*! 'Cause I ain't stepping *foot* in that motherfucker. Hell no!"

Autry ducked inside, grinning broadly. He seemed to be having great fun.

"That's what I thought," J.T. said, turning to me. "If you walk in there, the first time all these other niggers see you, then you're with Autry, not me. You didn't think about that, did you? You're a motherfucking impatient nigger. And an ignorant one, from where I stand. You walk in there and I can't do nothing for you. No more. So it's up to you."

"I didn't think about any of this," I apologized. "I didn't know how—"

"Yeah, nigger, you didn't *think*." J.T. started walking inside. "Like I said, you're with me or you're with someone else. You decide."

Inside, I could see Autry, giggling at me. "Come in, boy!" he yelled. "Come in, little baby! You scared?"

I decided I wasn't willing to jeopardize my relationship with J.T., even if it meant missing an opportunity to learn more about the community and the gangs. So I turned and walked away. I started toward the university, and then I stopped. The last time I'd had an uncomfortable episode with J.T.—his beat-down of C-Note—I'd made a mistake. I'd waited too long before speaking to him about it. That made it harder to get a satisfying explanation. So this time I headed straight for J.T.'s building, figuring he'd go there when the meeting was over.

He did. He still seemed upset and started yelling at his mother. "No one understands what I deal with!" he said. "No one listens and does what I say." He sent his bodyguards out to buy some beer. He sat on the recliner and grabbed the remote control. He barely glanced at me.

"You pissed at me?" I asked.

"What the fuck have you been doing around here?" he asked.

I explained that Ms. Bailey had introduced me to Autry and that I was interested in what went on at the club. He seemed surprised that he no longer knew all the specifics about the people I was meeting. "I guess you were going to make some friends while I was gone," he said, and then he asked a question I'd been hoping he'd never ask: "What exactly are you doing around here? I mean, what are you writing about?"

He started changing channels on the TV. It was the first time I'd ever been with him when he didn't look me in the eye.

"Well, honestly, I'm . . . I'm fascinated by how you do what you do," I stammered. "Like I said before, I'm trying to understand how your mind works, why you decided to come back to the neighborhood and run this organization, what you have to do to make it. But if I don't get out and see how others look at you, how you have this incredible effect on other people, then I'll never really understand what you do. So while you were gone, I thought I'd branch out."

"You mean you're asking people what they think about *me*?" Now he had turned to look at me again.

"Well, not really, because you know they would probably not feel comfortable telling me. I'm at stage one. I'm trying to understand what the organization does and how people have to deal with it. If you piss people off, how do they respond? Do they call the police? Do they call you?"

"Okay. So it's how others work *with me*."

He seemed appeased, so I was quick to affirm. "Yes! How others work with you. That's a great way of putting it." I hoped he wouldn't ask what "stage two" was, for I had no idea. I felt a little uneasy letting him think that I was actually writing his biography, but at the moment I just wanted to buy myself some time.

He checked his watch. "All right, I need to get some sleep." He got up and walked toward his bedroom without saying good-bye. In the kitchen Ms. Mae kissed me good night, and I walked to the bus stop.

J.T. was a little cool toward me the next few times I saw him. So to warm things up, I stopped going to the club and spent nearly all my time in and around J.T.'s building. I was unhappy to be missing the opportunity to see how Autry worked with other people behind the scenes on important community issues, but I didn't want to further anger J.T. I just told Autry that I'd be busy for a few weeks but I'd be back once I got settled in with my course work in the coming fall semester.

Soon after the school year began, a young boy and girl in Robert Taylor were shot, accidental victims of a drive-by gang shooting. The boy was eight, the girl nine. They both spent time in the hospital, and then the girl died. The shooting occurred at the border of Taylor A and Taylor B. J.T.'s gang had been on the receiving end of the shooting, with several members injured. The shooters were from the Disciples, who operated out of the projects near the Boys & Girls Club.

This single shooting had a widespread effect. Worried that a full-scale gang war would break out, parents began keeping their children inside, which meant taking time off from work or otherwise adjusting their schedules. Senior citizens worried about finding a safe way to get medical treatment. Local churches mobilized to deliver food to families too scared to walk to the store.

Ms. Bailey told me about a meeting at the Boys & Girls Club where the police would address concerned parents and tenant leaders. If I really wanted to see how the gang's actions affected the broader community, Ms. Bailey said, I should be there.

I asked J.T., and he thought it was a good idea, even though he never bothered with such things. "The police don't do nothing for us," he said. "You should understand that by now." Then he muttered something about how the community "takes care of its problems," mentioning the incident I'd seen with Boo-Boo, Price, and the Middle Eastern store manager.

The meeting was held late one weekday morning. The streets outside the club were quiet, populated by a smattering of unemployed people, gang members, and drug addicts. The leaves had already changed, but the day was unseasonably warm.

Autry was busy as usual, running to and fro making sure every-thing was ready. Although I hadn't seen him in some time, he shot me a friendly glance. The meeting was held in a large, windowless concrete room with a linoleum floor. There were perhaps forty ten-ants in attendance—all fanning themselves, since the heat was turned up too high. "If we turn it off, we can't get it back on right away," Autry told me. "And then it's May by the time you get it back on."

At the front of the room, several uniformed police officers and police officials sat behind a long table. Ms. Bailey nodded me toward a seat beside her, up front and off to one side.

The meeting was an exercise in chaos. Residents shouted past one another while the police officials begged for calm. A mother holding her infant yelled that she was "sick and tired of living like this." The younger and middle-aged parents were the most vocal. The senior citizens sat quietly, many of them with Bibles in their hands, looking as if they were ready for church. Nor did the police have much to say, other than platitudes about their continued efforts to disrupt the gangs and requests for tenants to start cooperating with them by reporting gang crimes.

After about forty-five minutes, the police looked very ready to leave. So did the tenants. As the meeting broke up, some of them waved their hands dismissively at the cops.

"Are these meetings always so crazy?" I asked Ms. Bailey.

"This is how it goes," she said. "We yell at them, they say noth-ing. Everyone goes back to doing what they were doing."

"I don't see what you get out of this. It seems like a waste of time."

Ms. Bailey just patted my knee and said, "Mm-hmm."

"I mean it," I said. "This is ridiculous. Where I grew up, you'd have an army of cops all over the place. But nothing is going on here. Doesn't that upset you?"

By now the room had cleared out except for Ms. Bailey and a few other tenant leaders, Autry, and one policeman, Officer Johnson, a tall black man who worked out of a nearby precinct. He was well groomed, with a short mustache and graying hair. They were all checking their watches and speaking quietly to one another.

I was about to leave when Ms. Bailey walked over. "In two hours come back here," she said. "But now you have to go."

Autry smiled and winked as he passed. What was he up to? I knew that Autry was still trying to groom himself as a local power broker, but I didn't know how much power, if any, he had actually accrued.

As instructed, I left for a while and took a walk around the neighborhood. When I returned to the club, Autry silently pointed me toward the room where the earlier meeting had been held. Inside, I saw Ms. Bailey and some other building presidents; Officer Johnson and Autry's friend Officer Reggie, a well-liked cop who had grown up in Robert Taylor; and Pastor Wilkins, who was said to be a long-standing expert in forging gang truces. Autry, I knew, saw himself as Pastor Wilkins's eventual successor.

They were all milling about, shaking hands and chatting softly before settling into the folding metal chairs Autry had arranged. A few of them looked at me with a bit of surprise as I sat down, but no one said anything.

And then, to *my* great surprise, I saw J.T., sitting with a few of his senior officers along one wall. Although our eyes didn't meet, I could tell that he noticed me.

Even more surprising was the group on the other side of the room: a gang leader named Mayne, who ran the Disciples, accompanied by *his* officers, leaning quietly against the wall.

I took a good look at Mayne. He was a heavyset man with a crumpled face, like a bulldog's. He appeared bored and irritated, and he kept issuing instructions to his men: "Nigger, get me a cigarette." "Boy, get me a chair."

Autry walked into the room. "Okay!" he shouted. "The club is closed, let's get going. Kids are going to come back at five."

Officer Reggie stood up. "Let's get moving," he said. "Ms. Bailey, you wanted to start. Go ahead." He walked toward the back of the room.

"First, J.T., get the other men out of the room," she said. "You, too, Mayne."

Mayne and J.T. both motioned for their senior officers to leave, and they did, walking out slowly with stoic faces. Ms. Bailey stood silently until they were gone. Then she took a deep breath. "Pastor, you said you had an idea, something you wanted to ask these young men?"

"Yes, Ms. Bailey," Pastor Wilkins said. He stood up. "Now, I know how this began. Shorties probably fighting over some girl, right? And it got all the way to shooting each other. That's crazy! I mean, I can understand if you were fighting over business, but you're killing people around here because of a spat in school!"

"We're defending our honor," Mayne said. "Ain't nothing more important than that."

"Yeah," said J.T. "And it *is* about business. Those guys come shooting down on our end, scaring people away."

Pastor Wilkins asked Mayne and J.T. to describe how the fight had escalated. Pastor Wilkins's original guess was mostly right: two teenage boys at DuSable High School got into a fight over a girl. One boy was in J.T.'s gang, the other in Mayne's. Over the course of a few weeks, the conflict escalated from unarmed to armed—first a knife fight and then the drive-by shooting. The shooting occurred during the afternoon, while kids were playing outside after school.

J.T. said that because his customers had been scared off since the shooting, and because tenants in his buildings were angry about their lives being interrupted, he wanted Mayne to pay a penalty.

Mayne argued that the shooting took place at the border of the two gangs' territory, near a park that neither gang claimed. Therefore, he argued, J.T. was ineligible for compensation.

My mind raced as they spoke. I couldn't believe that a religious leader and a police officer were not only watching this mediation but were actually *facilitating* it. What incentive did they have to do so—and what would happen if people from the community found out they were helping gang leaders settle their disputes? I was also struck by how levelheaded everyone seemed, even J.T. and Mayne, as if they'd been through this before. These were the same two gang leaders, after all, who had been trying to kill each other, quite literally, with drive-by shootings. I wondered if one of them might even pull a gun here at any moment. Perhaps the very strangest thing was how sanguine the community leaders were about the fact that these men sold crack cocaine for a living. But at this moment it seemed that pragmatism was more important than moralism.

After a while the conversation got bogged down, with J.T. and Mayne merely restating their positions. Autry jumped in to try to refocus things. "How much you think you lost?" he asked J.T. "I mean, you don't need to tell me the amount, but how many days did you lose business?"

"Probably a few days, maybe a week," J.T. said.

"Okay, well, we're going to bank this," Autry said. "Put it in the bank."

"What the fuck does that mean?" Mayne asked.

"Nigger, that means you messed up," Autry told him. "J.T. didn't retaliate, did he? I mean, he didn't shoot over at you. It was just you shooting down at his end, right? So J.T. gets to sell his shit in the park for a week. The next time this happens, and J.T. fucks up, you get to sell *your* shit in the park for a week."

Ms. Bailey spoke up. "You-all do not get to sell nothing when the kids are there, okay? Just late at night."

"Sounds fine to me," J.T. said. Mayne nodded in agreement.

"Then we have a truce," Pastor Wilkins said. He walked over to J.T. and Mayne. "Shake on it."

J.T. and Mayne shook hands, not warmly and not willing to look at each other. The pastor and Ms. Bailey each let out a sigh.

As J.T., Mayne, and Pastor Wilkins sat down to work out the details of the deal, I walked out front. There was Autry, smoking a cigarette on the sidewalk. He shook his head; he looked fatigued.

"This stuff is hard, isn't it?" I asked.

"Yeah, I try to block out the fact that they could get pissed at me and kill me if I say something they don't like. You never know if they'll go home and think you're working for the other side."

"You ever get hurt before?"

"I got my ass kicked a few times—one time real bad—'cause they thought I wasn't being fair. I'm not sure I want to have that happen again."

"You don't get paid enough," I said.

J.T. came out of the club and stopped beside me. His head was lowered. Autry moved away.

"You wanted this, right?" he asked.

"Yes," I said, "this is what I'm looking for." He knew I'd been eager to see how the community and the gang worked out their differences. But he'd also made it clear that I could do so only if I had a patron, and I had to choose between J.T. and Autry. I chose J.T.

"Just remember, *you* wanted this," he said. "I didn't make you come here today. I didn't tell you about this. *You* wanted this." He pressed his finger into my chest every time he said "you." I sensed that despite our last conversation J.T. felt I was slipping from his grasp.

"I know," I said. "Don't worry."

"*I'm* not worried." He let out a sinister laugh. "But you should really think about this. Just remember, I didn't bring you here. I can't protect you. Not all the time anyway. You did this on your own."

"I get it, I'm on my own."

J.T. smiled, pressed his finger into my chest one last time, with force, and walked away.

FOUR

Gang Leader for a Day

After nearly three years of hanging out with J.T., I began talking to several of my professors about my dissertation topic. As it happened, they weren't as enthusiastic as I was about an in-depth study of the Black Kings crack gang and its compelling leader. They were more interested in the standard sociological issues in the community: entrenched poverty, domestic violence, the prevalence of guns, residents' charged relations with the government—and, to a lesser extent, how the community dealt with the gang.

If I explored these subjects well, my professors said, I could explain how the Robert Taylor tenants really behaved, rather than simply arguing that they didn't act like middle-class people.

Bill Wilson in particular was adamant that I adopt a wider lens on the gang and its role in Robert Taylor. Because sociology had such a strong tradition of "community studies," he wanted me to write the definitive report on everyday life in high-rise housing projects.

He also said he'd started worrying about my safety in the projects. By this point I had taken up golf as a way to spend more time with Wilson, an avid golfer. "I'm having nightmares, Sudhir," he said once in the middle of the fairway, staring out blankly. "You're worrying me, and I really want you to think about spending some time with others." He drifted off, never instructing me about which "others" I should be observing, but I knew this was code for *anyone* besides the gang.

I knew he had my best interests in mind, but it still came as a shock to me that I would have to widen my focus if I still planned to base my dissertation on this community. It meant that J.T. wouldn't be the sole target of my attention, and perhaps not even the primary target. A few of my professors were seasoned ethnographers, experts in the methodology of firsthand observation. They were insistent that I avoid getting so close to any one source that I would be beholden to him.

Easier said than done. I hadn't forgotten how agitated J.T. became when he saw me branching out into the community. I really didn't feel I could tell him that my project was moving away from a focus on his leadership. By now J.T. wasn't my only access to the community, but he was certainly my best access. He was the one who had brought me in, and he was the one who could open—or shut—any door. But beyond all that lay one simple fact: J.T. was a charismatic man who led a fascinating life that I wanted to keep learning about.

J.T. seemed to appreciate having the ear of an outsider who would listen for hours to his tales of bravado and managerial prowess. He often expressed how hard it was to oversee the gang, to keep the drug economy running smoothly, and to deal with the law-abiding tenants who saw him as an adversary. Sometimes he spoke of his job with dispassion, as if he were the CEO of some widget manufacturer—an attitude that I found not only jarring but, given the violence and destruction his enterprise caused, irresponsible.

He fancied himself a philanthropist as much as a leader. He spoke proudly of quitting his mainstream sales job in downtown Chicago to return to the projects and use his drug profits "to help others." How did he help? He mandated that all his gang members get a high-school diploma and stay off drugs. He gave money to some local youth centers for sports equipment and computers. He willingly loaned out his gang members to Robert Taylor tenant leaders, who deployed them on such tasks as escorting the elderly on errands or beating up a domestic abuser. J.T. could even put a positive spin on the fact that he made money by selling drugs. A drug economy, he told me, was "useful for the community," since it redistributed the drug addicts' money back into the community via the gang's philanthropy.

I have to admit that J.T.'s rhetoric could be persuasive, even when I tried to play the skeptic. The fact was, I didn't yet have a good grip on how his gang really affected the broader community. On an even more basic level, I wondered if I really had a complete sense of what J.T. did on a daily level. What kind of gang activities *wasn't* he showing me?

One cold February morning, I stood with him on a street corner as he met with one of his drug-selling crews. I was shivering, still unaccustomed to the chilling lake winds, and trying hard to focus on what J.T. was saying. He spoke to his men about the need to take pride in their work. He was also trying to motivate the younger members to brave the cold and sell as much crack as they could. In weather like this, the youngest members had to stand outside and sell while the ones with more seniority hung out in a building lobby.

After addressing his troops, J.T. said he was going off to play basketball. He climbed into his Malibu and I climbed in with him. We were parked near a busy intersection at State Street, within view of a Robert Taylor high-rise, some low-rise stores, and the Boys & Girls Club. Before he even turned the key, I mentioned, half joking, that I thought he was seriously overpaid.

"I don't see what's so difficult about your job," I said. "I mean, you *say* how hard it is to do what you do, but I just can't see it being that difficult." All I ever saw him do, I said, was walk around and shake hands with people, spend money, drive nice cars—he owned at least three that I knew of—and party with his friends. J.T. just sat for a moment, making no move to drive off. "Okay, well, you want to give it a try? If you think it's so easy, you try it."

"I don't think that would be possible. I don't think graduate school is really training me to lead a gang."

"Yeah, but you don't think I need any skills at all to do this. So you should have no problem doing it, right?"

It was true that *sometimes* his job looked hard. When his gang was warring with another gang, for instance, J.T. had to coordinate his troops and motivate fifteen-year-old kids to stand out in the open and sell drugs despite the heightened risk of being shot, beaten up, or arrested. And it wasn't as though these kids were getting rich for their trouble. The BKs, like most other street gangs, had a small leadership class. J.T. kept only a few officers on his payroll: a treasurer, a couple of "enforcers," a security coordinator, and then a set of lesser-paid "directors" who managed the six-person teams that did the actual street-level selling of crack.

But for the most part, it seemed that J.T.'s gang members spent their time hanging around on street corners, selling drugs, shooting dice, playing sports, and talking about women. Did it really take a self-styled CEO to manage *that*?

I expressed this sentiment to J.T. "I could do it," I said. "Probably. I mean, I don't think I could handle a war and I've never shot a gun, so it depends what you mean when you say 'try it.' "

"Just that—try it. There's no war on right now, no fighting. So you don't even have to touch a gun. But I can't promise that you won't have to do something you may not like."

"Such as?"

"I'm not telling you. You said you think it's easy, so you do it, and you'll see what I mean."

"Is this an offer?"

"Nigger, this is the offer of a lifetime. Guaranteed that if you do this, you'll have a story for all your college friends."

He suggested that I try it for a day. This made me laugh: how could I possibly learn anything worthwhile in a single day?

From inside the car, I watched as parents gingerly stepped out of the high-rise lobby, kids in tow, trying to get to school and out of the unforgiving lake wind. A crossing guard motioned them to hurry up and cross the street, for there were a couple of eighteen-wheelers idling impatiently at a green light. As they passed his car, J.T. waved. Our breath was fogging up the windshield. He turned on the defroster, jacked the music a bit louder. "One day," he said. "Take it or leave it. That's all I'm saying. One day."

I met J.T. at seven-thirty the next morning at Kevin's Hamburger Heaven in Bridgeport, a predominantly Irish-American neighborhood across the expressway from the projects. This was his regular morning spot. "None of these white folks here know me," he said, "so I don't get any funny looks."

His steak and eggs arrived just as I sat down. He always ate alone, he said. Soon enough he'd be joined by two of his officers, Price and T-Bone. Even though J.T.'s gang was nearly twice as large as most others on the South Side, he kept his officer class small, because he trusted very few people. All of his officers were friends he'd known since high school.

"All right," he began, "let's talk a little about—"

"Listen," I blurted out, "I can't kill anybody, I can't sell shit to anybody." I had been awake much of the night worrying. "Or even *plan* any of that stuff! Not me!"

"Okay, nigger, first of all you need to stop shouting." He looked about the room. "And stop worrying. But let me tell you what *I'm* worried about, chief."

He twirled a piece of steak on his fork as he dabbed his mouth with a napkin.

"I can't let you do *everything,* right, because I'll get into trouble, you dig? So there's just going to be some stuff you *can't* do. And you already told me some of the other stuff you don't *want* to be doing. But all that doesn't matter, because I got plenty of stuff to keep you busy for the day. And only the cats coming for breakfast know what you'll be doing. So don't be acting like you run the place in front of everybody. Don't embarrass me."

It was his own bosses, J.T. explained, that he was worried about, the Black Kings' board of directors. The board, roughly two dozen men who controlled all the neighborhood BK gangs in Chicago, kept a close eye on drug revenues, since their generous skim came off the top. They were always concerned that local leaders like J.T. keep their troops in line. Young gang members who made trouble drew unwanted police attention, which made it harder to sell drugs; the fewer drugs that were sold, the less money the board collected. So the board was constantly reminding J.T. to minimize the friction of his operation.

As J.T. was explaining all this, he repeated that only his senior officers knew that I was gang leader for a day. It wouldn't do, he said, for the gang's rank and file to learn of our experiment, nor the community at large. I was excited at the thought of spending the day with J.T. I felt he might not be able to censor what I saw if I was with him for a full day. It was also an obvious sign that he trusted me. And I think he was flattered that I was interested in knowing what actually went into his work.

Impatient, I asked him what my first assignment was.

"You'll find out in a minute, as soon as I do. Eat up, you're going to need it."

I was nervous, to be sure, but not because I was implicating myself in an illegal enterprise. In fact, I hadn't even really thought about that angle. I probably should have. At most universities, faculty members solicit approval for their research from institutional review boards, which act as the main insurance against exploitative or unethical research. But the work of graduate students is largely overlooked. Only later, when I began sharing my experiences with my advisers and showing them my field notes, did I begin to understand—and adhere to—the reporting requirements for researchers who are privy to criminal conduct. But at the time, with little understanding of these protocols, I simply relied on my own moral compass.

This compass wasn't necessarily reliable. To be honest, I was a bit overwhelmed by the thrill of further entering J.T.'s world. I hoped he would someday introduce me to the powerful Black Kings leadership, the reputedly ruthless inner-city gang lords who had since transplanted themselves to the Chicago suburbs. I wondered if they were some kind of revolutionary vanguard, debating the theories of Karl Marx and W. E. B. Du Bois, Frantz Fanon and Kwame Nkrumah. (Probably not.) I also hoped that J.T. would bring me to some dark downtown tavern where large Italian men in large Italian suits met with black hustlers like J.T. to dream up a multiethnic, multigenerational, multimillion-dollar criminal plan. My mind, it was safe to say, was racing out of control.

Price and T-Bone soon arrived and sat down at our table. By now I knew these two pretty well—T-Bone, the gang's bookish and chatty treasurer (which meant he handled most of the gang's fiscal and organizational issues), and Price, the thuggish and hard-living security chief (a job that included the allocation of particular street corners to particular BK dealers). They were the two men most responsible for helping J.T. with day-to-day affairs. They both nodded in my direction as they sat down, then looked toward J.T.

"Okay, T-Bone," J.T. said, "you're up, nigger. Talk to me. What's happening today?"

"Whoa, whoa!" I said. "I'm in charge here, no? I should call this meeting to order, no?"

"Okay, nigger," J.T. said, again glancing around. He still seemed concerned that I was talking too loud. "Just be cool."

I tried to calm down. "T-Bone, you're up. Talk to me, nigger."

J.T. collapsed on the table, laughing hard. T-Bone and Price laughed along with him.

"If he calls me 'nigger' again, I'm giving him an ass whupping," T-Bone said. "I don't *care* if he's my leader."

J.T. told T-Bone to go ahead and start listing the day's tasks.

"Ms. Bailey needs about a dozen guys to clean up the building today," T-Bone said. "Last night Josie and them partied all night long, and there's shit everywhere. We need to send guys to her by eleven or she *will* be pissed. And I do not want to be dealing with her when she's pissed. Not me."

"Okay, Sudhir," J.T. said, "what do we do?" He folded his arms and sat back, as if he'd just set up a checkmate.

"What? Are you kidding me? Is this a joke?"

"Ain't no joke," said T-Bone flatly. "What do I do?" He looked at J.T., who pointed his finger at me. "C'mon, chief," T-Bone said to me. "I got about ten things I need to go over. Let's do this."

J.T. explained that he had to keep Ms. Bailey happy, since the gang sold crack in the lobby of her building and as building president she had the power to make things difficult. To appease her, J.T. regularly assigned his members to clean up her building and do other menial jobs. The young drug dealers hated these assignments not only because they were humiliating but because every hour of community service was one less hour earning money. Josie was a teenage member of J.T.'s gang who'd apparently thrown a party with some prostitutes and left the stairwells and gallery strewn with broken glass, trash, and used condoms.

"All right, who hasn't done cleanup in a while?" I asked.

"Well, you have Moochie's group and Kalia's group," T-Bone said. "Both of them ain't cleaned up for about three months." Moochie and Kalia were each in charge of a six-member sales force.

"Okay, how do we make a decision between the two?" I asked.

"Well, it depends on what you think is important," J.T. said. "Moochie's been making tall money, so you may not want to pull him off the streets. Kalia ain't been doing so hot lately, so maybe you want him to clean up, 'cause he isn't bringing in money anyway."

T-Bone countered by saying that maybe I should give the cleanup job to Moochie *because* he was making so much money lately. A little community service, T-Bone said, might ensure that "Moochie's head doesn't get too big." One of a leader's constant struggles was to keep younger members from feeling too powerful or independent.

Then Price threw in the fact that Moochie, who was in his early twenties, had been sleeping with Ms. Bailey, who was about fifty-five. This news shocked me: Was Moochie really attracted to a heavyset woman in her fifties? Price explained that younger guys often slept with older women, especially in winter, because otherwise they might not have a warm, safe place to spend the night. Also, a lease-holding woman might let her younger boyfriend stash drugs and cash in her apartment and maybe even use it as a freelance sales spot.

"Maybe Ms. Bailey gets to liking Moochie and she tells everyone not to buy shit from anyone but his boys," Price said. "You can't have that, because Moochie feels like he owns the building, and he doesn't."

"What if I flip a coin?" I asked, frustrated that I was spending so much time delegating janitorial duties. "I mean, you can't win one way or the other."

"Giving up already?" J.T. asked.

"Okay, let's send Moochie over there," I said. "It's better that his head doesn't get too big. Short run, you lose a little money."

"You got it," T-Bone said, and stepped away to make a phone call.

Price brought up the next item. The BKs had been trying to find a large space—a church or school or youth center—where they could hold meetings. There were several occasions, J.T. explained, when the gang needed to gather all its members. If a member violated a major gang rule, J.T. liked to mete out punishment in front of the entire membership in order to encourage solidarity and, just as important, provide deterrence. If a member was caught stealing drugs, for instance, he might be brutally beaten in front of the whole gang.

J.T. might also call a large meeting to go over practical matters like sales strategies or suspicions about who might be snitching to the police. A big meeting also gave J.T. a captive audience for his oratory. I had already been to a few meetings in which the only content was a two-hour speech by J.T. on the virtues of loyalty and bravery.

He often called the gang together on a street corner or in a park.

But this was far from ideal. There were about 250 young men in J.T.'s gang; summoning even 50 of them to the same street corner was sure to bring out the police, especially if a beating was on the agenda.

I was curious about the gang's relationship with the police, but it was very hard to fathom. Gang members brazenly sold drugs in public; why, I wondered, didn't the cops just shut down these open-air markets? But I couldn't get any solid answers to this question. J.T. was always evasive on the issue, and most people in the neighborhood were scared to talk about the cops at all—even more scared, it seemed to me, than to talk about the gang. As someone who grew up in a suburb where the police were a welcome presence, I found this bizarre. But there was plainly a lot that I didn't yet understand.

The Black Kings also needed to meet en masse if they were preparing for war with another gang. Once in a while, a war began when teenage members of different gangs got into a fight that then escalated. But leaders like J.T. had a strong incentive to thwart this sort of conflict, since it jeopardized moneymaking for no good reason. More typically, a war broke out when one gang tried to take over a sales location that belonged to another gang. Or one gang might do a drive-by shooting in another gang's territory, hoping to scare off its customers—perhaps right into the territory of the gang that did the shooting.

When this kind of spark occurred, J.T. might pick up the phone and call his counterpart in the other gang to arrange a compromise. But, more often, gang leaders ordered a retaliation in order to save face. One drive-by shooting begat a retaliatory drive-by; if a Black Kings dealer got robbed of his drugs or cash by someone from another gang, then the Black Kings would do at least the same.

The retaliation was what signaled the start of a war. In J.T.'s gang it was the security officer, Price, who oversaw the details of the war:

posting sentries, hiring mercenary gunmen if need be, planning the drive-bys. Price enjoyed this work, and was often happiest during gang wars.

I had never seen a war last beyond a few weeks; the higher-ups in each gang understood that public violence was, at the very least, bad for business. Usually, after a week or ten days of fighting, the leaders would find a mediator, someone like Autry, to help forge a truce.

"Pastor Wilkins says we can meet once a week at the church, at night," Price said. "I spoke to him yesterday. He says he would like a donation."

Price started to chuckle. So did T-Bone, who had returned from his phone call, and J.T.

"What's so funny?" I asked.

"Pastor Wilkins is a faggot, man," J.T. said. "That nigger sucks dick all night long!"

I had no idea whether Pastor Wilkins really did have sex with men, but I didn't think it much mattered. Price and the others enjoyed making fun of him, and that was that.

"I still don't see what's so funny," I said.

"Nigger, *you* have to meet with him," T-Bone said. "Alone!"

"Oh, I get it. Very funny. Well, how about this? Since I'm leader, then that meeting is now scheduled for tomorrow. Ha!"

"No, the pastor wants to meet today," J.T. said, suddenly stern. "And I need to find out today if we have a place to meet on Friday. So you're up, brown man. Get ready."

"All right, then. I'm delegating T-Bone to visit Pastor Wilkins. Now, you can't tell me that I can't delegate!"

"Actually, I can," J.T. said. "It says in the gang's rules that only the leader can make these kinds of meetings."

"Now you guys are making shit up. But fine, I'll do it. I say we give him fifty bucks for the use of the church."

"What!" Price said. "Are you crazy?"

"Fifty will just make sure the cops arrive on time," T-Bone said. "You better think a little higher."

"Well, what did we pay last time?" I asked.

"It depends," J.T. said, explaining that it was not uncommon for the less well-established clergy to rent out their storefront spaces to the gangs for business meetings. "Five hundred gets you the back room or the basement, but that's just one time. And the pastor stays in the building. Seven hundred fifty gets you the place to yourself. And sometimes you want to *be* by yourself, depending on what you're going to discuss."

"Yeah," Price chimed in. "If you have to beat somebody's ass, you might want to be alone."

I asked for a little time to think things over.

The four of us left the restaurant and got into J.T.'s Malibu for our next task: a meeting with Johnny, a man who owned a convenience store and no longer allowed members of the Black Kings inside. I already knew Johnny. He was a local historian of sorts who liked to regale me with stories of the 1960s and 1970s, when he was a gang leader himself. But he stressed how the gangs of that period were totally different. They were political organizations, he said, fighting police harassment and standing up for the community's right to a fair share of city services. In his view, today's gangs were mostly moneymaking outfits with little understanding of, or commitment to, the needs of Chicago's poor black population.

Johnny's store was on Forty-seventh Street, a busy commercial strip that bisected Robert Taylor. The strip was lined with liquor stores, check-cashing shops, party-supply and hardware stores, a few burned-out buildings and empty lots, a public-assistance center, two beauty salons, and a barbershop.

I wasn't very worried about meeting with Johnny until Price spoke up. "We've also got a problem with this nigger," he said, "because he's been charging us more than he charges other niggers."

"You mean he rips off only people in the Black Kings?" I asked.

"That's right," said J.T. "And this one is hard, because Johnny is T-Bone's uncle. He's also a dangerous motherfucker. He'll use a gun just like that. So you got to be careful."

"No, *you* have to be careful," I said. "I told you I won't use a gun."

"No one said *you* have to," Price offered, laughing from the backseat. "But *he* might!"

"What exactly is it that I'm supposed to do?" I asked. "You want me to make him charge you fair prices?"

"Well, this is a tough one," J.T. said, "because we can't have people taking advantage of us, you dig? But the thing is, we provide this nigger protection."

"Protection?"

"Yeah, say somebody steals something. Then we find out who did it and we deal with it."

"So he can't tell us that we can't come in his store," Price said. "Not if we're providing him a service."

"Right," said J.T. "We have to try and remind him that he's paying us to help him, and it doesn't look good if he doesn't let us come in his store. See, what he's doing is trying to make back the money that he's paying us for protection."

Johnny was out front when we pulled up, smoking a cigarette. "What's up, Sudhir?" he said. "I see you wasting your time again, hanging around these niggers."

Johnny looked like a caricature of a disco-era hustler: bright orange pants, a polyester shirt that appeared to be highly flammable, cowboy boots with fake diamond trim, and lots of ghetto glitter—fake rubies and other stones—on his fingers. A tattoo on his arm read BLACK BITCH, and another on his chest said PENTHOUSE KINGS, which was the name of his long-ago street gang.

J.T., Price, and I followed Johnny into the back of the store while T-Bone peeled off to attend to some other business. The back room was musty and unswept. The walls were plastered with pictures of naked black women and a big poster of Walter Payton, the beloved Chicago Bears running back. The sturdy shelves and even the floor were crammed with used TV sets, stereo components, and microwaves that Johnny fixed and sold. A big wooden table held the remnants of last night's poker game: cards and chips, cigar butts, some brandy, and a ledger tallying debts. Through the open back door, a small homeless encampment was visible. J.T. had told me that Johnny paid a homeless couple fifty dollars a week to sleep outside and watch over the store.

We all sat down around the table. Johnny seemed impatient. "All right," he said, "what are we going to do?"

"Well, we were thinking more like what *you* were going to do, nigger," Price said.

"Listen, big black," Johnny said, cigarette dancing in his lips, "you can take that mouth outside if you can't say something useful."

J.T. told Price to go back to the car, leaving just me, J.T., and Johnny.

"You're paying us, Johnny," J.T. said, "and now you're *charging* us. You trying to make your money back? Is that it?"

Johnny replied in a calm monotone. "You niggers charge me two hundred and fifty dollars a month, and that shit has to stop," he said. "A man can't run a business if he has to pay that kind of money.

And your boys keep coming in here demanding free shit. I told Moochie and the rest of them that if they come in here anymore, this .22 is going to find their back." He gestured to a rifle hanging behind him on the wall.

"See now, that's the kind of talk we don't need," J.T. said. "I mean, we need to cooperate."

"Cooperate, my ass!" said Johnny. "You can cooperate with my fist."

"Whoa, whoa!" I yelled, trying to be useful. "Let's calm down now, boys. What I think we need is a little—"

"Is this Arab going to sit here all day with us?" Johnny said.

"Leave that boy alone," J.T. said. "I'll explain later." He shot me a glance, a *Shut the fuck up* glance. "Listen, you pay me two hundred dollars a month and you'll get the same shit from us." He was talking about the protection the gang afforded. "And I'll talk to Moochie and everyone else, tell them they can't steal shit. Okay?"

"Bitch, you better tell him not to bring his girlfriends up in here."

"What?"

"You heard me. He brings them bitches in here when I'm not around, showing off and taking shit off the shelves, eating candy and drinking soda like he owns the place. When my man tried to do something about it, he pulled a gun on him. Let him bring that shit on me. Try it once, I'll kill the little bitch."

"All right," J.T. said, putting his hand in front of Johnny's face to shut him up. "I told you *I'll* deal with the nigger."

"I pay you two hundred dollars and your boys get to come in here, but they have to promise to spend at least two hundred dollars a month on shit," Johnny said.

"And you're not going to jack up prices, right?" I said.

"Goddamn, Arab, you still here?" Johnny said. "Yeah, that's right, they pay what everyone else pays."

"Okay, then," I said, "we got ourselves a deal, boys!" I stood up to go.

"Boy, sit your ass down," J.T. said. "Johnny, we'll get back with you."

"Yeah, we'll get back with you," I said. "We need to deliberate."

Johnny and J.T. started laughing.

"Goddamn!" Johnny shouted. "You bring this Arab with you wherever you go?"

"One day," J.T. muttered, clearly frustrated that I was taking my role a little too seriously. "One day, that's it."

We got back in the Malibu. Price drove, J.T. rode shotgun, and I sat in the back. My next duty, J.T. explained, was to settle a dispute between two gang members, Billy and Otis. Billy was the director of a six-man drug-selling crew. Otis, one of his six dealers, was claiming that Billy had underpaid him for a day's work. Billy, meanwhile, said that Otis lied about how much crack he sold and kept the extra money. My dilemma would be compounded by the fact that I already knew both Billy and Otis.

As we drove, Price explained my goal: to adjudicate the case and determine a fair punishment. "If Billy didn't pay Otis, then you have to punish Billy," he said. "The punishment for not paying one of your members would be two mouthshots, and Billy can't work for a week. And if you want, you get to make Otis the director for that week. But if Otis *stole* something, then we have a bigger problem. You have to beat the shit out of that nigger, not just hit him twice. *And* he has to work free for a month."

The thought of hitting someone in the face—delivering a "mouthshot"—made me nauseous. Growing up, I used to get picked on all the time. I was tall and athletic, but I was also a nerd, complete with pocket protector, bad haircut, and an armful of math and science books. I was a perfect target for the average football player or any other jock, especially since I played the less "manly" sports of tennis and soccer. I never even learned to throw a punch. In school most of the fights culminated with someone—most often a girl I was with—pleading for the bully to reconsider, or with me rolling up in a fetal ball, which I actually found to be quite a good strategy, since most bullies didn't want to fight someone who wouldn't fight back.

"Now, I don't mean to be picky," I said, "but isn't this why we have you here, Price? I mean, you're the security guy, no? *You* beat their ass—I mean, isn't that what you get paid for? And if I'm the leader, I can delegate, no?"

"Sudhir," J.T. said, "you have to realize that if you do that, then you lose respect. They need to see that you are the boss, which means that you hand out the beating."

"What if I make them do twenty pushups or fifty squat thrusts? Or maybe they have to clean my car."

"You don't own a car," J.T. said.

"That's right—so they have to clean *your* car for a month!"

"Listen, these guys already clean my car, wipe my ass, whatever I want, so that ain't happening," J.T. said calmly, as if wanting to make sure I understood the breadth of his power. "And if they can steal money or not pay somebody for working and they only have to clean a car, then think how much these guys will steal. You have to make sure they understand that they can't be stealing! Nigger, they need to *fear* you."

"So that's your leadership style? Fear?" I was trying to give the impression that I had my own style. Mostly, I was stalling out of worry that I'd have to throw a punch. "Fear, huh? Very interesting, very interesting."

We pulled up to the street corner where Billy and Otis had been told to meet us. It was cold, not quite noon, but the sun had broken through a bit. Aside from a nearby gas station, the corner was surrounded mostly by empty lots and abandoned buildings.

I watched Billy and Otis saunter over. Billy was about six foot six. He had been a star basketball player at Dunbar High School and won a scholarship to Southern Illinois at Carbondale, a small downstate school. He began using his connections with the Black Kings to deal marijuana and cocaine to students in his dorm. He eventually decided to quit the basketball team to sell drugs full-time. He once told me that the lure of cash "made my mouth water, and I couldn't get enough of it. Dumbest move I ever made." Now he was working in the gang to save money in hopes of returning to college.

I always liked Billy. He was one of thousands of people in this neighborhood who, by the time they turned eighteen, had made all sorts of important decisions by themselves. Fewer than 40 percent of the adults in the neighborhood had even graduated from high school, much less college, so Billy didn't have a lot of places to go for counsel. Even so, he was the first one to accept responsibility for the bad decisions he'd made. I'll never forget what he said when he moved back to the projects after dropping out of college: "I just needed someone to talk to. My mind was racing out of control, and I had no one to talk to."

I didn't want to think about hitting Billy today, because I really liked him—and because, at that height, his jaw was nearly out of reach.

Otis was a different story. He always wore dark sunglasses—even indoors, even in winter—and he kept a large knife underneath a long black jacket that he always wore, even in hot weather. He loved to cut people up and give them a scar. And he didn't like me at all.

This acrimony stemmed from a basketball game several months

earlier. I regularly attended the gang's midnight games at the Boys &
Girls Club. If Autry came up one referee short, he sometimes pressed
me into service. I had played basketball growing up, but not how it
was played in the ghetto. In my neighborhood we set picks, passed
the ball—and, perhaps most important, called fouls, even in pickup
games. In the gang games, if you called even half the fouls that were
actually committed, you'd run out of players by halftime. But during one game I refereed when Otis was playing, I called five quick
fouls on him because . . . well, because he fouled somebody five
times. He had to leave the game.

From the bench, with a cheap bottle of liquor in his hand, Otis
shouted at me, "I'm going to kill you, motherfucker! I'm going to
cut your balls off!" It was pretty hard to concentrate for the rest of
the game.

I left the gym immediately afterward, but Otis chased me down
in the parking lot. He was still in his uniform, so he didn't have his
machete with him. He picked up a bottle from the asphalt, smashed
it, and pressed the jagged edge to my neck. Just then Autry hustled
into the parking lot, pulled Otis back, and told me to run. I stood
there in shock while Autry kept yelling, "Run, nigger, run!" After
about thirty seconds, he and Otis both started laughing, because my
feet simply wouldn't move. They laughed so hard that they crumpled to the ground. I nearly threw up.

I was thinking of this incident now, as Otis walked toward us, and
I wondered if he was, too. I got out of the car along with J.T.
and Price.

"Okay, let's hear what happened," J.T. said. "I need to know who
fucked up last week. Billy, you first."

J.T. seemed preoccupied, maybe a little upset. I didn't know why,
and it wasn't the time to ask. It certainly didn't seem as if I had
much chance of leading the conversation.

"Like I already said," Billy began, "ain't nothing to say. Otis got a hundred-pack and was a hundred dollars short. I want my money." He was stubborn and defiant.

"Nigger, please," Otis said. "You ain't paid me for a week. You *owed* me that money." Otis's eyes were bloodshot, and he looked as if he might reach out and hit Billy at any moment.

"Didn't pay?" said Billy. "You're wrong on that. I paid you, and you went out that night partying. I remember."

The director of a sales team—in this case, Billy—usually gave his street dealers an allotment of prepackaged crack. A "100-pack" was the standard. A single bag sold for ten dollars, so once the dealer exhausted his inventory, he was supposed to give his director one thousand dollars. Billy was saying that Otis had turned over just nine hundred dollars. Otis's only defense seemed to be that Billy owed him money from an earlier transaction—a charge that Billy denied. Otis and Billy kept arguing with each other, but they were looking at J.T., Price, and me, pleading their cases.

"Okay, okay!" J.T. said. "This ain't going nowhere. Get the fuck out of here. I'll be back with you later."

Billy and Otis walked away, joining the rest of their crew near some Dumpsters where they stored their drugs and money. Once they were out of earshot, J.T. turned to me: "Well, what do you think? You heard enough?"

"Yes, I did!" I said proudly. "Here's my decision: Otis clearly took the money and pocketed it. You notice that he never actually denied taking something. He just said that he was owed the money by Billy. Now, I can't tell whether Billy never paid Otis for the day's work, but the fact that Otis didn't deny stealing the money makes me feel that Billy forgot to pay Otis—or maybe he didn't want to. But all that doesn't matter, because Otis *did* steal some money. And, I bet, Billy *didn't* pay."

There was silence for about thirty seconds. Finally Price spoke up. "Hey, I like it. Not bad. That was the smartest thing you said all day!"

"Yeah," said J.T. "Now, what's the penalty?"

"Well, in this case we borrow from the NFL and invoke the offsetting-penalty rule," I said. "Both guys screwed up, so the two penalties cancel each other out. I know that Otis's crime is more serious because he stole, but both of them messed up. So no one gets hurt or pays a fine. How about that?"

More silence. Price watched J.T. for his reaction. I did the same. "Tell Otis to come over here," J.T. finally said. Price went to fetch him.

"What are you going to do?" I asked J.T. He said nothing. "C'mon, tell me." He ignored me.

Price returned with Otis.

"Wait for me over there," J.T. told me quietly, nodding toward the car.

I did as he said. I climbed into the backseat, which faced away from J.T. and the others. Still, I was close enough to hear J.T. tell Otis to put his hands behind his back. Then I heard a punch, fist hitting cheekbone, and after about ten seconds another one. Then, slowly, two more punches. I looked behind me through the back window and saw Otis, bent over, holding his face. J.T. was slowly walking back toward the car, shaking his fist. He got in, and then Price did, too.

"You can't let them steal," J.T. told me. "I liked your take on what happened. You're right, they both fucked up. Since we don't really know if Billy didn't pay, I can't beat him. But like you said, we *do* know that Otis stole something, because he didn't deny it. So I had to punish him. I let him off easy, though. I told him he only had to work free for a week."

I could hear Otis moaning in pain, like a sick cow. I asked quietly if he was okay. Neither J.T. nor Price answered. As we drove past Billy and Otis, I was the only one who looked over. Otis still had his head down, and he turned away as we passed. Billy just watched us drive by, completely expressionless.

We spent the next several hours driving around the South Side, covering the great swath of territory controlled not just by J.T.'s faction of the Black Kings but by other gangs within the BK nation.

As J.T. rose within the BKs' citywide hierarchy, part of his broader duty was to monitor several BK factions besides his own to make sure that sales proceeded smoothly and that neighboring gangs cooperated with one another. This meant that he now oversaw, directly or indirectly, several hundred members of the Black Kings.

There was a constant reshuffling and realignment of gang factions. This typically had less to do with dramatic events like a gang war and more to do with basic economics. When one local gang withered, it was usually because it was unable to supply enough crack to meet the demand or because the gang leader set his street dealers' wages too low to attract motivated workers. In such cases a gang's leadership might transfer its distribution rights to a rival gang, a sort of merger in which the original gang got a small cut of the profits and a lower rank in the merged hierarchy. If running a drug gang wasn't quite business as usual, it was nevertheless very much a business.

Today was the day that J.T. needed to visit all the four- and six-man sales teams occupying the street corners, parks, alleyways, and abandoned buildings where the Black Kings sold crack. He did this once a week. Because these visits were perhaps J.T.'s most important work, it was pretty obvious that I wasn't going to have much input.

But as J.T. drove to his first stop, he told me that I could at least tag along.

By now a second car had joined us, occupied by four junior gang members. They were J.T.'s security detail, driving ahead to each location and paging him to say it was safe from rival gangs.

As I watched J.T. question his sales teams, one after the next, I began to realize that he truly was an accomplished manager. All his members knew the drill. As soon as J.T. reached a site, the sales team's director would approach him alone and instruct his troops to stop all sales activity. One member, taking all the cash and drugs, left the area entirely so that the police couldn't link J.T. directly to the drug sales. It was unclear to me whether this was J.T.'s idea or standard practice in gangland, but when it came to avoiding the police, J.T. was meticulous.

In order to keep himself clear, he never carried a gun, drugs, or large amounts of cash. Even though he occasionally alluded to cops he knew personally, men who'd grown up with him in the neighborhood, he was always sketchy as to whether he held any real influence among the police. Whatever the case, he didn't seem all that concerned about getting arrested. In his view the police could come after him whenever they wanted, but it was in their best interest to let familiar faces run the drug businesses. "They just want to control shit," he told me, "and that's why they really only come after us maybe once in a while."

His street dealers, however, were constantly getting arrested. From a legal standpoint this was mostly a nuisance; from a business standpoint, however, it posed a disastrous disruption of J.T.'s revenue flow. If a dealer went to prison, J.T. sometimes sent money to his family, but he was also worried that the dealer might decide to give testimony to the police in exchange for a reduced sentence. J.T. was more generous when it came to dealers killed in the line of duty. He nearly always paid their families a generous cash settlement.

As he met now with each sales director, J.T. would begin by grilling him with a standard set of questions: *You losing any of your regulars?* (In other words, customers.) *Anybody complaining?* (About the quality of the crack.) *You heard of people leaving you for others?* (Customers buying crack from other dealers.) *Anybody watching you?* (The police or tenant leaders.) *Any new hustlers been hanging around?* (Homeless people or street vendors.) *You seen any niggers come around?* (Enemy gangs.)

After answering these questions, the director had to report on the sales activity over the past week: a summary of the week's receipts, any drugs that had been lost or stolen, the names of any gang members who'd been causing trouble. J.T. was most concerned with the weekly drug revenues—not just because his own salary derived from these revenues but because of the tribute tax he had to send each month to his superiors. J.T. had told me earlier that his bosses occasionally changed their tax rate, even doubling it, for no good reason (at least no good reason that J.T. was ever told about). When this happened, J.T. had to dip into his own pocket. A few months before, he'd had to contribute five thousand dollars to help build up the gang's arsenal of weapons, and he wasn't at all happy about it.

These pressures, combined with his constant fear that his junior members were planning a coup d'état, made J.T. paranoid about being ripped off. He had told me of several such coups in other neighborhoods. So he practically interrogated his sales directors, asking the same question in a variety of ways or otherwise trying to trip them up.

"So you sold fifty bags, okay, that's fine," J.T. might start.

"No, I said we sold twenty-five," the director would answer.

"No, you said fifty, I could have sworn you said fifty. Everyone else heard fifty, right?"

"No, no, no. I said twenty-five."

Invariably J.T. and the young man directing his sales team—these directors were usually in their late teens or early twenties—would go back and forth like this for several minutes, often over a trivial detail, until J.T. felt confident that he was getting the truth. On this day, as the cold afternoon stretched into night, I watched several of these young men sweat under J.T.'s questioning. Surely they all knew by now what to expect of him. But even a hint of suspicion could earn them a "violation": J.T. was quick to physically punish them or suspend their privileges—the right to carry a gun, for instance, or the right to earn money.

J.T. also asked his directors about any behavior in the past week that might have attracted the attention of the police—a dispute between a customer and a dealer, perhaps, or any gunfire. If one of his members had been suspended from high school or had drawn complaints from a tenant leader, he would have to submit to even tougher questioning from J.T.

For the directors, the worst part of this interrogation was that J.T. maintained his own independent sources. He kept a roster of informants in every neighborhood where the Black Kings operated. He had begun this practice when he first became responsible for monitoring neighborhoods that he didn't know as well as his own. While he may have been familiar with the streets and stores in these neighborhoods, he didn't know every pastor, tenant leader, police officer, and hustler as he did in his own.

Most of his informants were homeless people, squatters, or other hard-up adults. They came cheap—J.T. paid most of them just ten or fifteen dollars a day—and these ghetto nomads could easily hang out in drug areas and spy on J.T.'s gang members without raising suspicion. J.T. generally dispatched his senior officers to debrief these informants, but sometimes he met with them personally. Although they couldn't tell him if his own members were stealing from him, they were valuable for reporting problems like street fights or customer complaints.

As we drove through the neighborhood, past the blighted storefronts on Forty-seventh Street, J.T. told me that one of his sales groups was selling diluted product. The BKs' crack-selling chain began with J.T.'s senior officers buying large quantities of powder cocaine from a distributor in the outlying suburbs or a neighborhood at the city's edge. The officers usually cooked up the cocaine into crack themselves, using a vacant apartment or paying a tenant perhaps a hundred dollars a month to use her kitchen. Then the officers would deliver the prepackaged allocations to the sales directors.

Sometimes, however, the street crews were allowed to cook up the crack themselves. In such a case, J.T. explained, they might surreptitiously use an additive to stretch their cocaine allotment into more crack. They could turn each 100-pack of $10 bags into a 125-pack, which meant earning an extra $250. This money obviously wouldn't be susceptible to collection by J.T., since he could account only for 100-packs.

I was surprised that J.T. would give anyone a chance to rip him off like this. But he now had so many crews under management, with such overwhelming volume, that he occasionally farmed out the production. It was a relatively simple process: you mixed together powder cocaine with baking soda and water, then boiled off the water until all that remained were the crystallized nuggets of crack. Subcontracting the production also provided J.T. a hedge of sorts: even if the police raided one of the apartments where the crack was being processed, he wouldn't lose his entire supply of cocaine.

The sale of diluted crack troubled J.T. for reasons beyond the obvious fact that his members were stealing from him. Such entrepreneurial energy could be infectious. If other factions of the gang thought up schemes to increase their revenues, not only would J.T. lose taxable receipts but his sales directors might feel empowered to try to knock him off his throne. He was also concerned about the physical dangers of diluted crack cocaine. Not long ago a teenager in Robert Taylor had nearly died of an overdose, and rumor had it that one of J.T.'s dealers had sold him crack that had been processed with a dangerous additive. As a result the building president got the police to post a twenty-four-hour patrol for two weeks, which shut down drug sales. J.T.'s superiors nearly demoted him because of this incident, out of concern that he couldn't control his members.

J.T.'s other worry about altered crack was a simple matter of competitive practice: if word got out that the Black Kings were selling an inferior product, they would lose customers to other gangs. This was what troubled him most, J.T. told me now as we drove to meet with Michael, a twenty-year-old gang member who had recently been promoted to run a six-man sales team.

One of J.T.'s informants had told him that Michael's crew was selling diluted product. The informant was in fact a crack addict; J.T. had him buy the crack and turn it over to J.T., who could tell from its color and brittle texture that the crack had indeed been stretched.

J.T. asked me what I would do if I were the gang boss and had to deal with Michael.

"Kick him out!" I said.

J.T. explained that this decision couldn't be so straightforward. "Most guys wouldn't even think of these ways to make money," he said. "Here's a guy who is looking to make an extra buck. I have hundreds of people working for me, but only a few who think like that. You don't want to lose people like that." What he needed to do, J.T.

told me, was quash Michael's tactic but not the spirit that lay at its root.

When we reached Michael, J.T. told his officers and security detail to leave him alone with Michael. He asked me to stay. We went into the alleyway behind a fast-food restaurant.

"See this?" J.T. said, holding up a tiny Ziploc bag to Michael's face. "What is it?"

"It's mine," Michael said. I had no idea how he could tell that the crack was his, and I wondered if he said so simply as a reflex.

Michael had a stoic look about him, as if he were expecting to be punished. The rest of his crew watched from perhaps ten yards away.

"Yeah, that's right, and it's half what it should be," J.T. said.

"You want us to fill it up with more than that?"

"Don't play with me, nigger. I know you been putting some shit in the product. I have the shit with me right here. How are you going to deny it?"

Michael was silent.

"I'm going to tell you what we're going to do," J.T. said. "I'm not going to put you on the spot. You're going to finish selling this, and next week you're not earning shit. Your take goes to all the other guys. And you know what? You're going to tell them, too. You're going to tell them why it's no good to make this weaker. You know why, right?"

Michael, his head down, nodded.

"Okay, then, you're going to tell them it's not right because we lose customers and then we don't have no work. And you're going to tell them that it was your idea, that you fucked up, and that as a way of dealing with it, you want them to have the money you would have made."

Michael was by now visibly upset, his face set in a sort of angry mope. Finally he looked up, groaned, shook his head, glanced away, kicked a few stones on the ground. It seemed as if he wanted to challenge J.T., but he had obviously been caught. So he said nothing. After a while J.T. called over the other members of Michael's group and finished obtaining his weekly report.

It had been dark for a few hours now. My stint as gang leader for a day—albeit in a very limited capacity—was finally over. It was both more banal and more dramatic than I could have envisioned. I was exhausted. My head was spinning with details, settled and unsettled. I never did manage to decide how much the Black Kings should pay Pastor Wilkins for the use of his church.

I had accompanied J.T. on site visits to roughly twenty Black Kings sales teams. Two sales directors had been taken off to a secluded area and given mouthshots for their transgressions. Another one, who had failed to make his weekly payment to J.T., was levied a 10 percent fine and a 50 percent deduction of his next week's pay. But J.T. used the carrot as well as the stick. The workers in one group who had done particularly well were allowed to carry guns over the weekend. (J.T. usually didn't let his members walk around armed unless there was a war going on; he also required that members buy guns directly from the gang.) And he gave a $250 bonus to the members of another group that had several weeks of above-average sales.

There seemed to be no end to the problems that J.T. encountered during this weekly reconnaissance, problems he'd have to fix before they spun out of control. There were several incidents of customers fighting in public with a BK member who sold them drugs; in each case the customer complained that the bag of crack was too small or that the product was not of suitable quality. A store owner reported to J.T. that several gang members demanded he give *them* his monthly "protection" payment; this couldn't have been a legitimate request, since J.T. allowed only his senior officers to pick up extortion receipts. A pastor called the police on one of J.T.'s members who used the church parking lot to receive oral sex (in lieu of cash payment) from a local drug user. And two gang members had been suspended from school for fighting, one of them for having a gun in his locker.

The next day I would wake up free of the hundreds of obligations and judgments I'd been witness to. But J.T. wouldn't. He'd still bear all the burdens of running a successful underground economy: enforcing contracts, motivating his members to risk their lives for low wages, dealing with capricious bosses. I was no less critical of what he did for a living. I also wanted to know more about his professed benevolence and how his gang acted on behalf of Robert Taylor's tenants. And I still knew very little about J.T.'s bosses.

But all that would take some time. My next set of answers about life in Robert Taylor came from the *second*-most-powerful force in my orbit, the woman known to one and all as Ms. Bailey.

FIVE

Ms. Bailey's Neighborhood

I ran into Ms. Bailey pretty regularly. Sometimes she accompanied J.T. as he made his rounds of the building; sometimes I'd see her with a police officer or a CHA official. She always said hello and politely introduced me to whomever she was with. But I didn't really know what she did or how she did it. Although she was present at the backroom gang negotiation I witnessed at the Boys & Girls Club, she hadn't gotten very involved. So I was curious to learn more about her.

Specifically, I wanted to know why residents spoke of her with a mixture of reverence and fear, much as they spoke of J.T. "Oh, you don't want to mess with Ms. Bailey," they'd say. Or, "Yeah, Ms. Bailey can tell you a lot about what's happening, but make sure you have five dollars with you." Even J.T., who agreed that I should spend some time with Ms. Bailey, vaguely hinted that I ought to be careful around her.

Part of my motivation to observe Ms. Bailey came from my advisers at the University of Chicago. Jean Comaroff, an accomplished ethnographer, said that I was spending too much time with men. Since two-thirds of the community were women raising children, she suggested that I try to better understand how women managed households, secured services from the CHA, and otherwise helped families get by. Bill Wilson told me that poverty scholars knew little about the role women played in community affairs, and he encouraged me to spend time with household leaders like Ms. Mae but also tenant leaders like Ms. Bailey. Wilson and Comaroff both advised me to exercise the same sort of caution with Ms. Bailey as I would with other powerful people, never taking what they told me at face value.

Ms. Bailey was of average height and stout. Because of arthritis in her knees, she walked slowly, but always looking straight ahead with great focus, like Washington crossing the Delaware. She had a tattoo on her right arm that read MO-JO—the nickname, Ms. Mae told me, of a son who'd passed away. Ms. Bailey had pudgy fingers and, when she shook your hand, the tightest grip I've ever felt.

Her title was building president of the Local Advisory Council (LAC). This was an elected position that paid a part-time wage of a few hundred dollars a month. The official duties of a building president included lobbying the CHA for better building maintenance, obtaining funds for tenant activities, and so on. Elections were held every four years, and incumbents were rarely deposed. Some LAC presidents were much more powerful than others, and from what I'd heard, Ms. Bailey was on the upper end of the power scale. She had actually fought for the creation of the LAC many years ago, and she kept her fighting spirit. I'd heard stories about Ms. Bailey getting medical clinics to give free checkups to the children in her building and local stores to donate food.

I witnessed this fighting spirit firsthand when I visited her small, decrepit office one day. I wanted to explain why I'd been hanging around her building and also explain my research. I began by discussing the prevailing academic wisdom about urban poverty and the factors that contributed to it.

"You planning on talking with white people in your study?" she snapped, waving her hand at me as if she'd heard my spiel a hundred times already.

I was confused. "This is a study of the Robert Taylor Homes, and I suppose that most of the people I'll be talking to are black. Unless there are whites who live here that I'm not aware of."

"If I gave you only *one* piece of bread to eat each day and asked why you're starving, what would you say?"

I was thrown off by this seeming non sequitur. I thought for a minute. "I guess I would say I'm starving because I'm not eating enough," I answered.

"You got a lot to learn, Mr. Professor," she said. "Again, *if I gave you* one piece of bread to eat each day and asked why you're starving, what would you say?"

I was getting even more confused. I took a chance. "Because you're not feeding me?"

"Yes! Very good!"

I felt relieved. I hoped no more tests were coming my way, but Ms. Bailey kept going. "Let's say I took away your house key and you had to sleep outside," she said. "A man from the city comes over and counts you as 'homeless.' What would you say?"

"Umm." This one seemed even harder. "I'd say you're wrong. I *have* a place to stay, so . . . no! I'm not homeless!" I thought I had nailed this one.

But she looked exasperated at my answer. "Wow, have you ever had to do *anything* for yourself?" she said.

I was at least smart enough to know that she wasn't literally asking me to reply.

"If I took your house key away," she barked, "what does that make you?" She leaned across the desk, and I could feel her breath on my face.

"Well, I guess you robbed me. So I'm not homeless, I'm a victim."

"Okay, we're getting somewhere. Now let's say I tell the police to stop coming to *your* block and to go only where *I* live. And then I write that you live in a crime-infested neighborhood, that there's more crime on your block than mine. What would you say?"

"Well, I guess I'd say that it's not really fair because you have all the police, so—"

"Mr. Professor, we're really getting moving now!" Ms. Bailey threw up her hands in mock celebration. "Okay, so let's go back to the original question. You want to understand how black folks live in the projects. Why we are poor. Why we have so much crime. Why we can't feed our families. Why our kids can't get work when they grow up. So will you be studying white people?"

"Yes," I said. I understood, finally, that she also wanted me to focus on the people outside Robert Taylor who determined how the tenants lived day to day.

"But don't make us the victim," she said. "We'll take responsibility for what we can control. It's just that not everything is in our hands."

Our subsequent meetings were much the same. I would walk in to discuss an issue—the 60 percent dropout rate, for instance, among the project's high-school kids. "Research today says that if kids can get through high school, they have a twenty-five percent greater likelihood of escaping poverty," I said, as if giving a lecture. "So *early* education—keeping them in school—is the key. Also—"

Ms. Bailey interrupted. "If your family is starving and I tell you that I'll give you a chance to make some money, what are you going to do?"

"Make the money. I have to help my family."

"But what about school?" she said.

"I guess it will have to wait."

"Until what?"

"Until my family gets enough to eat."

"But you should stay in school, right?" she said, sarcasm rising in her voice. "That's what will help you leave poverty." She paused. Then she smiled triumphantly and made no effort to hide her patronizing tone. "So . . . you said you wanted to talk with me about high-school dropouts?"

It took a while, but I eventually realized there was no point in trying to act even remotely authoritative around Ms. Bailey. There was part of me that felt like the expert researcher, but only a very small part. Once I learned that there was no way around Ms. Bailey's Socratic browbeating, I decided to give in and just let her teach me.

I usually dropped by her office during the hours she reserved for open visitation from tenants; otherwise it could be hard to track her down. When a tenant came by, Ms. Bailey would ask me to step out. Our longest conversations, therefore, rarely lasted beyond fifteen minutes. Ms. Bailey remained formal with me, as if she were keeping her guard up. She never shared details about specific tenants; instead she spoke in generalities about "families who live around here."

After a few months of this, I told J.T. that I was frustrated by my interactions with Ms. Bailey. I couldn't tell if she trusted me.

J.T. enjoyed seeing me struggle. He had warned me that getting to know her wouldn't be easy and perhaps wasn't even worth trying. "It took a while before I let you talk with my boys," he said.

"What makes you think she'll just walk you around and show you everybody? Things don't go so fast around here."

He had a point. If Ms. Bailey needed time to feel comfortable with me, then I would just have to wait.

As the Chicago winter began to settle in, Ms. Bailey asked me to help her with a clothing drive. Tenants and squatters in her building needed winter coats, she said, as well as blankets and portable heaters. She wanted me to collect donations with her from several stores that had agreed to contribute.

A friend of mine let me borrow his car, a battered yellow and brown station wagon. When I went to collect Ms. Bailey at her building, she was carrying a large plastic bag. She grunted as she bent over to pick it up and again as she set it down on the floor of the car. With labored breaths, she directed me to our first stop: a liquor store a few blocks from her building.

She instructed me to drive around the back. She told me she didn't want the manager to see me, but she didn't explain why.

I parked in the alley as Ms. Bailey went inside. Five minutes later a few employees came out the back door and began loading the station wagon with cases of beer and bottles of liquor. Nothing expressly for winter, I noted, although a stiff bourbon could certainly help take the sting off the Chicago cold. Ms. Bailey climbed into the car. This donation, she told me, was made with the understanding that she would direct her tenants to visit this liquor store exclusively when they needed booze.

We drove a few miles to a grocery store on Stony Island Avenue. We went in the back way and met with a man who appeared to be the manager.

"Hey, sweetheart," Ms. Bailey said. She introduced me to Mr.

Baldwin, a large, pear-shaped black man with a round face and a wide grin. He had a clipboard in his hand, marking off the sides of beef hanging from a ceiling rack.

Mr. Baldwin gave Ms. Bailey a hug. "I got what you want, babe," he said. "All in the back. I got them ready for you yesterday."

He pointed us toward a younger man, who led us over to a few big garbage bags filled with puffy black jackets. At first glance they looked exactly like the jacket the young man was wearing, which had the name of the grocery store prominently displayed on the sleeves and chest. *Were* they the same jackets? I wondered if Ms. Bailey's tenants would wear clothing with a grocery store's name on it.

As I hauled the bags to the car, Ms. Bailey shouted at me. "And bring three cases of beer in here, Sudhir!"

I did as I was told. Even I, middle-class naïf that I was, could sense a horse trade.

Back in the car, Ms. Bailey anticipated my question. "I know you're wondering what we were doing at the food store," she said. "Take a look at the jackets." I reached into the backseat and grabbed one. It smelled distinctly of bleach, as if it had been disinfected. The store's patch had been either removed or covered up with another, even larger patch. It read ROBERT TAYLOR PRIDE.

Ms. Bailey smiled. "Those jackets are warmer than what most families can buy in the stores. These workers are sitting in a meat locker all day, so you know they have to stay warm. The manager donates about twenty to me each Christmas."

"And the patches?" I asked.

"The guy who makes the jackets for him does it for free—for us."

"And the beer?"

Ms. Bailey just smiled and told me where to drive next.

We hit several more stores that day. At Sears, Ms. Bailey exchanged pleasantries with the manager, and they asked about each other's families. Then he handed over a few boxes of children's coats; Ms. Bailey directed me to put the rest of the beer in his car. At a dollar store, Ms. Bailey traded some of the liquor for a bundle of blankets. At a hardware store, Ms. Bailey gave the manager the heavy plastic bag she'd brought along, and he gave her three portable heaters.

"Don't ask what's in the bag," she told me as I carried the heaters back to the car. "When I know you better, I'll tell you."

Only once did Ms. Bailey receive a donation that was actually a donation—that is, something for free. At one grocery store, she got some canned food without having to exchange any beer or liquor.

By the time we finished, we were on the far southern edge of the city. We hit traffic on the drive back to Robert Taylor, which gave me the opportunity to pepper Ms. Bailey with questions.

"When did you start doing this?" I asked.

Ms. Bailey told me that she had grown up in public housing herself. Back then, charities, churches, city agencies, and individual volunteers all helped out in the projects. "But the volunteers don't come around anymore," she said wistfully. "Have you seen any of those nice white people since you've been around? I didn't think so. Nobody gives us money, nobody runs programs. Not a lot of people are doing the free-food thing anymore. Even the churches really don't do what they did in the past."

"But I don't understand why the people we saw today want to give you things. I mean, how did you get to know them?"

"Well, first of all, most of them grew up in Robert Taylor or they have family in the projects. Lots of middle-class people don't like to talk about it, but they came from the projects. It's easy to forget where you came from. But I try and remind these people that they were once like us. And a few times a year, they do the right thing."

"So why give them beer and liquor?" I asked. "If it's a donation, it should be for free, no?"

"Well, things ain't always that simple," Ms. Bailey said. She brought up the incident I'd seen some months back, when the woman named Boo-Boo wanted to kill the Middle Eastern shopkeeper who'd slept with her teenage daughter. "That's what a *lot* of women have to do around here to get some free food," she said. "I don't want to see it come to that. So if I have to give away a few bottles of gin, that's fine with me."

Back at her office, Ms. Bailey organized the winter gear and prepared large baskets filled with canned food and meat. Word spread quickly, and families from her building soon began to drop by. Some were shy, others excited. But everyone seemed happy, and I watched as children smiled when they tried on a new coat or a warm sweater.

I noticed that some people received food but no clothing. Others got a jacket but no food. And some people just stood around until Ms. Bailey told them, "We don't have anything for you today." She said this even though the food baskets and clothing were in plain view, so I didn't know why she was withholding the gifts from them. Did she play favorites with some families?

One day Clarisse, the prostitute, walked into Ms. Bailey's office. There were several women already in front of her. Ms. Bailey's assistant, Catrina, was writing their names and noting exactly what each of them received.

"You got something for me today?" Clarisse asked, a lilt in her voice. Then her eyes landed on me briefly, but I didn't seem to register. She smelled like liquor; her blouse was undone so that one of her breasts was nearly popping out. Despite the cold weather, Clarisse was wearing a black miniskirt and sliding around perilously on high heels. Her face looked vacant, and her mouth was frothy. I had never seen her in this condition before. She had told me herself that she didn't do drugs.

"You're messed up," Catrina said, peering over her thick glasses. "You need to shower."

Ms. Bailey was in the next room, speaking with a tenant. "Ms. Bailey, look who's here!" Catrina called out. "Ms. Bailey, you need to tell her to get out of the office!" Catrina turned back to Clarisse and shot her a disapproving look.

Ms. Bailey came out and told Catrina to calm down. Then she motioned for Clarisse to come inside. As she closed the door, she rolled her eyes at me and sighed. I couldn't make out the whole conversation—it was unclear, in fact, if Clarisse was talking at all—but some of Ms. Bailey's proclamations were plainly audible.

"Get yourself clean or you ain't getting nothing! . . . Don't embarrass yourself, coming in here high on that shit! . . . You call yourself a mother? You ain't no mother. You *could* be one, if you stopped smoking that junk!"

The door opened, and Clarisse stumbled out, tears in her eyes. She dropped her purse and then, as she stopped to pick it up, tripped and fell, ramming into the pile of donation baskets. As she tried getting up, Clarisse vomited, some of it landing on the baskets.

Catrina and I jumped over to help her. Both of us slipped on the vomit. A strong wind blew in from outside, and the smell filled the room. Clarisse resisted our help, but she couldn't manage to get up by herself. Her pretty face had turned pale and pasty.

"Grab her and get her out of here!" Catrina yelled. She had to say this two more times before I realized that she was talking to me. "Sudhir! Grab her and take her home. Now!"

I tried being delicate with Clarisse. She was falling out of her clothes, and I didn't quite know how to touch her. She began throwing up again, and this time it landed on my arm.

"Sudhir!" Catrina yelled.

Clarisse was on all fours by now. She was drooling and heaving, but nothing came out. This time I wrapped my arms around her stomach and yanked her up. I figured I'd better get her out of the office even if I had to drag her.

"That bitch don't want me to feed my babies," Clarisse moaned. "I need food to feed my babies!" She started looking around frantically—for her purse, I realized.

"Clarisse, just a few more feet," I said. "I'll get your bag, don't worry. But let's get you out of the office."

"My bag!" she wailed. "My bag, I need my bag!"

She started kicking and flailing, trying to make her way back inside the office. With one last effort, I heaved her upright, causing us both to stumble and slam against the gallery's chain-link fencing. She sank back to the floor. I hoped I hadn't hurt her, but I couldn't tell.

As I turned to retrieve her purse, I saw Ms. Bailey, standing in the doorway. She held the purse in her hands.

"Is this what she wants?" Ms. Bailey asked. "Is it?!" I nodded. "Look inside. You want to help this lady, then look and see why she wants her bag."

I shook my head, staring at the floor.

"Look!" Ms. Bailey snapped at me. She strode over and held the bag up to my face. I saw a few condoms, some lipsticks, pictures of her daughters, and a few bags of either heroin or cocaine.

"Have to have that fix, don't you, baby?" Ms. Bailey asked Clarisse, sneering. We all stood there for what felt like an hour but was probably only a few seconds. Catrina tried to interrupt, but Ms. Bailey waved her off.

"Go ahead, Sudhir, take her home," Ms. Bailey said. She bent over to stare down at Clarisse. "If I see your babies coming over and telling me that they ain't eaten no food in three days, I'm taking them away. You hear?"

Ms. Bailey turned and left. Catrina, with a disinterested look, handed me some paper towels. I bent down to wipe the vomit and tears from Clarisse's face. She didn't resist this time when I helped her up.

I walked Clarisse upstairs to her apartment and led her to the couch. The apartment was dark, and I figured it would be best to let her sleep. In a back room, her two daughters were sitting on a queen-size bed. They looked to be about two and four years old and were watching the TV intently. I closed the door to their room and put a glass of water on the table next to Clarisse. The scene was a study in contrasts. The apartment was neat and cozy, with wall hangings and framed pictures throughout, some of Jesus Christ and some of family members. It smelled as if it had just been cleaned. And then there was Clarisse on the couch, breathing heavily, eyelids drooping, a total mess.

When I had first met her, on the gallery outside J.T.'s apartment, Clarisse had set herself apart from other prostitutes—the "hypes and rock stars"—who sold sex for drugs. Plainly, she had lied to me about not using drugs; I guess she'd wanted to make a decent impression. At this moment I wasn't too concerned about her lies. She needed help, after all. But it was pretty clear that I had to be careful about blindly accepting what people told me.

I sat on a recliner next to the couch. "I'm afraid to leave you here alone," I said. In the dim light, I couldn't really make out her facial expression. But she was breathing heavily, as if she'd just gone through battle. "Let me call an ambulance."

"I'm okay. I just need it to wear off."

"What about the kids? Have they eaten?"

"Ms. Bailey wouldn't give us nothing," she whimpered, a stage past crying. "Why she treat me like that? Why she treat me like that?"

I felt a sudden urge to make sure her kids were fed. I went into the bedroom, asked them to grab their jackets, and walked them over to a local sandwich shop. I bought them cheeseburgers, chips, and soda, and on the way home we stopped at a small grocery store. I had only fifteen dollars with me, but I told the owner, a Middle Eastern man, that the family hadn't eaten in a while. He shook his head—as if he'd heard this story a million times—and instructed me to get what I needed and just take it with me. When I told Clarisse's girls that we were going to fill up a shopping cart, they looked like I'd just given them free passes to Disney World. While they grabbed candy, I tried to sneak in a few cans of spaghetti—alas, one of the most nutritious items on the shelves—and some milk, cereal, and frozen dinners. When we got back, Clarisse was asleep. I put the food away, broke out a few Ring Dings for the kids, and put them in front of the TV again. They fixed on the cartoon images as if they'd never been gone. Since Clarisse was still sleeping, I left.

Two days later I returned to the building. Walking through the crowded lobby, nodding at the people I knew, I felt someone grab my arm and pull me into a corner. It was Ms. Bailey.

"You're sweet, you're young, you're good-looking, and these women will take advantage of you," she said. "Be careful when you help them."

"Her kids hadn't eaten," I said. "What could I do?"

"Her kids ate at my place *that morning*!" Ms. Bailey said. She tightened her grip on my arm and moved in even closer. "*I* make sure they eat. *No* children go hungry in my building. No, sir." She tightened her grip even further, and it hurt. "These women need to do the right thing if they have a baby. You remember that if you have a child someday."

"I will."

"Mm-hmm, we'll see about that. For now, be careful when you help the women. They'll take advantage of you, and you won't know what hit you. And I can't be there to protect you." I wasn't sure exactly what Ms. Bailey meant.

I nodded anyway, mostly so Ms. Bailey would loosen her grip. When she finally let go, I walked up to J.T.'s apartment to wait for him. It was the second time I'd been warned that I couldn't be "protected." First J.T. and now Ms. Bailey. I decided not to tell anyone, including J.T., about the conversation I'd just had with Ms. Bailey. In fact, the conversation had put me so out of sorts that by the time I got upstairs, I told Ms. Mae I had some schoolwork to do and had to get going. She fixed me a plate of food for the bus ride home.

A few weeks later, Ms. Bailey invited me to the building's monthly meeting. It was open to all tenants and posed one of the few opportunities for people to publicly voice their problems.

There were about 150 tenant families in Ms. Bailey's building. That included perhaps six hundred people living there legally and another four hundred living off the books. These were either boarders who paid rent to the leaseholders or husbands and boyfriends who kept their names off the leases so the women qualified for welfare. There were likely another few hundred squatters or people living temporarily with friends, but they were unlikely to attend a tenant meeting.

Ms. Bailey didn't seem all that enthusiastic about these meetings, but she let me know that she well understood their symbolic value. "They need to see that something is going on," she said, "even if nothing is going on."

The meeting was held in Ms. Bailey's office on a Saturday afternoon in December. Although it wasn't very cold outside, the radiator was at full blast and the windows were closed. Ms. Bailey entered the steaming room and calmly walked past the few dozen people assembled on folding chairs, parking herself up front. She always sat down in the same awkward way. Because she was so heavyset, and because she had arthritis in her legs, she usually had to grab someone or something to help ease herself into a chair.

I was surprised at the small turnout. The attendees were mostly women and mostly in their mid-fifties like Ms. Bailey. There were, however, a few younger women with children and a few men as well.

Ms. Bailey deliberately arranged a sheaf of papers in front of her. She motioned for a young woman to open up the window, but it wouldn't budge.

"Okay, this meeting is in session," Ms. Bailey said.

A well-dressed man toward the back of the room immediately jumped up. "I thought you said you'd talk with those boys!" he said. "They're still hanging out there, making all that damn noise. I can't get no sleep."

I assumed he was talking about the parties the Black Kings threw inside and outside the building.

"Did you make a note of that, Millie?" Ms. Bailey asked an old woman to her left. She was the official LAC recording secretary. Millie nodded while scribbling away.

"Okay," Ms. Bailey said, "go on, young man."

"Go on? I've *been* going on. I'm *tired* of going on. Each time I *come* here, I go on. I'm tired of it. Can you do something?"

"You got that, Millie?" Ms. Bailey asked, looking over the rims of her glasses.

"Mm-hmm," Millie answered. "He's tired of it, he's been going on, and he wants you to do something."

"You can probably leave out the tired part," Ms. Bailey said in a serious tone.

"Yes, okay," Millie said, scratching away in her notes.

"Will there be anything else, young man?" Ms. Bailey asked. He didn't say anything. "Okay, then, I'm figuring you don't want to talk about the fact that you're living here illegally. Is that right? Now, who's next? Nobody? Okay, then, we have some *serious* business to discuss. Before I take questions, let me tell you that Pride will be here on Tuesday registering all of you to vote. Please make sure to show up. It's very important we have a good turnout for them."

Pride was the organization I'd come across earlier, made up of ex–gang members and devoted to gang truces and voter registration. Ms. Bailey had already told me that she worked closely with them.

"What are we voting for?" asked a young woman in the front row.

"We're not actually voting, sweetheart. You need to register first. If you're already registered, you don't need to come. But I want every apartment in this building registered."

"Ain't you even a little bit concerned that we're just helping J.T. and the rest of them?" an older woman asked. "I mean, they're the only ones who seem to be getting something out of this."

"You want these boys to turn themselves around?" Ms. Bailey answered. "Then you got to take them seriously when they try to do right. It's better than them shooting each other."

"The voting hasn't done a damn thing for us!" someone cried out. "So why are you so accepting of what they're doing?" A chorus of "oohs" followed the question.

Ms. Bailey shushed the crowd. "Excuse me, Ms. Cartwright," she said. "If you're suggesting that I may be benefiting in any way by the voting stuff going on, you can just come out and say it."

"I'm not saying you *may* be benefiting," Ms. Cartwright said. "I'm saying you *are* benefiting. You get that new TV on your own, Ms. Bailey?"

This produced some more "oohs" and a round of outright giggling.

"Let me remind you," Ms. Bailey yelled, trying to reestablish order, "that we ain't had no harassment, no shooting, no killing for six months. And that's because these young men are getting right. So you can help them or you can just sit and moan. And about my TV. Who was the one that give you fifty bucks for your new fridge? And you, Ms. Elder, how exactly did you get that new mattress?"

No one answered.

"That's what I thought. You-all can keep up the bitchin' or you can realize that every one of us is benefiting from me helping these young men."

The rest of the meeting was similarly animated and followed this same pattern. Tenants accused Ms. Bailey of going easy on J.T.'s gang and personally benefiting from her alliance with them. She replied that her job was to help the tenants, period, and if that meant finding creative solutions to a multitude of problems, then she needed to be allowed such flexibility. To nearly every resident who complained, Ms. Bailey could cite an instance of giving money to that person for rent, for a utility bill, or to buy food or furniture. She plainly knew how to play the influence game. I'd been to her apartment a few times and, although she never let me stay for long, it was a testament to her skills: There were photos of her with political officials, several new refrigerators from the CHA, and cases of donated food and liquor. One bedroom was practically overrun with stacks of small appliances that she would give to tenants in her favor.

At one point during the meeting, Ms. Bailey mentioned the "donations" that she regularly procured from the gang, to be applied to various tenants' causes. J.T. had repeatedly told me that he had to keep Ms. Bailey happy—having his junior members carry out her orders, for instance, and paying her each month for the right to sell drugs in the lobby. But this was the first time I ever heard Ms. Bailey admit to this largesse. In fact, she discussed it with a measure of pride, highlighting her ability to put the gang's ill-gotten gains to good use. Although none of the tenants said so, I also knew from J.T. that some of *them* received payoffs from the gang—in exchange for their silence or for allowing the gang to stash drugs, cash, or weapons in their apartments. For a poor family, it was hard to turn down the gang's money.

"Why are we even talking about J.T.?" asked an older man. "Why don't we just go to the police? Can you tell me what you get from taking their help—or their money?"

"You-all want this place clean," Ms. Bailey said. "You want this place safe. You want this and that. And you want it right away. Well, the CHA ain't doing nothing. So I have to find ways to take care of it."

"But we can't walk around safely," the man said. "My car got the windows shot out last year."

"Right," Ms. Bailey countered. "That was *last* year, and sometimes that happens. But you see this place getting cleaned up. You see people getting rides to the store. Who do you think is doing that? Before you go yelling at J.T. and the rest of them, you better understand that they're family, too. And they're *helping*—which is more than I can say for you."

That a tenant leader—one who was respected by politicians,

shop owners, the police, and others—would praise a crack gang and work so closely with *its* leader made me realize just how desperate people could become in the projects. But I was learning that Ms. Bailey's compromising position also arose out of her own personal ambitions: in order to retain her authority, she had to collaborate with the other power groups, in this case the gangs, who helped shape the status quo. This resulted in the bizarre spectacle of Ms. Bailey's publicly defending the very people who were shooting and causing trouble for her tenant families. Even though it was obvious that tenant leaders had few good choices, I still wasn't convinced that they needed to operate in such murky ethical waters. Nevertheless I found myself wondering how much Ms. Bailey's actions were actually a response to hardships that limited her options and how much arose from her own desire to have power.

As the meeting broke up, people approached Ms. Bailey for one-on-one conversations. They all had their grievances: no hot water or a broken sink, a child getting in trouble, prostitutes taking clients into the stairwell, crack addicts partying the whole night.

Afterward Ms. Bailey motioned me into her office. Catrina was looking over some notes she'd taken at the meeting. Ms. Bailey asked her to get together with Millie, the LAC secretary, to prepare a list of tenant concerns to pass along to the CHA.

Ms. Bailey opened a small refrigerator and took out sodas for all of us. Grabbing a small blue rag, she wiped her sweaty forehead. "Did that live up to your expectations?" she asked me with a wink.

"Well, I thought you were just going to make a few announcements!" I said, laughing. "What do you do with everything you heard? I mean, a lot of it was directed at you. They were saying some pretty harsh things."

"We tell the CHA that things ain't working in the building, and we try to get them to fix it. That's it."

"And do you tell them about residents accusing you of taking gang money?"

"We tell the CHA that things ain't working in the building, and we try to get them to fix it."

She smiled cunningly and looked over to Catrina, who returned the dutiful glance of an ever-loyal junior officer.

"Sudhir, you have to remember something," Ms. Bailey continued. "In the projects it's more important that you take care of the problem first. Then you worry about *how* you took care of the problem." I opened my mouth to object, but she stopped me. "If no one dies, then all the complaining don't mean nothing, because I'm doing my job. If all I got to worry about is a few people wondering where the money's coming from, then around here that's a good day! No one dies, no one gets hurt, I'm doing my job."

"That's an awful way to live," I blurted out.

"Now you're starting to understand," she said in a tone somewhere between pedantic and patronizing. "Maybe you're even starting to learn."

Someone knocked on the door, and Ms. Bailey got up to answer it. Catrina leaned in toward me. "Watch how she helps people," she whispered. "She says it don't matter, but she's amazing. Have you seen how she gets apartments fixed around here?"

I told her that I hadn't.

"Have you seen how she helps women around here?" Catrina pushed her glasses up the bridge of her nose and kept her voice low. I felt as if we were in high school and I was sneaking a conversation with the teacher's pet.

"Well, Ms. Bailey gives away food to the mothers, right?" I whispered back.

Catrina shook her head and inhaled deeply, looking disappointed in me. "That's not what I'm talking about. You watch what she does when she helps women. Pay attention to *that*." Her voice was insistent, but she offered no more details. "She is *the* most amazing person I know."

As I spent more time with Ms. Bailey over the coming months, I found that most tenants were less suspicious of me than they'd been in the past. Sometimes, when a tenant came into Ms. Bailey's office to talk about a problem, the tenant would say, "It's okay, I don't mind if Sudhir listens."

Like J.T., Ms. Bailey seemed to enjoy the fact that I was interested in her. Perhaps she, too, thought I was going to be her personal biographer. I could see why she might make this assumption. I took every opportunity to express my fascination for her life, which seemed more fascinating the more I hung around.

One cold winter morning, I sat in Ms. Bailey's office with Catrina. It was a slow day, and only a few tenants visited. Ms. Bailey asked if I would go out and get her some coffee, and Catrina came with me. We bundled up and trudged through eight inches of fresh snow. The wind was nearly strong enough to blow you over; it was too cold for even a conversation. Catrina and I just concentrated on stepping in the footprints of people who'd made a first pass in the snow. Catrina wondered aloud what kind of God would make the earth so cold.

As we slogged our way back to the building, coffee and doughnuts in hand, a young woman hurried over to us as best as she could. "Catrina, you got to come quick," she said. "Ms. Bailey ran upstairs to Taneesha's apartment. She said you have to call Officer Reggie."

Catrina shoved the coffee at me and ran off as fast as possible under the circumstances. Since tenants had a tough time getting the police to respond, Ms. Bailey summoned Officer Reggie, the cop who'd grown up in Robert Taylor, when the situation warranted.

"Where's Taneesha live?" I yelled.

The young woman who'd summoned Catrina shouted back over her shoulder, "Twelve-oh-four!"

Approaching the building, I encountered a couple of J.T.'s gang members. They wore brown work boots and thick down jackets with the Oakland Raiders' distinctive silver-and-black insignia. To me it seemed too cold for business, but I could see a steady stream of cars coming down the alley to buy drugs. White and black addicts jumped out of their cars and ran into the lobby to buy crack. As I walked inside, one of J.T.'s men shouted to me, "They're up on the twelfth. Elevator's broken."

The stairwells were brutally cold. I had to stop a few times to catch my breath. I came across quite a few other people, all of them upset by the broken elevators. "Merry fucking Christmas," one said to me bitterly as he passed by with a heavy laundry bag.

As I stepped into the gallery on the twelfth floor, I saw a group of men standing outside Apartment 1204. I recognized C-Note and a few other squatters among them. They were all moving about, trying to keep warm, some of them jumping up and down. The gallery floor was concrete, so even if you were wearing thick-soled shoes, the cold still shot up your legs.

The door of 1204 was partially open. Ms. Bailey stood over the sofa and, when she caught sight of me, beckoned me inside. I had met Taneesha a few times, most recently at her twenty-first birthday party, which J.T. had thrown. She was tall and very pretty, with long, straight black hair, and she was trying to make a career as a model. She currently modeled clothes at various nightclubs—so-called lingerie parties—and also went to college at night. She had a baby boy,

Justin, named for her favorite high-school teacher, who had encouraged her to pursue modeling.

Everyone suspected that J.T. was the baby's father. He had told me never to ask him about the baby.

The light in her apartment was dim, but bright enough to show that her face was beaten badly and her white T-shirt was stained with blood. Her breathing was labored, her eyes closed; you could hear the blood gurgling in her mouth. Another young woman held her hand and comforted her. "They're coming," she said, "the ambulance is coming. Just relax, 'Neesha."

Ms. Bailey pulled me aside and asked if I would drive Taneesha to the hospital.

"I don't have a car, Ms. Bailey," I said. "Didn't you call the ambulance?"

"Okay, then, do me a favor," she said. "Ask C-Note to tell the boys in the lobby to take her."

"What about the ambulance?"

"Oh, no, baby," Ms. Bailey said softly. "They never come."

I wasn't sure whether to believe her, but at least fifteen minutes had passed since I'd arrived and there was no ambulance. Provident Hospital was only two miles away.

I walked out to the gallery and told C-Note, who simply leaned over and yelled down to the street twelve floors below. "Cheetah! Yo, Cheetah! Ms. Bailey says bring the car 'round! You got to take her to the hospital!"

"C-Note!" Ms. Bailey shouted out. "Don't yell! He's still in the building. Damn, we can't have him leaving the building."

I was confused. *Whom didn't she want to leave the building?* Before I could ask, she rounded up the men and addressed them as if she were a general and they, however ragged, were her troops. "She got hurt pretty bad. She'll make it, but she don't look so good. I need you-all to find him. He goes by 'Bee-Bee.' He may be in 407, inside that vacant apartment, or at his cousin's. I want to see him before you do anything to him."

I figured out that the man who had beat up Taneesha was hiding in the building.

"What if he starts to run or gets crazy?" one of the men asked. "Can we get him then?"

"Yeah, I suppose, but don't hurt him too bad before I talk to the fool. And *don't* let him get away. Sudhir, could you call J.T.?"

I nodded and followed C-Note and the others as they made for the stairwell. I recognized most of them as squatters who helped C-Note fix cars in the warmer months.

As soon as we were out of Ms. Bailey's earshot, I told C-Note I wanted to come with him.

"Call J.T.," he said, shaking his head. "Don't mess around with this. Do what Ms. Bailey says, *boy*."

C-Note had called me "boy" only a few times, the last one when a friend of his was caught in a knife fight and C-Note instructed me to watch from inside a car, where I couldn't get hurt.

"I will, I will," I insisted. "But I want to go."

C-Note realized I wouldn't take no for an answer. "Just stay near me," he said. "But if shit gets crazy and I tell you to leave, you go, right? You hear me?"

Eight of us made our way down the stairwell, our breath leaving trails of hot steam in the frigid air. There were a lot of questions I wanted to ask. Who was Bee-Bee and what was his relationship with Taneesha? Did C-Note and the other men know him? But we were moving too fast, and C-Note was preoccupied, his eyes ablaze.

We stopped just above the fourth-floor stairwell, since it was thought that Bee-Bee had taken refuge in Number 407. "Charlie, you and Blue go ahead," C-Note said. "Shorty, you and them go to the other stairwell in case he runs past. Sudhir and me will stay in the back. Charlie, I'm right behind you, so if he got a knife, just let him go. I'll get him."

It struck me that I might not be as far out of the way as I'd planned.

All the men hurried to their positions. I could see the door to Number 407 from where I stood in the stairwell with C-Note. Charlie and Blue approached it. Like C-Note, they wore secondhand clothes and ill-fitting shoes. Charlie had a crowbar in his hand. Blue's fist was clenched, but I couldn't tell what he was holding.

Charlie knocked. The thin wooden door gave a hollow sound. All the other apartments on the floor had thick steel doors, but the CHA used wooden doors to designate which apartments were vacant. "Yo, nigger!" Charlie called out. "Hey, Bee-Bee! Taneesha says she wants to talk with you. Come on out. She says she's cool with everything." He looked back at us. C-Note waved his hands, signaling him to shout again. "Yo, Bee-Bee! Taneesha says she just wants to talk, nigger! I'll take you up there." *Why would Bee-Bee need an escort to go back upstairs?* I thought. *And why on earth would he believe any of this?*

Just then a voice rang out from the stairwell above us. "He's on eleven, and he's coming down the stairs! Get him, he's coming down!"

C-Note instinctively pinned me against the gallery, letting Charlie and Blue go past. They stopped just inside the stairwell. C-Note and I crouched down a few feet behind them. The intense cold made me shiver. Charlie pressed his hand toward the floor a few times, motioning us to stand still. I had never heard the building so quiet. Apart from the wind and some cars in the distance, the only sound I could make out was a mouse or rat scratching around in the incinerator room.

Then, from above, I heard some distant footsteps turning into a rumble. Someone was running down the stairs, breathing heavily. I found myself grabbing onto the back of C-Note's jacket. Charlie and Blue were crouched just in front of us. I made out what was in Blue's hand: brass knuckles.

Just as the footsteps reached the fourth floor, Charlie jumped up and swung the crowbar, waist high. He struck Bee-Bee full-on, bowling him over.

"Yeah, nigger!" Blue shouted, then jumped over and started pounding Bee-Bee in the side. His head hit the wall of the stairwell and snapped back. "Leave that bitch alone, you hear me?" Blue shouted, punching him repeatedly in the gut. "You better leave her alone, nigger!"

Bee-Bee was tall and strong, and he threw Charlie off him. He stood up and began shouting, but Blue tackled him, smashing Bee-Bee into the wall. The two of them started tumbling down the stairs. Charlie grabbed Bee-Bee's leg, so he, too, fell down the stairwell.

"Grab his other leg!" Charlie yelled in our direction. C-Note jumped down the stairs and made a grab. Blue, meanwhile, was struggling to get out from under Bee-Bee, who had Blue's head in a choke hold. I could see that Blue was struggling to breathe; he looked like he might pass out, or worse. I felt as if I had to do something. Running over to them, I kicked Bee-Bee in the stomach, which made him relax his grip on Blue. The other men smothered him, and I could hear his muffled words: "Okay, okay. All right, enough."

Blue, the strongest of them, bent Bee-Bee's arms behind his back, bringing him to his knees. I don't know whether it was the cold air, the adrenaline, or the swift kick I'd delivered, but I was badly out of breath. I leaned against the wall near the incinerator room. "Charlie, run back up the stairs and make sure he didn't drop nothing," C-Note said. "We'll meet you at the office."

The rest of us walked Bee-Bee downstairs to Ms. Bailey's office. She wasn't in, so C-Note sent another squatter to fetch her. We all stood outside the office, silent. No one seemed to worry that Bee-Bee would run away.

He sat down on the floor with his head pitched back, resting against the wall. This was my first opportunity to get a good look at him. He was young, his face light-skinned and boyish but with a menacing air. And he appeared to be aging fast. His nostrils were black, his eyes hollow and glazed, telltale signs of crack use. He wore a brown sweatshirt over a stained white tank top, with loose jeans and unlaced sneakers dirtied by the winter slush. I saw a gang tattoo on his neck, the crescent-and-star pattern of the Black P. Stone Nation. The Stones had been largely dismantled in the 1980s by the feds, with some remaining factions now aligned with the Black Kings. Why, I wondered, was Taneesha hanging around with *this* guy?

C-Note had caught his breath by now. "You really fucked up this time, Bee-Bee."

Bee-Bee said nothing. He wiped the sweat from his face.

I heard Ms. Bailey coming. I'd never seen her move so fast before—she was practically galloping, trailed by Catrina and a few older women in blue Tenant Patrol jackets.

Ms. Bailey hurried past without looking at me. Catrina, however, gave me one of her signature looks that I now recognized as meaning this: *Ms. Bailey's got the situation under control, and all will soon be right with the world.* Ms. Bailey unlocked her office door and went inside. Blue and Charlie, who'd returned from upstairs, picked up Bee-Bee and brought him into the office. Bee-Bee seemed cooperative. The three of them entered the back room in Ms. Bailey's office, and then someone shut the front door. I stayed outside, along with the other squatters and the Tenant Patrol women. C-Note, his work done, took off.

Then Catrina poked her head out the door and waved me inside. *Get in here!* she mouthed silently. I did, and she pointed me to a chair.

It was hard to make out the full conversation behind Ms. Bailey's closed door, but once in a while her voice was loud enough for me to hear: "You got some nerve, young man! . . . Beat her like that. . . . Where do you live, huh, where do you live?! . . . She's a good girl. She owe you money? She wouldn't fuck you? Why did you do that? . . . Say something!"

Then came the beating. Charlie or Blue, or maybe both of them, started hitting Bee-Bee. I also heard Ms. Bailey cry out in a muffled tone. *Maybe Ms. Bailey is hitting him as well,* I thought. I heard chairs scuffing the floor. Then, for the first time, I heard Bee-Bee's voice: "Oh, shit! . . . Get off me. . . . Fuck that! She deserved it."

Ms. Bailey started to yell louder. "Deserved it? . . . You'll get worse if you come around here. . . . Don't ever, don't *ever* touch her again, you hear me? *You hear me?* Don't ever come in this building again."

Ms. Bailey threw open the door. Blue dragged Bee-Bee out. His face was badly worked over; he was drooling and mumbling something unintelligible. Blue hustled him past Catrina and me and threw him to the floor on the gallery. Two other men grabbed him and led him toward the stairwell. Ms. Bailey followed them, with the members of the Tenant Patrol right behind.

I started to get up, but Catrina stopped me. "Sudhir! No, let them go! They're just taking him in the car, and they'll leave him on State Street. Come up with me and see how Taneesha's doing."

Taneesha's aunt answered our knock. She and Taneesha's mother told us that Taneesha was at the hospital; she had some bad bruises, but it seemed as if she'd be okay. "I don't know what she's going to *look* like, though," said the aunt. "He beat her pretty good." Tanee-sha's mother promised to call Ms. Bailey later that night.

We went back downstairs to Ms. Bailey's office. She hadn't re-turned yet—she was apparently visiting Taneesha at the hospital—so Catrina told me what she knew. Bee-Bee had been managing Taneesha's modeling career, booking her at lingerie shows and dances. For this, he received a 25 percent cut—and, according to Cat-rina, he made Taneesha sleep with him. When Bee-Bee heard that Taneesha was going to sign up with a legitimate modeling agency, he got mad and started beating her. Today wasn't the first time this had happened. In fact, Ms. Bailey had repeatedly warned Bee-Bee to stop. But he kept harassing Taneesha, even stealing money from her apartment. It was only because Ms. Bailey felt there was no other recourse, Catrina explained, that today she had rounded up C-Note and the others to form a sort of militia. In the projects this was a long-standing practice. Militias were regularly put together to track down stolen property, mete out punishment, or simply obtain an apology for a victim.

In a neighborhood like this one, with poor police response and no shelter for abused women, the militias sometimes represented the best defense. "It's hard when you can't get nobody to come around," Catrina said solemnly. She was sitting in Ms. Bailey's chair, a soda in hand and her voice assured, seeming for all the world like the heiress to Ms. Bailey's throne. "No police, nobody from the hospital. We can't live like this! That's why Ms. Bailey is so important. And espe-cially for women. She makes sure we're safe."

"I suppose," I said. "But it's a horrible way to live. And wouldn't you rather have the police come around?"

"I'd rather not live in the projects," Catrina shot back. "But women are always getting beat on, getting sent to the hospital. I mean, you have to take care of yourself. Ms. Bailey makes these men take care of us. I don't see what's wrong with that. Unless you live here, you can't judge us, Sudhir."

For some reason I couldn't restrain the judgmental voice of my middle-class self. "You all didn't call the police, did you?" I blurted out.

For the first time since I knew Catrina, she couldn't look me in the eye. "No, we didn't."

"Why?"

She took a deep breath and raised her head. "Because we're scared of them."

"*You* are scared? *Women* are scared? *Everyone* is scared?" I asked. "Who *exactly* is scared? I hear this all the time."

"Everybody. But for women it's different. You wouldn't understand." She paused. "At least we have C-Note and the rest of them when things go crazy." It was clear that Catrina didn't want to talk further. I decided to ask Ms. Bailey about this when things calmed down.

I'd seen some police around the neighborhood, and I'd seen them work with Autry at the Boys & Girls Club. But since most tenants were so distrustful of the cops, I kept my interactions with them to a minimum, since I didn't want to be thought of as being "with" the cops.

Still, I had a hard time accepting the idea that tenants wouldn't call the police for something as serious as an assault. I also found it tough to believe that the police wouldn't show up—or, for that matter, that an ambulance wouldn't respond either. But as Catrina sat now in total silence, staring at me expressionlessly, I realized I might well be wrong.

I told her that I'd better get back to my apartment. She didn't acknowledge me. I wanted to do something to help her.

"Would you like to get something to eat?" I asked meekly.

She shook her head.

"Do you want to write me another essay?" I asked. "Do you want to write about what just happened?"

Catrina liked to write essays, which I read so that we could discuss them. This was a good way for her to talk through her aspirations as well as the shadows of her past: intense poverty and a bad family situation that I was just starting to learn about.

She shrugged. I couldn't tell if that meant yes or no.

"Well, I'm happy to read it if you do write something. Whenever."

"Thanks," she said. The barest hint of a smile came to her face, and she pushed her thick, black-framed glasses up on her nose. She started sniffling and reaching for a tissue. She looked no more than twelve years old. "I'll see you around," she said. "I'm sure things will be okay."

With Catrina having gone quiet and Ms. Bailey at the hospital and C-Note and the other squatters nowhere to be seen, there wasn't anyone left for me to talk with. I thought about visiting J.T., but every time I asked him anything about Ms. Bailey, he'd shut me down. "You want to know what she's like, *you* hang out with her," he said. "I ain't telling you shit." J.T. didn't care much for Ms. Bailey's authority, as it occasionally challenged his own. It was well within her power, for instance, to close off the lobby to his sales crew. J.T. wanted me to experience Ms. Bailey for myself to see what he had to deal with.

took the bus back to my apartment but decided to stop first at Jimmy's, a local bar where a lot of U of C professors and students hung out. No one knew me there, and I could sit quietly and process what had just happened in my fieldwork. Sometimes I would go there to write up my notes, but more often I just sat and stared blankly into my glass. With increasing frequency, Jimmy's was a ritual stop on my way home. At Jimmy's, as at the best bars, no one cared what troubles I brought to the table. Most of the people were sitting alone, like me, and I figured they were dealing with their own problems.

Jimmy's gave me a place to take off one hat (the fieldworker) and put on the other (the student). I needed this break, because I was starting to feel schizophrenic, as if I were one person in the projects—sometimes I caught myself even talking in a different way—and another back in Hyde Park.

Increasingly I found that I was angry at the entire field of social science—which meant, to some degree, that I was angry at myself. I resented the fact that the standard tools of sociologists seemed powerless to prevent the hardships I was seeing. The abstract social policies that my colleagues were developing to house, educate, and employ the poor seemed woefully out of touch. On the other hand, life in the projects was starting to seem too wild, too hard, and too chaotic for the staid prescriptions that social scientists could muster. It struck me as only partially helpful to convince youth to stay in school: what was the value in giving kids low-paying, menial jobs when they could probably be making more money on the streets?

In the poverty seminars that Bill Wilson sponsored, where some of the best academic minds congregated to discuss the latest research, I acted as if I had a unique insight into poverty by virtue of my proximity to families. I prefaced my questions by blurting out a self-serving objection: "No one here seems to have spent much time with the poor, but if you did, you would see that . . ." or, "If you actually watched poor people instead of just reading census tables, you would understand that . . ." I felt as though the other scholars were living in a bubble, but my arrogant tone did little to help anyone hear what I was trying to say. I worried that my behavior might embarrass Wilson, but I was too bitter to take a moderate stance.

I wouldn't say that I was disillusioned with the academic life per se. I still attended classes, worked with professors and met my deadlines, earned pretty good grades, and even received a few prestigious fellowships. I still saw myself on the road to being a professor like Wilson. But day by day, it was getting harder to reconcile my life at the U of C with my life in the projects.

Rather than sharing my frustration with my girlfriend, my roommates, and my friends—most of whom were actually quite supportive and curious about my research—I just kept my experiences to myself. How could I explain the vigilante justice that C-Note and the others had just delivered? How could I explain my own role in the beating? I didn't understand it myself, and I feared that I'd open myself up to my friends' advice: *You need to call the police if they don't. . . . You're getting too involved. . . . You've gone too far. . . .*

When I did try talking about my fieldwork, I felt awkward. In fact, I sometimes came off as defending the gangs and their violent practices or as romanticizing the conditions in the projects. So, to stay sane, I'd usually just tell people about Autry's work at the Boys & Girls Club or, if pushed, a few stories about life in the gang.

I was growing quieter and more solitary. My fellow graduate students and even some faculty members thought of me as unapproachable. Rumors circulated that I was too ambitious, too aloof, but I figured I'd just have to live with them. A small part of me hoped that life would get back to normal once my fieldwork was over. But the end didn't seem very near, so I just kept to myself.

was eager to know more about the incident with Bee-Bee. Why had Ms. Bailey sicced the squatters on him instead of leaving it to the police? *Had* the police been called—Catrina said they hadn't, but I wanted to be sure—and if so, why didn't they respond? What were the consequences for Ms. Bailey of taking such matters into her own hands?

I waited until "check day" to go see Ms. Bailey. That's when welfare checks were distributed, which meant that most tenants were out buying food and clothing and household items—and not, therefore, coming to Ms. Bailey with demands.

On the way up to her office, I stopped in to see J.T. He was lying on the sofa, watching TV. Ms. Mae gave me a big hug and told me to sit down for lunch. She had cooked some of my favorites—okra, greens, mac and cheese—and so I gladly obliged. J.T. quipped that I was eating his share of food. "You're becoming the little brother I never wanted," he said.

I told him about Ms. Bailey and the Bee-Bee incident. "Oh, man!" he said with a laugh. "That's why she's so upset. She keeps asking if I've seen you."

"Why's she upset at *me*?"

"Because you beat the shit out of that man, the one who beat Taneesha. I told you to be careful with Ms. Bailey, not to do things for her."

"First of all, I didn't do anything. Blue was choking, so I kicked the guy to help him."

"That's not *really* why she's upset." J.T. sat up. "She thinks that you were spying for us. Remember when I said that she doesn't use us as much anymore? We could've taken care of the man who did that, but she didn't ask us. She asked those fools, C-Note and those crackheads."

I knew that J.T. had tried to persuade Ms. Bailey to call him when a woman in the building got beat up. But I also knew, from Catrina, that Ms. Bailey wouldn't call J.T. because his gang members were known to physically and sexually abuse women.

By now J.T. was in lecture mode. "*That's* why I told you not to do things with her. Because I can't be there to protect you. She already knows that you're with me, so she doesn't trust you." According to this theory, Ms. Bailey must have thought I was spying for the gang, keeping track of how often she used non-gang affiliates for enforcing justice in the building.

I was taken aback when J.T. said that I was "with" him. I hadn't thought my relationship with J.T. would affect my work with Ms. Bailey—and I certainly wouldn't have predicted she would see me as a spy. His casual aside left me unsure of how to talk with different people in the projects. Once again I was being asked to pick sides. Was it possible, I wondered, to be in the projects for any length of time and remain neutral, an outsider, an objective observer?

J.T. urged me to go see Ms. Bailey immediately. "You might as well deal with this shit," he said. "It's not going away." He changed the channel.

As I headed for Ms. Bailey's office, I thought that I should probably just confess the truth: I hadn't asked her permission to join C-Note, and I had participated—however minimally—in the beating of Bee-Bee.

Catrina was leaving as I entered. She said nothing, just shook her head as if in disapproval. I stepped into Ms. Bailey's office. "Ms. Bailey, I have to apologize." I told her about my involvement with Bee-Bee.

She stared at me for a while. I fidgeted.

"That's not really what bothers me, Sudhir," she finally said. "What bothers me is that you are seeing things and you may not be ready for it."

"I'm not sure I understand."

"See, if you were in a war and you were a reporter, you could just say what's going on. No one would be mad at you. But this ain't a war. I try to tell you that all the time. It's *every day.* Every day something happens like what happened to 'Neesha. And you're getting yourself in the middle. People are saying, 'Sudhir's tough, he beat up that man almost by himself. He'll do things for us.' You understand why that's a problem?"

"I'm not sure. You think they'll hire me to beat up people?"

"They might, they might not. But they *will* start talking about you. Sometimes they'll give you credit, and sometimes they'll blame you. Understand?"

I didn't answer.

"And when you say, 'No, I can't help you with that,' they'll say, 'But you helped 'Neesha, so why won't you help me?' Then they'll say, 'Sudhir don't care about *us,*' or 'Sudhir is 'Neesha's manager.' Then they'll say, 'Sudhir is working for Ms. Bailey, and he don't do nothing unless he gets paid.' Get it?"

"I think I get it." I sat silently and stared into my hands. "When do you think I *should* see these things?"

"Well, *why* do you want to see what we do? I mean, why don't you hang around the police? You should figure out why they don't come."

"Ms. Bailey, I wanted to ask you about that. Did you really call the police? Or the ambulance?"

"Sudhir, the hardest thing for middle-class white folk to understand is why those people don't come when we call."

Ms. Bailey didn't think I was actually white, but she always tried to show me how my middle-class background got in the way of understanding life in the projects.

"They just don't come around all the time. And so we have to find ways to deal with it. I'm not sure how much better I can explain it to you. Why don't you watch out for the next few months? See how much they come around."

"What about Officer Reggie?"

"Yes, he's a friend. But can I tell you how he can be helpful? Not by coming and putting Bee-Bee in jail. Because he'll be out in the morning. But Officer Reggie *can* visit Bee-Bee after we're through with him. Maybe put the fear in him."

"Put the fear in him? I don't understand."

"He could visit Bee-Bee and tell him that we won't be so nice the next time he does that to 'Neesha. If Bee-Bee knows that the cop don't care if we kick his ass, that may make him think twice. *That* is what we need Officer Reggie for."

"Ms. Bailey, I have to tell you that I just don't get it. I've been watching you for a while, and it just seems to me that you shouldn't have to be doing everything you're doing. If you got the help you needed, you wouldn't have to act like this."

"Sudhir, what's the first thing I told you when you asked about my job?"

I smiled as I thought of something she'd told me months earlier: "As long as I'm helping people, something ain't right about this community. When they don't need me no more, that's when I know they're okay."

But she'd been helping for three decades and didn't see any end in sight.

One day in the middle of February, the Wilson family lost their front door. The Wilsons lived on the twelfth floor, just down the hall from Ms. Bailey. Their door simply fell off its hinges, leaving the family exposed to the brutal cold of a Chicago winter.

Even *with* a front door, the Robert Taylor Homes weren't very comfortable in the winter. Because the galleries are outdoors, you can practically get blown over by the lake wind as you walk from the elevator to your apartment. Inside, the winter wind inevitably finds its way through the seams in the doorframe.

Chris Wilson worked for the city and moved in and out of Robert Taylor, living off-the-lease with his wife, Mari, and her six children. Chris and Mari were, unsurprisingly, pretty anxious when they lost their door. It wasn't just the cold; they were worried about being robbed. It was common knowledge that drug addicts would pounce on any opportunity to steal a TV or anything else of value.

The Wilsons tried calling the CHA but got no response. They put up a makeshift door of wooden planks and plastic sheeting, but it didn't keep out the cold. Neighbors who said they'd keep an eye on the apartment didn't show up reliably. So after a few days, the Wilsons called Ms. Bailey.

Ms. Bailey leaped into action. She asked J.T. to station a few of his gang members in the twelfth-floor stairwells to keep out potential burglars. As a preventive measure, J.T. also shut down a nearby vacant apartment that was being used as a crack den. Then Ms. Bailey contacted two people she knew at the CHA. The first was a man who obtained a voucher so the Wilsons could stay at an inexpensive motel until their door was fixed. The second person was able to speed up the requisition process for obtaining a new door. It arrived two days after Ms. Bailey placed her first call.

The door didn't come cheap for the Wilsons. They had to pay Ms. Bailey several hundred dollars, which covered the fees that she paid to her CHA friends, as well as an electrician's bill, since some of the wiring in the Wilsons' apartment went bad because of the cold. Ms. Bailey presumably pocketed the rest of the money. Mari Wilson was, on balance, unperturbed. "Last summer we didn't have running water for a month," she told me, "so one week without a door was nothing."

Having watched Ms. Bailey help women like Taneesha and families like the Wilsons, I was left with deeply mixed feelings about her methodology—often ingenious and just as often morally questionable. With such scarce resources available, I understood why she believed that the ends justified the means. But collaborating with gangs, bribing officials for services, and redistributing drug money did little to help the typical family in her building. Ms. Bailey had told me that she would much rather play by the rules if only the rules worked. But in the end I concluded that what really drove Ms. Bailey was a thirst for power. She liked the fact she could get things done (and get paid for it), and she wasn't about to give that up, even if it meant that sometimes her families might get short shrift. Many families, meanwhile, were too scared to challenge her and invite the consequences of her wrath.

I was left discouraged by the sort of power bestowed upon building presidents like Ms. Bailey. People in this community shouldn't have to wait more than a week to get a new front door. People in this community shouldn't have to wonder if the ambulance or police would bother responding. People in this community shouldn't have to pay a go-between like Ms. Bailey to get the services that most Americans barely bother to think about. No one in the suburb where I grew up would tolerate such inconvenience and neglect.

But life in the projects wasn't like my life in the suburbs. Not only was it harder, but it was utterly unpredictable, which necessitated a different set of rules for getting by. And living in a building with a powerful tenant leader, as hard as that life could be, was slightly less hard. It may have cost a little more to get what you needed, but at least you had a chance.

SIX

The Hustler and the Hustled

Four years deep into my research, it came to my attention that I might get into a lot of trouble if I kept doing what I'd been doing.

During a casual conversation with a couple of my professors, in which I apprised them of how J.T.'s gang went about planning a drive-by shooting—they often sent a young woman to surreptitiously cozy up to the rival gang and learn enough information to prepare a surprise attack—my professors duly apprised *me* that I needed to consult a lawyer. Apparently the research I was doing lay a bit out of bounds of the typical academic research.

Bill Wilson told me to stop visiting the projects until I got some legal advice. I tried to convince Wilson to let me at least hang out around the Boys & Girls Club, but he shot me a look indicating that his position was not negotiable.

I did see a lawyer, and I learned a few important things.

First, if I became aware of a plan to physically harm somebody,

I was obliged to tell the police. Meaning I could no longer watch the gang plan a drive-by shooting, although I could speak with them about drive-bys in the abstract.

Second, there was no such thing as "researcher-client confidentiality," akin to the privilege conferred upon lawyers, doctors, or priests. This meant that if I were ever subpoenaed to testify against the gang, I would be legally obligated to participate. If I withheld information, I could be cited for contempt. While some states offer so-called shield laws that allow journalists to protect their confidential sources, no such protection exists for academic researchers.

It wasn't as if I had any intention of joining the gang in an actual drive-by shooting (nor would they ever invite me). But since I could get in trouble just for driving around with them while they *talked* about shooting somebody, I had to rethink my approach. I would especially have to be clearer with J.T. We had spoken several times about my involvement; when I was gang leader for a day, for instance, he knew my limits and I understood his. But now I would need to tell him, and perhaps a few others, about the fact that I was legally obligated to share my notes if I was ever subpoenaed.

This legal advice was ultimately helpful in that it led me to seriously take stock of my research. It was getting to be time for me to start thinking about the next stage: writing up my notes into a dissertation. I had become so involved in the daily drama of tagging along with Ms. Bailey and J.T. that I'd nearly abandoned my study of the broader underground economy my professors wanted to be the backbone of my research.

So I returned to Robert Taylor armed with two objectives: let people know about my legal issues and glean more details of the tenants' illegal economic activities.

I figured that most people would balk at revealing the economics of hustling, but when I presented the idea to J.T., Ms. Bailey, and several others, nearly everyone agreed to cooperate. Most of the hustlers liked being taken seriously as businesspeople—and, it should be said, they were eager to know if they earned more than their competitors. I emphasized that I wouldn't be able to share the details of anyone else's business, but most people just shrugged off my caveat as a technicality that could be gotten around.

So with the blessing of J.T. and Ms. Bailey, I began devoting my time to interviewing the local hustlers: candy sellers, pimps and prostitutes, tailors, psychics, squeegee men.

I also told J.T. and Ms. Bailey about my second problem, my legal obligation to share notes with the police.

"You mean you didn't know this all along?" Ms. Bailey said. "Even *I* knew that you have to tell police what you're doing—unless you give them information on the sly."

"Oh, no!" I protested. "I'm not going to be an informant."

"Sweetheart, we're all informants around here. Nothing to be ashamed of. Just make sure that you get what you need, I always say. And don't let them beat you up."

"I'm not sharing my data with them—that's what I mean."

"You mean you'll go to prison?"

"Well, not exactly. I just mean I won't share my data with them."

"Do you know what being in contempt means?"

When I didn't reply, Ms. Bailey shook her head in disgust. I had seen this look before: she was wondering how I had qualified for higher education given my lack of street smarts.

"Any nigger around here can tell you that you got two choices," she said. "Tell them what they want or sit in Cook County Jail."

I was silent, trying to think of a third option.

"I'll ask you again," she said. "Will you give up your information, or will you agree to go to jail?"

"You need to know that? That's important to you?"

"Sudhir, let me explain something to you. You think we were born yesterday around here. Haven't we had this conversation a hundred times? You think we don't know what you do? You think we don't know that you keep all your notebooks in Ms. Mae's apartment?"

I shuddered. Ms. Mae had made me feel so comfortable in her apartment that I'd never even entertained the possibility that someone like Ms. Bailey would think about—and perhaps even page through—my notebooks.

"So why let me hang out?" I asked.

"Why do you *want* to hang out?"

"I suppose I'm learning. That's what I do, study the poor."

"Okay, well, you want to act like a saint, then you go ahead," Ms. Bailey said, laughing. "Of course you're learning! But you are also *hustling.* And we're all hustlers. So when we see another one of us, we gravitate toward them. Because we need other hustlers to survive."

"You mean that people think I can do something for them if they talk to me?"

"They *know* you can do something for them!" she yelped, leaning across the table and practically spitting out her words. "And they know you *will,* because you need to get your information. You're a hustler, I can see it. You'll do anything to get what you want. Just don't be ashamed of it."

I tried to turn the conversation back to the narrow legal issue, but Ms. Bailey kept on lecturing me.

"I'll be honest with you," she said, sitting back in her chair. "If you *do* tell the police, everyone here will find you and beat the shit out of you. So that's why we know you won't tell nobody." She smiled as if she'd won the battle.

So who should I be worried about? I wondered. *The police or Ms. Bailey and the tenants?*

When I told J.T. about my legal concerns, he looked at me with some surprise. "I could've told you all that!" he said. "Listen, I'm never going to tell you anything that's going to land me in jail—or get me killed. So it don't bother me what you write down, because I can take care of myself. But that's really not what you should be worried about."

I waited.

"What you should be asking yourself is this: 'Am I going to be on the side of black folks or the cops?' Once you decide, you'll do whatever it takes. You understand?"

I didn't.

"Let me try again. Either you're with us—you feel like you're in this with us and you respect that—or you're just here to look around. So far these niggers can tell that you've been with us. You come back every day. Just don't change, and nothing will go wrong, at least not around here."

J.T.'s advice seemed vague and a bit too philosophical. Ms. Bailey's warning—that I would get beat up if I betrayed confidences—made more sense. But maybe J.T. was saying the same thing, in his own way.

I decided to focus my study of the underground economy on the three high-rise buildings that formed the core of J.T.'s territory. I already knew quite a bit—that squatters fixed cars in the alleys, people sold meals out of their homes, and prostitutes took clients to vacant apartments—but I had never asked people how much money they made, what kind of expenses they incurred, and so on.

J.T. was far more enthusiastic about my project than I'd imagined he would be, although I couldn't figure out why.

"I have a great idea," he told me one day. "I think you should talk to all the pimps. Then you can go to all the whores. Then I'll let you talk to all the people stealing cars. Oh, yeah! And you also have folks selling stolen stuff. I mean, there's a whole bunch of people you can talk to about selling shoes or shirts! And I'll make sure they cooperate with you. Don't worry, they won't say no."

"Well, we don't want to force anyone to talk to me," I said, even though I was excited about meeting all these people. "I can't *make* anyone talk to me."

"I know," J.T. said, breaking into a smile. "But *I* can."

I laughed. "No, you can't do that. That's what I'm saying. That wouldn't be good for my research."

"Fine, fine," he said. "I'll do it, but I won't tell you."

J.T. arranged for me to start interviewing the pimps. He explained that he taxed all the pimps working in or around his buildings: some paid a flat fee, others paid a percentage of their take, and all paid in kind by providing women to J.T.'s members at no cost. The pimps had to pay extra, of course, if they used a vacant apartment as a brothel; they even paid a fee to use the stairwells or a parking lot.

As I began interviewing the pimps, I also befriended some of the freelance prostitutes like Clarisse who lived and worked in the building. "Oh, my ladies will love the attention," Clarisse said when I asked for help in talking to these women. Within two weeks I had interviewed more than twenty of them.

Between these conversations and my interviews with the pimps, some distinctions began to emerge. The prostitutes who were managed by pimps (these women were known as "affiliates") had some clear advantages over the "independents" who worked for themselves. The typical affiliate was beaten up far less frequently—about once a year, as against roughly four times a year for the independents. The affiliates also earned about twenty dollars per week more than the independents, even though their pimps took a 33 percent cut. (Twenty dollars wasn't a small sum, considering that the average Robert Taylor prostitute earned only about one hundred dollars per week.) And I never heard of an affiliate being killed in the line of work, whereas in one recent two-year stretch three independents were killed.

But the two types of prostitutes had much in common. Both groups had high rates of heroin and crack use, and they were bound to the projects, where the demand for sex came mostly from low-income customers. At the truck stops on the other side of the Dan Ryan Expressway—barely a mile away from Robert Taylor but a different ecosystem entirely—a different set of pimps catered to a clientele of white truckers who paid more than the typical black customer in a housing project. Around Robert Taylor a prostitute usually earned ten to twenty dollars for oral sex, sometimes as little as twenty-five dollars for intercourse, and at least fifty dollars for anal sex. But if she was in need of drugs, she would drop her price significantly or accept a few bags of drugs in lieu of any cash.

Once my prostitute research was under way, I asked Ms. Bailey if she would help me meet female hustlers who sold something other than sex. I had casual knowledge of any number of off-the-books businesses: women who sold food out of their apartments or catered parties; women who made clothing, offered marital counseling or baby-sitting; women who read horoscopes, styled hair, prepared taxes, drove gypsy cabs, and sold anything from candy to used appliances to stolen goods. But since most of these activities were conducted out of public view, I needed Ms. Bailey to open some doors.

She was cautious. For the first week, she selectively introduced me to a few women but refused to let me meet others. I'd suggest a name, and she'd mull it over. "Well," she'd say, "let me think about whether I want you to meet with her." Or, just as often, "No, she's not good. But I got someone else for you." Once, after Ms. Bailey introduced me to a psychic, I asked if many other psychics worked in the building. "Maybe, maybe," she said, then changed the subject and left the room.

I eventually figured out why she was reluctant to let me explore the underground economy. As it turned out, tenant leaders like Ms. Bailey always got their cut from such activities. If you sold food out of your kitchen or took in other people's children to baby-sit, you'd better give Ms. Bailey a few dollars, or you might find a CHA manager knocking on your door. If you occasionally cut hair in your apartment, it was probably a good idea to give Ms. Bailey a free styling once in a while. In these parts Ms. Bailey was like the local IRS—and probably a whole lot more successful at collecting her due.

So the people she let me talk to were the ones she probably trusted most not to speak out of line. But I didn't have much choice: Without Ms. Bailey's say-so, *no one* was going to speak with me about any illegal activities.

Truth be told, nearly everyone Ms. Bailey introduced me to had a fascinating story to tell. One of the most fascinating women I met was Cordella Levy, a close friend of Ms. Bailey. She was sixty-three years old and had lived in public housing her entire life, the past thirty years in Robert Taylor. (She had a Jewish surname, she said, because her grandmother had married a Jewish man; someone else in her family, however, told me that they were descended from black Hebrew Israelites.) Cordella had raised seven children, all but one of whom had moved out of Robert Taylor. Although she used a walking crutch to get around, Cordella had the fight of a bulldog in-side her.

She now ran a small candy store inside her apartment. All day long she sat on a stool by the door and waited for children to stop by. Her living room was barren except for the candy: boxes and boxes of lollipops, gum, and candy bars stacked invitingly on a few tables. If you peeked around the corner, you could see into the back bedroom, where Cordella had a TV, couches, and so on. But she liked to keep her candy room sparse, she told me, because if customers saw her furniture, they might decide to come back and rob her.

"You know," she told me, "I didn't always sell candy."

"You mean you didn't go to school for this?" I joked.

"Sweetheart, I never made it past the fourth grade. Black folks weren't really allowed to go to school in the South. What I meant was that I used to be somebody different. Ms. Bailey didn't tell you?" I shook my head. "She told me you wanted to know how I used to hustle."

"I'd love to hear," I said. Cordella seemed itching to tell her story.

"Sweetheart, I've made money around here every which way you can. You know, I started out working for Ms. Bailey's mother, Ella Bailey. Ella was a madam, used to have parties in the building. Oh, Lord! She could throw a party!"

"Ms. Bailey's mother was a madam?" I laughed. "That explains a lot!"

"Yes, sir, and when she passed, I took over from her. Three apart-ments on the fourteenth floor. Cordella's Place, they used to call it. Come in for a drink, play some cards, make a friend, have a nice time."

"Make a friend? Is that what they used to call it?"

"Ain't nothing wrong with friendship. And then I started mak-ing clothes, and then I sold some food, drove people around for a while to the store. My mother taught me how to sew wedding dresses, so I was doing a lot of—"

"Wait!" I said. "Slow down, please. Let's get back to helping people make friends. I'm curious why you stopped running the parties. What happened? I ask because all the people doing that today are men: J.T. and the pimps. I haven't heard about any women."

"That's because they took over. The men ruined everything for us. The first one was J.T.'s mama's cousin, Miss Mae's cousin. He just decided to start harassing all the women who were making money. I think it was around 1981. He would beat us up if we didn't pay him money to work out of the building. I had to pay him a few dollars each week to manage my women and throw my parties. He nearly killed my friend because she wouldn't give him money for doing hairstyling in her apartment. He was real awful. On heroin, used to carry around a big gun, like he was in the movies. And he was a very violent man."

"So what happened, he took over your parties?"

"Well, all of a sudden, he told me I had to give him fifty percent of what I was making, and he'd protect me—keep the cops away. But I knew he couldn't keep any cops away. The man was a thug and wasn't even no good at that. I figured I had been doing it for a while, and so I just gave up and let him have the whole thing. But what I'm saying is that the women ran things around here, before the gangs and the rest of them took over. It was different, because we also helped people."

"How?"

"See, people like me had a little power. I could get your apartment fixed or get you out of jail, because the cops were my best customers. These folks today, like J.T., they can't do that."

"What about Ms. Bailey?"

"Yeah, she can, but she's just one person. Imagine if you had about fifty people like her doing their thing! Now, that was a sight. Fifty women, all powerful women with no shame. It was a different time. It was a time for women, a place for women."

For several days after I interviewed Cordella, I kept thinking of what she said: "It was a time for women, a place for women." Her nostalgia reminded me of how Catrina, Ms. Bailey's assistant, spoke so reverently of women helping each other in the building.

I spent the next three months focused on meeting the matriarchs of the high-rises. There were plenty to choose from: more than 90 percent of the four thousand households in Robert Taylor were headed by a female. Whenever Ms. Bailey introduced me to an elderly dressmaker or a grandmother who offered day care to working parents, I tried to solicit stories about the past as well as details of her current enterprise.

Many of these women had protested for civil rights in the 1960s and campaigned for black political candidates in the 1970s; they took the need to fight for their community very seriously. But during the 1980s and 1990s, as their plight was worsened by gangs, drugs, and even deeper poverty, they struggled just to keep their families together. By then the housing authority had grown corrupt and unsupportive, the police were largely unresponsive, and the tribe of strong women had been severely marginalized.

While the official statistics said that 96 percent of Robert Taylor's adult population was unemployed, many tenants did have part-time legitimate jobs—as restaurant workers, cabdrivers, cleaning ladies in downtown corporate offices, and nannies to middle-class families. But nearly all of them tried to hide any legitimate income from the CHA, lest they lose their lease or other welfare benefits.

There were also working men living in Robert Taylor, perhaps a few dozen in each building. But they stayed largely out of sight, again because of the CHA limits on how much money a tenant family could earn. Sometimes a man would leave home for a few weeks just to keep the CHA inspectors off guard. So when I or someone else they didn't recognize came into an apartment, the men might head for the back room. They didn't attend many tenant meetings, and for the most part they let the women handle the battle for better living conditions. The absence of men in Robert Taylor had made it that much easier for the gang members and pimps to essentially have the run of the place.

As I began compiling statistics on the illicit earnings generated by women throughout Robert Taylor, it became obvious that all their illicit earnings combined hardly constituted a lucrative economy. Selling food or candy out of your apartment might net you about twenty dollars per week. (Cordella Levy managed to do better than that, having persuaded a local grocery store to sell her candy wholesale in return for steering her customers to that store for their groceries.) Day care brought in five or ten dollars per day per child, but business wasn't steady. A woman could earn more selling sex, but that was risky in a few ways. One of the favored moneymaking options, therefore, was to take in a boarder, which could generate a hundred dollars a month. There was never any shortage of people who needed a place to stay.

But I also discovered something more interesting, and probably more important, than the money that changed hands in these various transactions. Many households participated in a vast web of exchange in which women borrowed, bartered, and pooled their resources to survive. One woman might offer day care for a large group of women, another might have a car and contribute by driving folks to buy groceries, and other women might take turns cooking for various families. In some cases the members of a network maintained a fixed formula of exchange: If you cook my family five dinners, I'll take care of your kids for two days.

Often a network of women would share their apartments as well. Let's say there were five women on one floor whose apartments had maintenance problems (which, given the condition of the buildings, wasn't uncommon). There was little chance that the CHA would respond to all their repair requests, and the women couldn't afford to pay five different bribes to Ms. Bailey or the CHA building manager. These women would pool their money to make sure they *could* pay the necessary bribes so that at least one apartment in their network had hot water and at least two had working refrigerators and stoves; perhaps one of them would also pay for pirated cable TV. Everyone would shower in one apartment, cook in another apartment, keep their food elsewhere, sit in the one air-conditioned room to watch the one TV with cable, and so on. To have your own apartment with all utilities functioning was a luxury that few people expected in Robert Taylor.

I met most of the neighborhood's male hustlers by hanging out in the local parking lot with C-Note. He let people know that it was safe to speak with me. There were always a lot of men milling around, talking and drinking, who represented the diversity of the neighborhood hustlers: carpenters who did inexpensive home repairs, freelance preachers, truck drivers who worked off the books for local factories, car thieves, rappers and musicians, cooks and cleaners. All of them made their money under the table.

Most of them had once held legitimate jobs that they lost out of either misfortune or misbehavior. Until a few years earlier, they could have gotten a few hundred dollars a month in welfare money, but by

1990, Illinois and many other states eliminated such aid for adult men. The conservative revolution launched by President Ronald Reagan would lead eventually to a complete welfare overhaul, culminating in the 1996 directive by President Bill Clinton that made welfare a temporary program by setting time limits on just about every form of public aid—for men, women, and children.

For men like the ones in Robert Taylor, the welfare changes only exacerbated their poverty. They all learned to keep track of which restaurants and churches offered free food and which abandoned buildings were available for sleeping. Like the women, the men also had a network: One would cook while another looked for work while yet another tried to find a place for all of them to sleep. If they heard of a vacant apartment, they'd pool their resources to bribe the CHA building manager, gang leader, tenant leader, or whoever else happened to have the key. These men also passed along information to cops in exchange for "get out of jail free" promises, and they could always make a few dollars from CHA janitors—who regularly paid off hustlers to clean the buildings when they felt like taking a day off.

C-Note introduced me to Porter Harris, a bone-thin man, sixty-five years old, who spent much of his time scouring the South Side for recyclable junk. When I met him, he was pushing a shopping cart filled with wire, cans, and metal scrap, trolling the tall grass between the high-rises and the railroad tracks. Years ago, Porter told me, *he* was the one who dictated where various hustlers in Robert Taylor could work, sell, and trade, much as C-Note did now. But he'd had to leave because of a battle with a gang leader.

"Booty Caldwell, real name was Carter," he told me in a southern drawl. "That was the one who kicked me out of here for good." Porter picked at his few remaining teeth with a blade of grass. He wore a floppy straw hat that made him look as if he'd stepped out of a faded photograph from the Old South. "There were about ten of us. I controlled Forty-seventh Street to Fifty-first. I had this whole area—you couldn't sell your *soul* without letting me know about it, yessir."

"Sounds like a good living," I said, smiling. "You were the king of hustlers?"

"Lord, king, and chief. Call it what you want, I ran that area. And then one day it all was taken away. By Booty Caldwell. He was part of the El Rukn gang." By the late 1960s, El Rukn had become the most powerful gang in Chicago. They were widely credited with uniting many independent gangs, making peace treaties and coop- erative arrangements that resulted in a few El Rukn "supergangs." But a federal indictment in the mid-1980s weakened El Rukn, al- lowing other gangs, including the Black Kings, to take over the bur- geoning crack trade.

From Porter, C-Note, and others, I learned that the most prof- itable hustling jobs for men were in manual labor: you could earn five hundred dollars a month fixing cars in a parking lot or roughly three hundred dollars a month cleaning up at the local schools. The worst-paying jobs, meanwhile, often required the longest hours: gathering up scrap metal or aluminum (a hundred dollars a month) or selling stolen clothes or cigarettes (about seventy-five dollars a month). While just about every hustler I interviewed told me that he was hoping for a legit job and a better life, I rarely saw anyone get out of the hustling racket unless he died or went to jail.

One day, after I'd spent hours interviewing Porter and some of the other male hustlers, I was summoned to Ms. Bailey's office. I'd been so busy that I hadn't seen her in a while. It was probably a good idea, I thought, to have a catch-up session.

I said hello to Catrina on my way in, and she gave me a smile. She was assuming more and more duties and seemed to be acting nearly as a junior officer to Ms. Bailey. Inside, J.T. and Ms. Bailey were laughing together and greeted me heartily.

"Mr. Professor!" J.T. said. "My mother says you haven't been by in a month! What, you don't like us anymore? You found somebody who cooks better?"

"You better not piss off Ms. Mae," Ms. Bailey said. "You'll never be able to come back in the building again."

"Sorry, all this interviewing has kept me really busy," I said, exasperated. "I just haven't had time to do much of anything else."

"Well, then, sit down, baby," Ms. Bailey said. "We won't keep you long. We just wanted to know who you've been meeting. We're curious about what you've learned."

"Hey, you know what, I could actually use the chance to tell you what I've been finding," I said, taking out my notebooks. "I've been meeting so many people, and I can't be sure whether they're telling me the truth about how much they earn. I suppose I want to know whether I'm really understanding what it's like to hustle around here."

"Sure," J.T. said. "We were just talking about that. You used to ask us to find you people. Now you do it yourself. We feel like you don't need us no more." He started laughing, and so did Ms. Bailey.

"Yeah," Ms. Bailey said. "Don't leave us behind, Mr. Professor, when you start to be successful! Go ahead, tell me who you've been talking to. If you tell us who you met and what they're doing, maybe we can check for you and see if folks are being straight."

For the next three hours, I went through my notebooks and told them what I'd learned about dozens of hustlers, male and female. There was Bird, the guy who sold license plates, Social Security cards, and small appliances out of his van. Doritha the tax preparer.

Candy, one of the only female carpenters in the neighborhood. Prince, the man who could pirate gas and electricity for your apartment. J.T. and Ms. Bailey rarely seemed surprised, although every now and then one of them perked up when I mentioned a particularly enterprising hustler or a woman who had recently started taking in boarders.

I finally left, riding the bus home to my apartment. I was grateful for having had the opportunity to discuss my findings with two of the neighborhood's most formidable power brokers. As I looked out the bus windows, I realized just how much I owed Ms. Bailey and J.T. If it weren't for the two of them, and a few other people like C-Note and Autry, I wouldn't ever have made any progress in learning how things really worked around Robert Taylor.

I spent the next few weeks turning the information in my notebooks into statistical tables and graphs that showed how much different hustlers made. I figured that J.T. would appreciate this data at least as much as my professors would, since he was always talking about the importance of data analysis within his managerial technique. So I headed over to Robert Taylor to show him my research.

In the parking lot, I ran into C-Note, who was in his usual spot with a few other squatters, fixing flat tires and washing cars.

"Hey, what's up, guys?" I shouted out. "Long time—how you been?"

Nobody replied. They looked at me, then turned away. I walked closer and stood a few feet from them. "What's up?" I said. "Everything all right?"

One of the men, Pootie, picked up a tool and started to loosen a tire from the rim. "Man, sometimes you just learn the hard way," he said to no one in particular. "That's life, isn't it? Sometimes you realize you can't trust nobody. They could be a cop, a snitch—who knows?"

C-Note simply shrugged. "Mm–hmm," he said.

"Yup, you just learn you can't trust *nobody*," Pootie continued. "You tell them something, and then they turn on you. Just like *that*! You can't predict it. Especially if they're not from around here."

Once again C-Note shrugged. "Mm–hmm," he muttered. "You got that right."

They kept ignoring me, so I walked over to J.T.'s building. A young woman I knew named Keisha was standing on the grass with her kids. They looked like they were waiting for a ride.

"Hey, Keisha," I said. "How are you doing?"

"How am I *doing*?" she asked, shaking her head. "I was doing a lot better before I started talking to *you*." She picked up her things and walked her kids a few yards away.

In the lobby some of J.T.'s gang members were hanging out. We shook hands and said hello. I went upstairs to see Ms. Bailey and J.T., but neither of them was home.

Down in the lobby again, I could feel people staring at me, but I couldn't figure out why. I felt myself growing paranoid. Did people suddenly think I was a cop? What was up with Pootie, C-Note, and Keisha? I decided to go back home.

I spent a few days trying to track down J.T., but nobody knew where he was. I couldn't wait any longer, so I went back to Robert Taylor and found C-Note in the parking lot. He and two other men were working on a car.

"C-Note, please," I begged, "what did I do? Tell me."

C-Note stood up and wiped the oil off a wrench. He motioned for the two other men to leave us alone. One of them gave me a nasty look and muttered something that sounded equally nasty, but I couldn't quite make it out.

"You need to learn to shut your mouth," C-Note finally said.

"Shut my mouth? I don't know what you're talking about."

"Don't play with me. All that shit I told you. All them niggers I introduced you to. If you told me you were going to tell J.T. they were making that money, I wouldn't have told you nothing."

My heart sank. I thought of my long debriefing with J.T. and Ms. Bailey. I had given them breakdowns on each hustler's earnings: how much every one of them made, when and where they worked, what they planned for the future. I didn't hand over my written data, but I'd done the next-best thing.

"J.T. is all *over* these niggers," C-Note said. He looked disgusted and spit on the ground. I could tell he was angry but that he wasn't comfortable expressing it to me. Until now our relationship had been based on trust; I rarely, if ever, spoke to anyone about what I learned from C-Note.

"He's taxing every one of them now," he said. "And he beat the shit out of Parnell and his brother because he thought they were hiding what they were doing. They weren't, but you can't convince J.T. of nothing. When he gets his mind to something, that's it. And then he tells Jo-Jo and his guys that they can't come around no more because *they* were hiding things from him. Jo-Jo's daughter lives up in here. So now he can't see *her*." C-Note kept talking, getting angrier and angrier as he listed all the people that J.T. was cracking down on. "There's no way he could've found out if you didn't say nothing."

There was an awkward silence. I thought about lying, and I began to drum up an excuse. But something came over me. During the years I'd been in this community, people were always telling me that I was different from all the journalists and other outsiders who came by, hunting up stories. They didn't eat dinner with families or hang around at night to share a beer; they typically asked a lot of questions and then left with their story, never to return. I prided myself on this difference.

But now it was time to accept my fate. "I was sitting in Ms. Bailey's office," I told C-Note. "She and J.T. always help me, just like you. And I fucked up. I told them things, and I had no idea that they would use that information. Man, I had no idea that it would even be useful to them."

"That has to be one of the stupidest things I *ever* heard you say." C-Note began putting away his tools.

"Honestly, C-Note, I had no idea when I was talking to them—"

"No!" C-Note's voice grew sharp. "You knew. Yes you did. But you were too busy thinking about your own self. That's what happened. You got some shit for your professors, and you were getting high on that. I know you ain't *that* naïve, man."

"I'm sorry, C-Note. I don't know what else to say. I fucked up."

"Yeah, you fucked up. You need to think about *why* you're doing your work. You always tell me you want to help us. Well, we ain't never asked for your help, and we sure don't need it now."

C-Note walked away toward the other men. They stood quietly drinking beer and watching me. I headed toward the building. I wanted to see if Ms. Bailey was in her office.

Then an obvious thought hit me: If J.T. had acted on my information to tax the male street hustlers, Ms. Bailey might have started taxing the women I told her about. Worse yet, she might have had some of them evicted for hiding their income. How could I find out what had happened because of my stupidity? As I stood in the grassy expanse, staring up at the high-rise, I tried to think of someone who might possibly help me. I needed a tenant who was relatively independent of Ms. Bailey, someone who might still trust me enough to talk. I thought of Clarisse.

I hustled over to the liquor store and bought a few bottles of Boone's Farm wine. Clarisse wasn't going to talk for free.

I walked quickly through the building lobby and took the stairs up. I didn't want to get trapped in the elevator with women who might be angry with me for selling them out to Ms. Bailey. Clarisse opened her door and greeted me with a loud burst of laughter.

"Oooh! Boy, you fucked up this time, you surely did."

"So it's all over the building? Everyone knows?"

"Sweetheart, ain't no secrets in this place. What did Clarisse tell you when we first met? *Shut the fuck up.* Don't tell them nothing about who you are and what you do. Clarisse should have been there with you. You were spying for Ms. Bailey?"

"Spying! No way. I wasn't spying, I was just doing my research, asking questions and—"

"Sweetheart, it don't matter what you call it. Ms. Bailey got pissed off and went running up in people's houses, claiming they owed her money. I mean, you probably doubled her income, just like that. And you're really not getting *any* kickbacks? Just a little something from her?"

"Wait a minute," I said. "How do they know I was the one who gave Ms. Bailey the information?"

"Because, you fool, she *told* everyone! Even if she didn't tell them, she was running around saying, 'You made twenty-five dollars last month,' 'You made fifty dollars last week,' 'You made ten dollars this week, and you owe me ten percent plus a penalty for not telling me.' I mean, the only folks we told all this information to was you!"

"But did she charge you, too?"

"No, no! She don't charge the hos, remember? J.T. already charges us."

I sat and listened with my head down as Clarisse listed all the women who'd been confronted by Ms. Bailey. I had a sinking feeling that I'd have a hard time coming back to this building to continue my research. I also had to face the small matter of managing to leave here today still in one piece.

Clarisse sensed my anxiety. As she talked—laughing heartily all the while, at my expense—she started massaging my shoulder. "Don't worry, little baby! You probably never had an ass whuppin', have you? Well, sometimes that helps clear the air. Just don't take the stairs when you leave, 'cause if you get caught there, they may never find your body."

I must have looked truly frightened, for Clarisse stopped laughing and took a sincere tone.

"Folks forgive around here," she said gently. "We're all religious people, sweetheart. We have to put up with a lot of shit from our own families, so nothing you did to us will make things much worse."

At that moment, sitting with Clarisse, I didn't think that even the Good Lord himself could, or would, help me. It was embarrassing to think that I had been so wrapped up in my desire to obtain good data that I couldn't anticipate the consequences of my actions. After several years in the projects, I had become attuned to each and every opportunity to get information from the tenants. This obsession was primarily fueled by a desire to make my dissertation stand out and increase my stature in the eyes of my advisers. After I'd talked with C-Note and Clarisse, it was clear to me that other people were paying a price for my success.

I began to feel deeply ambivalent about my own reasons for being in the projects. Would I really advance society with my research, as Bill Wilson had promised I could do if I worked hard?

Could I change our stereotypes of the poor by getting so deep inside the lives of the families? I suddenly felt deluged by these kinds of questions.

Looking back, I was probably being a little melodramatic. I had been so naïve up to this point about how others perceived my presence that any sort of shake-up at all was bound to send me reeling.

I couldn't think of a way to rectify the situation other than to stop coming to Robert Taylor entirely. But I was close to finishing my fieldwork, and I didn't want to quit prematurely. In the coming weeks, I spoke to Clarisse and Autry a few times for advice. Both suggested that the tenants I had angered would eventually stop being so angry, but they couldn't promise much more than that. When I asked Autry whether I'd be able to get back to collecting data, he just shrugged and walked off.

I eventually came back to the building to face the tenants. No one declined to speak with me outright, but I didn't exactly receive a hero's welcome either. Everyone knew I had J.T.'s support, so it was unlikely that anyone would confront me in a hostile manner. When I went to visit C-Note in the parking lot, he simply nodded at me and then went about his work, talking with customers and singing along with the radio. It felt like people in the building looked at me strangely when I passed by, but I wondered if I was just being paranoid. Perhaps the best indicator of my change in status was that I wasn't doing much of anything *casual*—hearing jokes, sharing a beer, loaning someone a dollar.

One sultry summer day not long after my fiasco with the hustlers, I attended the funeral of Catrina, Ms. Bailey's dutiful assistant. On the printed announcement, her full name was rendered as Catrina Eugenia Washington. But I knew this was not her real name.

Catrina had once told me that her father had sexually abused her when she was a teenager, so she ran away from home. She wound up living in Robert Taylor with a distant relative. She changed her name so her father wouldn't find her and enrolled in a GED program at DuSable High School. She took a few part-time jobs to help pay for rent and groceries. She was also saving money to go to community college; she was trying to start over. I never did find out her real name.

As a kid she had wanted to study math. But her father, she told me, said that higher education was inappropriate for a young black woman. He advised her instead just to get married and have children.

Catrina had a love of knowledge and would participate in a discussion about nearly anything. I enjoyed talking with her about science, African-American history, and Chicago politics. She always wore a studious look, intense and focused. Working as Ms. Bailey's assistant, she received just a few dollars a week. But, far more significant, she was receiving an apprenticeship in Chicago politics. "I will do something important one day," she liked to tell me, in her most serious voice. "Like Ms. Bailey, I *will* make a difference for black people. Especially black women."

By this time Catrina had been living in Robert Taylor for a few years. But over the July Fourth holiday, she decided to visit her siblings in Chicago's south suburbs, an area increasingly populated with African-American families who'd made it out of the ghetto. From what I was told, her father heard that she was visiting and tracked her down. A skirmish followed. Catrina got caught between her brother, who was protecting her, and her angry father. A gun went off, and the bullet hit Catrina, killing her instantly. No one around Robert Taylor knew if either the brother or the father had been arrested.

The funeral was held in the back room of a large African Methodist Episcopal church on the grounds of Robert Taylor. The hot air was stifling, the sun streaming in shafts through dusty windows. There were perhaps fifty people in attendance, mostly women from Ms. Bailey's building. A few members of Catrina's family were also there, but they came surreptitiously because they didn't want her father to hear about the funeral. Ms. Bailey stationed herself at the room's entrance, welcoming the mourners. She looked as if she were presiding over a tenant meeting: upright, authoritarian, refusing to cry while consoling those who were. She had the air of someone who did this regularly, who mourned for someone every week.

Sitting in a corner up front was T-Bone, his head down, still as stone. He and Catrina had been seeing each other for a few months. Although T-Bone had a steady girlfriend—it wasn't uncommon for gang members, or practically any other young man in the projects, to have multiple girlfriends—he and Catrina had struck up a friendship and, over time, become lovers. I sometimes came upon the two of them studying together at a local diner. T-Bone was about to leave his girlfriend for Catrina when she was killed.

Any loss of life is mourned in the projects, but there are degrees. Young men and women who choose a life of drugs and street gangs may, understandably, not be long for this world. When one of them dies, he or she is certainly mourned, but without any great sense of shock; there is a general feeling that death was always a good possibility. But for someone like Catrina, who had refused to follow such a path, death came with a deep sense of shock and disbelief. She was one of thousands of young people who had escaped the attention of social workers, the police, and just about everyone else. Adults in the projects pile up their hopes on people like Catrina, young men and women who take a sincere interest in education, work, and self-betterment. And I guess I did, too. Her death left me with a sting that would never fade.

The essays that Catrina used to write covered the difficulties of family life in the projects, the need for women to be independent, the stereotypes about poor people. Writing seemed to provide Catrina a sense of relief, as though she were finally acknowledging the hurdles of her own past; it also helped her develop a strong, assertive voice, not unlike that of her hero, Ms. Bailey.

In tribute to Catrina, I thought I'd try to broaden this idea by starting a writing workshop for young women in the building who were interested in going back to school. I brought up the possibility with Ms. Bailey. "Good idea," she said, "but take it slow, especially when you're dealing with *these* young women."

I was nervous about teaching the workshop, but I was also eager. My relationship with tenants up to this point had largely been a one-way street; after all this time in Robert Taylor, I felt as though I should give something back. On a few occasions, I had managed to solicit donations from my professors, fifty or a hundred dollars, for some kind of program in the neighborhood. This money might do a great deal of good, but it seemed to me a fairly impersonal way of helping. I was hoping to do something more direct.

In the past I hadn't been drawn to standard charitable activities like coaching basketball or volunteering at a school, because I wanted to differentiate myself from the people who helped families and ran programs in the community. I had heard many tenants criticize the patronizing attitudes of such volunteers. The writing workshop, however, seemed like a good fit. Having hung out in the community for several years, I believed I could avoid the kind of fate—

exclusion, cold stares, condescending responses—that often greeted the people who rode into town to do good.

I was also still reeling from the fact that I had alienated so many people around J.T.'s territory. I was feeling guilty, and I needed to get people back on my side again.

Of all the people in the projects, I had the least experience spending time with young women, particularly single mothers. I was a bit nervous, particularly because Ms. Bailey, Ms. Mae, and other older women warned me not to get too close to the young women. They felt that the women would begin looking to me as a source of support.

In the beginning the group convened wherever we could—in someone's apartment, at a diner, outside under a tree. At first there were five women in the group, and then we grew to roughly a dozen as more people heard about it. The meetings were pretty casual, and attendance could be spotty, since the women had family and work obligations.

From the outset it was an emotional experience. The women wrote and spoke openly about their struggles. Each of them had at least a couple of children, which generally meant at least one "baby daddy" who wasn't in the picture. Each of them had a man in her life who'd been either jailed or killed. They spoke of in-laws who demanded that the women give up their children to the father's family, some of whom were willing to use physical force to claim the children.

Their material hardships were overwhelming. Most of them earned no more than ten thousand dollars a year, a combination of welfare payments and food stamps. Some worked part-time, and others took in boarders who paid cash or, nearly as valuable, provided day care so the young women could work, run errands, or just have a little time for themselves.

The most forceful stories were the tales of abuse. Every single woman had been beaten up by a boyfriend (who was usually drunk at the time), some almost fatally. Every one of them had lived in fear for days or weeks, waiting for the same man to return.

One cold autumn evening, we congregated at a local diner. We found a large table in the back, where it was quiet. The owner was by now accustomed to our presence, and he didn't mind that we stayed for hours. If business was particularly good, he'd feed us all night long and then waive the tab. He and I had struck up a friendship—I often came to the diner to write up my field notes— and he liked the fact that I was trying to help tenants.

The theme of this week's essay was "How I Survive." Tanya was the first to read from her journal. She was twenty years old, a high-school dropout with two children. She'd stayed with her mother after the first child was born but eventually got her own apartment in the same building, then had a second baby. She didn't know the whereabouts of the first father; the second had died in a gang shooting. In her essay she bragged about how she earned twice her welfare income by taking in boarders.

"But sometimes it doesn't go so well, Sudhir," said one of the other women, Sarina, who liked to be the voice of reason. She stared down Tanya as she spoke. Sarina had three children, the fathers of whom were, respectively, in jail, dead, and unwilling to pay child support. So she, too, had taken in boarders. "I remember when my brother came into the house, he started dealing dope and they caught him. Almost took my lease away."

"Yeah, but that's just because you didn't pay the building manager enough money," Tanya said. "Or I think that it was because you didn't sleep with him!"

"Well, I'm not doing either one of those things," Sarina said in a moralistic tone, shaking her head.

"You got some nerve," interrupted Keisha. "Sarina, you put your ass out there for any man who comes looking." At twenty-six, Keisha was one of the oldest women in the group. Even though she had grown angry with me for sharing information about hustlers with Ms. Bailey, she hadn't held the grudge for long. She had two daughters and was the best writer in the group, a high-school graduate now planning to apply to Roosevelt College. "Hell, there ain't no difference between some ho selling her shit and you taking some man in your house for money."

"Hey, *that's* survival!" Tanya said. "I mean, that's what we're here to talk about, right?"

"Okay," I jumped in, trying to establish some order. "What's the best way for you to take care of whatever you need to? Give me the top ten ways you survive."

Sarina began. "Always make sure you know someone at the CHA you can turn to when you can't make rent. It helps, because you could get evicted."

"Yeah, and if you have to sleep with a nigger downtown, then you got to do it," said Keisha. "Because if you don't, they *will* put your kids on the street."

Sarina went on, ignoring Keisha. "You got to make sure you can get clothes and food and diapers for your kids," she said. "Even if you don't have money. So you need to have good relations with stores."

"Make sure Ms. Bailey's always getting some dick!" Keisha shouted, laughing hard.

"You know, one time I had to let her sleep with *my* man so I wouldn't get kicked out of the building," Chantelle said.

"That's awful," I said.

"Yeah," Chantelle said. "And he almost left me, too, when he found out that Ms. Bailey could get him a job and would let him stay up there and eat all her food." Chantelle was twenty-one. Her son had learning disabilities, so she was struggling to find a school that could help him. She worked part-time at a fast-food restaurant and depended on her mother and grandmother for day care and cash.

Chantelle's hardships weren't uncommon in the projects. Unfortunately, neither was her need to appease Ms. Bailey. The thought that a tenant had to let the building president sleep with her partner was alarming to me. But among these women such indignities weren't rare. To keep your own household intact, they said, you had to keep Ms. Bailey happy and well paid. As I heard more stories similar to Chantelle's, I found myself growing angry at Ms. Bailey and the other LAC officials. I asked Chantelle and the other women why they didn't challenge Ms. Bailey. Their answer made perfect sense: When it became obvious that the housing authority supported a management system based on extortion and corruption, the women decided their best option was to shrug their shoulders and accept their fate.

I found it unconscionable that such a regime existed, but I wasn't going to confront Ms. Bailey either. She was too powerful. And so while the women's anger turned into despair, my disgust began to morph into bitterness.

The women's list of survival techniques went well beyond ten. Keep cigarettes in your apartment so you can pay off a squatter to fix things when they break. Let your child pee in the stairwell to keep prostitutes from congregating there at night. Let the gangs pay you to store drugs and cash in your apartment. (The risk of apprehension, the women concurred, was slim.)

Then there were all the resources to be procured in exchange for sex: groceries from the bodega owner, rent forgiveness from the CHA, assistance from a welfare bureaucrat, preferential treatment from a police officer for a jailed relative. The women's explanation for using sex as currency was consistent and pragmatic: If your child was in danger of going hungry, then you did whatever it took to fix the problem. The women looked pained when they discussed using their bodies to obtain these necessities; it was clear that this wasn't their first—or even their hundredth—preference.

"Always know somebody at the hospital," Tanya blurted out. "Always have somebody you can call, because that ambulance never comes. And when you get there, you need to pay somebody, or else you'll be waiting in line forever!"

"Yes, that's true, and the people at the hospital can give you free baby food," Sarina said. "Usually you need to meet them in the back alley. And I'd say you should keep a gun or a knife hidden, in case your man starts beating you. Because sometimes you have to do something to get him to stop."

"You've had to use a knife before?" I asked. No one had spoken or written about this yet. "How often?"

"Many times!" Sarina looked at me as if I'd grown up on Mars. "When these men start drinking, you can't talk to them. You just need to protect yourself—and don't forget, they'll beat up the kids, too."

Keisha started to cry. She dropped her head into her lap and covered up so no one could see. Sarina leaned over and hugged her.

"The easiest time is when they're asleep," Tanya said. "They're lying there, mostly because they've passed out drunk. That's when it runs through your mind. You start thinking, 'I could end it right here. I could kill the motherfucker, right now. Then he can't beat me no more.' I think about it a lot."

Keisha wiped her eyes. "I stabbed that nigger because I couldn't take it no more. Wasn't anybody helping me. Ms. Bailey said she couldn't do nothing, the police said they couldn't do nothing. And this man was coming around beating me and beating my baby for no reason. I couldn't think of any other way, couldn't think of nothing else to do. . . ."

She began to sob again. Sarina escorted her to the bathroom.

"She sent her man to the hospital," Tanya quietly explained. "Almost killed him. One night he was asleep on the couch—he had already sent *her* to the hospital a few times, broke her ribs, she got stitches and bruises all over her body. She grabbed that knife and kept putting it in his stomach. He got up and ran out the apartment. I think one of J.T.'s boys took him to the hospital. He's a BK."

Because the boyfriend was a senior gang member, Tanya said, J.T. refused to pressure him to stop beating Keisha. She still lived in fear that the man would return.

One day Ms. Bailey called and asked that I come to a building-wide meeting with her tenants. She hadn't invited me to such a meeting in more than a year, so I figured something important was afoot.

I hadn't been keeping up with Ms. Bailey's tenant meetings in part because I'd already amassed sufficient information on these gatherings and also because, in all honesty, I'd grown uncomfortable watching the horse-trading schemes that she and other tenant leaders used to manage the community.

My own life was also starting to evolve. I had moved in with my girlfriend, Katchen, and we were thinking about getting married. Visiting our relatives—mine in California and hers in Montana—took time away from my fieldwork, including much of our summers and vacations. My parents were thrilled, and they pushed me to think seriously about starting a family along with a career. Katchen was applying to law school; neither of us was ready for children just yet.

And then there was the matter of my dissertation, which I still had to write. I began to meet more regularly with Bill Wilson and other advisers to see whether I could plausibly move toward wrapping up my graduate study.

Ms. Bailey's office was packed for the meeting when I arrived, with a few dozen people in attendance, all talking excitedly. As usual, most of them were older women, but there were also several men standing in the back. I recognized a couple of them as the partners of women in the building; it was unusual to see these men at a public meeting. Ms. Bailey waved me up front, pointing me to the chair next to hers.

"Okay," she said, "Sudhir has agreed to come here today so we can clear this up."

I was taken aback. Clear *what* up? Everyone was suddenly staring at me, and they didn't look happy.

"Why are you sleeping with my daughter?" shouted a woman I didn't recognize. "Tell me, goddamn it! Why are you fucking my baby?"

"Answer the woman!" someone else hollered. I couldn't tell who was talking, but it didn't matter: I was in a state of shock.

One man, addressing me as "Arab," told me I should get out of the neighborhood for good and especially leave alone their young women. Other people joined in:

"Nigger, get out of here!"

"Arab, go home!"

"Get the fuck out, Julio!"

Ms. Bailey tried to restore order. Amid the shouting she yelled out that I would explain myself.

I was still confused. "Let Sudhir tell you why he's meeting them!"

Ms. Bailey said, and then I understood: It was the writing workshop. People had seen me picking up the young women and driving away with them. Apparently they thought I was sleeping with them, or maybe pimping them out.

As I tried to explain the writing workshop, I kept getting drowned out. I began to feel scared. I had seen how a mob of tenants nearly tore apart the Middle Eastern shopkeeper who'd slept with Boo-Boo's daughter.

Ms. Bailey finally made herself heard above the riot. "He's trying to tell you that he's just helping them with homework!"

That quieted everyone down a little bit. But still, I was stung: Why weren't any of the women from the workshop in attendance? Why hadn't anyone come to defend me, to tell the truth?

After a few more minutes, things having calmed down a bit, Ms. Bailey told me to leave. There was other business to take care of, she said, laughing—at me—and clearly enjoying herself at my expense.

Leaving the building that night, I wondered how much more time I could afford to spend in J.T.'s territory. It was hard to think of any tenants who *weren't* angry with me.

SEVEN

Black and Blue

Of all the relationships I'd developed during my time at Robert Taylor, it turned out that the strongest one by far was my bond with J.T. As unusual and as morally murky as this relationship may have been, it was also undeniably powerful. Our years together had produced a close relationship. This bond would become even more intimate, to the point that J.T. felt personally indebted to me, when I had the opportunity to help save the life of one of his closest friends.

It was a classic Chicago summer afternoon: a cloudless sky, the muggy air broken occasionally by a soft lake breeze. I was hanging around at Robert Taylor, outside J.T.'s building, along with perhaps a hundred other people. Tenants were barbecuing, playing softball, and taking comfort in the cool shadow of the building. Few apartments had a working air conditioner, so on a day like this the lawn got more and more crowded as the day wore on.

I was sitting on the lawn next to Darryl Young, one of J.T.'s uncles, who relaxed on a lawn chair with a six-pack of beer. Since the beer was warm, Darryl sent a niece or nephew inside every now and then to fetch some ice for his cup. Darryl was in his late forties and had long ago lost most of his teeth. He had unkempt salt-and-pepper hair, walked with a stiff limp, and always wore his State of Illinois ID on a chain around his neck. He left the project grounds so rarely that his friends called him "a lifer." He knew every inch of Robert Taylor, and he loved to tell stories about the most dramatic police busts and the most memorable baseball games between competing buildings. He told me about the project's famous pimps and infamous murderers as well as about one tenant who tried to raise a tiger in his apartment and another who kept a hundred snakes in her apartment—until the day she let them loose in the building.

Suddenly Darryl sat up, staring at an old beater of a Ford sedan cruising slowly past the building. The driver was a young white man, looking up at the building as if he expected someone to come down.

"Get the fuck out of here, boy!" Darryl shouted. "We don't need you around here. Go and sleep with your own women!" Darryl turned and hollered to a teenage boy playing basketball nearby. "Cheetah! Go and get Price, tell him to come here."

"Why do you want Price?" I asked.

"Price is the only one who can take care of this," Darryl said. His face was tight, and he kept his eyes on the Ford. By now the car had come to a stop.

"Take care of what?" I asked.

"Damn white boys come around here for our women," Darryl said. "It's disgusting. This ain't no goddamn brothel."

"You think he's a john?"

"I *know* he's a john," Darryl said, scowling, and then went back to shouting at the Ford. "Boy! Hey, boy, get on home, we don't want your money!"

Price sauntered out of the building, trailed by a few other members of the BK security squad. Darryl stood up and hobbled over to Price.

"Get that boy out of here, Price!" he said. "I'm tired of them coming around here. This ain't no goddamn whorehouse!"

"All right, old man," Price said, irritated by Darryl's enthusiasm but clearly a bit concerned. "Don't worry. We'll take care of him."

Price and his entourage approached the car. I could hear Price speaking gruffly to the driver while the other BKs surrounded the car so that it couldn't drive off. Then Price opened the door and gestured for the white guy to get out.

Just then I heard the loud squeal of a car rounding the corner of Twenty-fifth and Federal. Some kids shouted at people to get out of its path. It was a gray sedan, and I could see it roaring toward us, but unsteadily, as if one of the wheels were loose.

The first shots sounded like machine-gun fire. Everyone seemed to duck instinctively, except for me. I was frozen upright; my legs were stuck in place and everything turned to slow motion. The car came closer. Price and the other BK security men ran toward the building as more shots were fired. The car flew past, and I could see four people inside, all black. It looked as if two of them were shooting, one from either side.

Price got hit and dropped to the ground. The rest of his entourage reached the lobby safely. Price wasn't moving. I saw Darryl lying flat on the grass, while other tenants were crawling toward shelter—a car, a tree, the building itself—and grabbing children as they went. I was still standing, in shock, though I had managed to at least hunch over. The gray car had vanished.

Then I heard a second car screeching down the back alleyway. I was puzzled. In most drive-by shootings, a gang wouldn't risk a second pass, since the element of surprise had been used up. Indeed, looking around now at the expanse in front of the building, I saw perhaps a dozen young men with guns in their hands, crouching behind cars or along the sides of the building. I had never seen so many guns in Robert Taylor.

Price still hadn't gotten up. I could see that he was gripping his leg. Somehow the sight of him lying motionless moved me to action. I headed toward him and saw that one of the BKs had come back outside to do the same. We grabbed Price and started to drag him toward the building.

"Get Serena! Get Serena!" someone shouted down from an upper floor. "She's out there with her baby!"

The BK helping me with Price ran over to help Serena and her children to a safe spot. I dragged Price the rest of the way by myself and made it to the lobby just as the second car emerged from the alley. I heard some shouts and some more gunshots. I saw that the BK who'd gone to help Serena had draped his body atop her and her kids.

In the dim light of the lobby, I could see that Price's leg was bleeding badly, just above the knee. J.T.'s men pushed me out of the way. They carried Price farther inside the building, toward one of the ground-floor apartments. I wondered where J.T. was.

"Sudhir, get inside, go upstairs to Ms. Mae's—now!" It was Ms. Bailey. I gestured toward Price, to show that I wanted to help. She just yelled at me again to get upstairs.

About five flights up the stairs, I ran into a group of J.T.'s men on the gallery, looking out. "I don't see no more!" one of them shouted to some BKs on the ground outside. "It don't look like there's any more! Just get everyone inside and put four in the lobby."

I heard a stream of footsteps in the stairwell. Parents yelled at their children to hurry up, and a few mothers asked for help carrying their strollers. I heard someone say that J.T. was in the lobby, so I hustled back downstairs.

He stood at the center of a small mob, taking reports from his men. There was a lot of commotion, all of them talking past one another:

"Niggers will do it again, I know they will!"

"We need to get Price to the hospital, he's still bleeding."

"No, we need to secure the building."

"I say we drive by and shoot back, now!"

As instructed, four young men now stood armed guard in the lobby, two at each entrance. Under normal circumstances young gang members like these bragged about their toughness, their willingness to kill for the family. But now, with the danger real, they looked shaky, eyes wide and fearful.

J.T. stood calmly, wearing dark sunglasses, picking his teeth. When his eyes fell upon me, he fixed me with a glare. I didn't know what he was trying to communicate. Then he pointed toward the ceiling. He wanted me upstairs, at his mother's place, out of the way.

Instead I walked even farther into the lobby, out of his view. I asked a rank-and-file BK where Price was. He pointed down the hall. J.T. approached, patted me on the back, and pulled me in close. "Price isn't doing so hot," he whispered. "He's bleeding real bad, and I need to get him to the hospital."

"Call the ambulance," I said instinctively.

"They won't come. Listen, we need your car. If they see one of our cars come up to Provident, they may call the police. We need to borrow your car."

"Sure, of course," I said, reaching for my keys. I had recently bought a junker, a 1982 Cutlass Ciera. "Let me get it."

"No," J.T. said, grabbing my hand. "You can't leave the building for a while. Go upstairs, but let me have the keys. Cherise will take him."

I gave J.T. my keys and watched him walk toward the apartment where Price was being looked after. It was common practice to have a woman drive a BK to the hospital so that he wouldn't immediately be tagged as a gangster. Cherise lived in the building and let the Black Kings use her apartment to make crack cocaine. J.T. sometimes joked that the young women in the projects would never turn on their stoves if it weren't for his gang cooking up crack.

J.T. commandeered a vacant apartment on the fourteenth floor to use as a temporary headquarters. The scene was surreal, like watching an army prepare for war. I sat in a corner and watched as J.T. issued commands. Small groups of men would come inside, receive their orders, and hurry off. J.T. assigned several men to take up rifles and sit in the windows of the third, fifth, and seventh floors. He instructed other groups of men to go door-to-door and warn tenants to stay away from the west-facing windows.

He told one young BK that there probably wouldn't be another shooting for at least a few hours. "Get some of the older people out of here," he ordered. "Take them to 2325." A BK foot soldier told me that Price had made it to the emergency room but was said to be still bleeding badly.

J.T. came over and told me what he knew. The first car, the beat-up Ford, was a decoy to lure some Black Kings out of the building. The attack appeared to be a collaboration between the MCs and the Stones. They were deeply envious, J.T. told me, that the BKs had been able to attract so many customers to their territory. The MCs and the Stones were a constant source of worry for J.T., since they were led by "crazy niggers," his term for the kind of bad business-men who thought that a drive-by shooting was the best way to compete in a drug market. J.T. much preferred the more established rival gangs, since a shared interest in maintaining the status quo decreased their appetite for violence.

Every so often J.T. sent out an entourage to buy food for people in the building. A few tenants carried on as usual, paying little attention to the Black Kings' dramatic show of security in the lobby. But except for a couple of stereos and some shouting in the stairwells, the building was eerily quiet. We all baked in the still, hot air.

Occasionally one of J.T.'s more senior members would throw out a plan for retaliation. J.T. listened to every proposal but was noncommittal. "We got time for all that," he kept saying. "Let's just see what happens tonight."

Every half hour Cherise called from the hospital to report on Price's condition. J.T. looked tense as he took these reports. Price was a friend since high school, one of the few people J.T. allowed in his inner circle.

I was just nodding off to sleep on the floor when J.T. walked over.

"Thanks, man," he said quietly.

"For what?"

"You didn't have to get mixed up in this shit."

He must have heard that I'd helped drag Price into the lobby. I didn't say anything. J.T. slapped my leg, asked if I wanted a Coke, and walked off to the fridge.

There were no more shootings that night, but the tension didn't let up. I never went home.

Within a few days, once he figured out exactly who was responsible for the attack, J.T. rounded up T-Bone and several other officers and went after the shooters. J.T. personally helped beat them up; the BKs also took their guns and money. Because these young rivals had "no business sense," as J.T. told me later, there was no hope of a compromise. Physical retaliation was the only measure to consider.

Price stayed in the hospital for a few days, but the bullet caused no irreparable damage, and he was soon back in action.

T-Bone called me one day with big news: J.T. was on the verge of receiving another important promotion within the citywide Black Kings organization. If all went according to plan, J.T., T-Bone, and Price would be responsible for taking on even more BK factions, which meant managing a considerably larger drug-trafficking operation. I could hear the excitement in T-Bone's voice. For him, too, the promotion meant more money as well as a boost in status. "Two years, that's it," he told me. "Two more years of this shit, and I'm getting out of the game." Ever practical, T-Bone was saving for his future—a house, full-time college, and a legal job.

J.T. wouldn't be around Robert Taylor much for the next several weeks, T-Bone told me, since his new assignment required a lot of preparation and legwork. But he had asked T-Bone to give me a message: "J.T. wants you to go with him to the next regional BK meeting. You up for it?"

I had been waiting for this phone call for a few years. I desperately wanted to learn about the gang's senior leadership, and now that J.T. was one of them, it looked like I'd finally have my chance.

By this point in my research, I still felt guilty sometimes for being as much of a hustler, in my own way, as the other hustlers in the neighborhood. C-Note had called me on it, and C-Note was right. I constantly hustled people for information—stories, data, interviews, facts—anything that might make my research more interesting.

So I was happy whenever I had the chance to give a little bit back. The writing workshop hadn't worked out as well as I'd wanted, and I was searching for another way to act charitably. An opportunity fell into my lap when the Chicago public-school teachers went on strike. Since BK rules stipulated that each member graduate from high school, J.T. asked Autry to set up a program during the strike so that J.T.'s members could stay off the streets and do some homework. Autry had set up a similar program at the Boys & Girls Club, but gang boundaries forbade J.T.'s members to go there.

Autry agreed, and he asked me to run a classroom in J.T.'s building. I obliged, pretty sure that lecturing high-schoolers on history, politics, and math shouldn't be too hard.

We met in a dingy, darkened apartment with a bathroom that didn't work. On a given day, there were anywhere from twenty to fifty teenage gang members on my watch. The air was so foul that I let them smoke to cover the odor. There weren't enough seats, so the kids forcibly claimed some chairs from neighboring apartments, with no promise of returning them.

On the first day, as the students talked loudly through my lecture on history and politics, J.T. walked in unannounced and shouted at them to pay attention. He ordered Price to take one particularly noisy foot soldier into the hallway and beat him.

Later I asked J.T. not to interrupt again. The kids would never learn anything, I insisted, if they knew that he was going to be monitoring them. J.T. and Autry both thought I was crazy. They didn't think I had any chance of controlling the unruly teens without the threat of an occasional visit by J.T.

They were right. Within a day the "classroom" had descended

into anarchy. In one corner a few guys were admiring a gun that one of them had just bought. (He was thoughtful enough to remove the bullets during class.) In another corner several teenagers had organized a dice game. The winner would get not only the cash but also the right to rob the homeless people sleeping in a nearby vacant apartment. One kid brought in a radio and improvised a rap song about their "Injun teacher," replete with references to Custer, Geronimo, and "the smelly Ay-Rab." (It never seemed to occur to anyone that "Arab" and "Indian" were not in fact interchangeable; in my case they were equally valuable put-downs.) The most harmless kids in the room were the ones who patiently waited for their friends to return from the store with some beer.

Things got worse from there. Some of my students started selling marijuana in the classroom; others would casually leave the building to find a prostitute. When I conveyed all this to J.T., he said that as long as the guys showed up, they weren't hanging out on the street and getting into any real trouble.

Given that they were using my "classroom" to deal drugs, gamble, and play with guns, I wondered exactly what J.T. meant by "real" trouble.

My role was quickly downgraded from teacher to baby-sitter. The sessions lasted about two weeks, until news came that the teachers' strike was being settled. By this time my admiration for Autry's skill with the neighborhood kids had increased exponentially.

Despite my utter failure as a teacher, Autry called me again for help. The stakes were a little higher this time—and, for me, so was the reward.

Autry and the other staffers at the Boys & Girls Club wanted me to help write a grant proposal for the U.S. Department of Justice, which had advertised special funds being allocated for youth programs. The proposal needed to include in-depth crime statistics for the projects and the surrounding neighborhood, data that was typically hard to get, since the police didn't like to make such information public. But if I took on the project, I'd get direct access to Officer Reggie Marcus—"Officer Reggie" to tenants—the local cop who had grown up in Robert Taylor himself and was devoted to making life there better. I jumped at the chance.

I had met Reggie on several occasions, but now I had an opportunity to work closely with him and cultivate a genuine friendship. He was about six feet tall, as muscular and fit as a football player; he always dressed well and carried himself with a quiet determination. I knew that Reggie often dealt directly with gang leaders in the hopes of keeping violence to a minimum and that he was a diplomatic force among the project's street hustlers. Now I would be able to ask as many questions as I wanted about the particulars of his work.

Why, for instance, did he try to reduce gun violence by making sure that the *gangs* were the only ones who had guns?

"They don't like gun violence any more than the tenants, because it scares away customers," he explained. "So they try to keep things quiet."

One wintry afternoon I met Reggie at the police station in the Grand Boulevard neighborhood, a few blocks from J.T.'s territory. When I arrived, he told me he still had some phone calls to make, so I went to find a water fountain. The police station was drab, row after row of bland gray cubicles; the air was cold and damp, the tile floor slippery from the tracked-in snow.

Near the water fountain, I came upon a wall covered with Polaroid pictures. They were all of black men in their teens and twenties, most of them looking dazed or defiant. Beneath each photo was a caption with the person's name and gang affiliation.

Taped next to the photos was a party flyer headlined "MC South-side Fest." J.T.'s gang hung similar flyers all around the buildings when they were sponsoring a party or a basketball tournament. On the MC flyer, there were several names handwritten along the right margin, as if it were a sign-up sheet: "Watson," "O'Neill," "Brown."

Reggie came by as I was inspecting the flyer.

"Let's not hang out here," he said, looking concerned. "And let's not talk about that. I'll explain later."

We were heading over to the Boys & Girls Club to talk to Autry about the Department of Justice grant. As we walked to Reggie's SUV, parked behind the police station, I was still thinking about the MC flyer.

I recalled a party the Black Kings had thrown a few years back, having rented out the second floor of an Elks Lodge. The women were dressed up, and the men wore spiffy tracksuits or pressed jeans. They drank beer and wine coolers, danced, and passed marijuana joints around the room.

As J.T. and I stood talking in a corner, a group of five men suddenly busted into the room, all dressed in black. One of them held up a gun for everyone to see. The other four ran to the corners of the room, one of them shouting for everyone to get up against the wall. Four of the men were black, one white. J.T. whispered to me, "Cops." He and I took our places against the wall.

One of the partying gangsters, a huge man, at least six foot two and 250 pounds, started to resist. "Fuck you, nigger!" he shouted. Two of the men in black promptly yanked him into the bathroom— where, from the sound of it, they beat him brutally. We all stood silently against the wall, listening to his grunts and groans.

"Who's next?" shouted one of the men in black. "Who wants some of this?"

Two of them pulled out black trash bags. "Cash and jewels, I want everything in the bag!" one shouted. "Now!"

When the bag reached us, J.T. calmly deposited his necklace and his money clip, fat with twenties. I put the cash from my pocket, about fifteen dollars, into the bag. As I did so, the man holding the bag looked up and stared at me. He didn't say anything, but he kept glancing over at me as he continued his collection rounds. He seemed puzzled as to what I, plainly an outsider, was doing there.

When they were done, the five men dropped the bags out the window and calmly filed out. After a time J.T. motioned for me to follow him outside. We walked to his car, parked in the adjoining lot. Some other BK leaders joined him, commiserating over the robbery.

"Fucking cops do this all the time," J.T. told me. "As soon as they find out we're having a party, they raid it."

"Why? And why don't they arrest you?" I asked. "And how do you know they were cops?"

"It's a game!" shouted one of the other BK leaders. "*We* make all this fucking money, and they want some."

"They're jealous," J.T. said calmly. "We make more than them, and they can't stand it. So this is how they get back at us."

I had a hard time believing that the police would so brazenly rob a street gang. But it didn't seem like the kind of thing that J.T. would lie about; most of his exaggerations served the purpose of making him look *more* powerful, not less so.

I had forgotten the incident entirely until I saw the MC flyer at the police station. I wondered if the names written in the margin were the cops who had signed up to raid the party. So I told Reggie about the BK party and J.T.'s claim that the robbers were cops.

He took a deep breath and looked straight ahead as he drove. "You know, Sudhir, you have to be careful about what you hear," he said. Reggie drove fast, barreling over the unplowed snow as if he were off-roading. Our breath was fogging up the windshield. "I'm not going to say that all the people I work with are always doing the right thing. Hell, *I* don't do the right thing all the time. But—"

"You don't have to tell me anything if you don't want to."

"I know that, I know that. But you *should* know what's going on. Yes, some of the people I work with raid the parties. And you know, sometimes I feel like I should do it, too! I mean, guys like J.T. are making a killing off people. And for what? *Peddling* stuff that kills. But it's not for me. I don't participate—I just don't see the point."

"I've ridden along with J.T. and a few of his friends in their sports cars," I said. "Sometimes a cop will pull us over for no reason. And then—"

"He asks to see a paycheck stub, right?"

"Yeah! How did you know I was going to say that?"

"Think about how frustrating it is to do policing," Reggie said. "You've been hanging out with these guys. You know that they never hold the cash that they make. They have all these investments in other people's names. So what can we do? We can't arrest their mothers for living in a nice house. But when we stop them in their fancy cars, we can legitimately ask whether they stole the car or not. Now, again, I don't do that stuff. But some other people do."

"But *I* don't have to carry around a paycheck stub. Why should they?" I knew this was a naïve-sounding question, and I was fully aware that there was a big difference between me and the gang members. But because naïveté had worked in the past, I'd stuck with this strategy.

"*You* are not peddling that shit," Reggie said, stating the obvious. I wasn't sure if his explanation was meant to be sarcastic, whether he was humoring me, or whether he just wanted to make sure I understood precisely the police officers' rationale. "*You* aren't making millions by killing people. Sometimes we'll take their car away."

"What do you do with it?" I asked. I knew Reggie didn't believe that the drug dealers were each "making millions," but some of their earnings were still sufficiently greater than the cops' to make Reggie upset.

"A lot of times, we'll sell it at the police auction, and the money goes to charity. I figure it's a way of getting back at those fools."

On a few occasions, I'd been riding in a car with some gang members when a cop stopped the car, made everyone get out, and summarily called for a tow truck. On a few other occasions, the cop let the driver keep the car but took everyone's jewelry and cash. To me the strangest thing was that the gang members barely protested. It was as if they were playing a life-size board game, the rules of which were well established and immutable, and on this occasion they'd simply gotten a bad roll of the dice.

A few weeks later, Reggie invited me to a South Side bar frequented by black cops. "I think you're getting a real one-sided view of our work," he said.

His offer surprised me. Reggie was a reserved man, and he rarely introduced me to other police officers even if they were standing nearby. He preferred to speak with me behind closed doors—in Ms. Bailey's office, inside the Boys & Girls Club, or in his car.

We met at the bar on a Saturday afternoon. It was located a few blocks from the precinct and Robert Taylor. It was nondescript on the outside, marked only by some neon beer signs. On either side of it lay fast-food restaurants, liquor stores, and check-cashing shops. Even Reggie didn't know the bar's actual name. "I've been coming

here for fifteen years," he said, "and I never even bothered to ask."
He and the other cops just called it "the Lounge." The place was
just as nondescript inside: a long wooden bar, several tables, dim
lighting, some Bears and Bulls posters. It had the feel of a well-worn
den in a working-class home. All the patrons were black and at least
in their mid-thirties, with a few old-timers nursing an afternoon beer.

Reggie sat us down at a table and introduced me to three of his
off-duty colleagues. From the outset they seemed wary of speaking
about their work. And since I never liked to question people too
much until I got to know them, the conversation was stiff to say the
least. In a short time, we covered my ethnic background, the Chicago
Bears, and the strange beliefs of the university crowd in Hyde Park.
The cops, like most working-class Chicagoans, thought that Hyde
Park liberals—myself included, presumably—held quaint, unrealis-
tic views of reality, especially in terms of racial integration. To these
men Hyde Park was known as the "why can't everyone just get
along?" part of town.

One of the cops, a man named Jerry, sat staring at me the entire
time. I felt sure I'd seen him before. He was quietly drinking whiskey
shots with beer chasers. Once in a while, he'd spit out a question:
"So you think you know a lot about gangs, huh?" or "What are you
going to write about, Mr. Professor?" I got a little nervous when he
started calling me "Mr. Professor," since that's how I was known in
J.T.'s building. Was this just a coincidence?

The more Officer Jerry drank, the more belligerent he became.
"You university types like to talk about how much you know, don't
you?" he said. "You like to talk about how you're going to solve all
these problems, don't you?"

Reggie shot me a glance as if to say that I'd better defend myself.

"Well, if you think I don't know something, why don't you teach me?" I said. I'd had a few beers myself by now, and I probably sounded more aggressive than I'd intended.

"Motherfucker!" Jerry leaned in hard toward me. "You think I don't know who you fucking are? You think we *all* don't know what you're doing? If you want to play with us, you better be real careful. If you like watching, you may get caught."

A shiver ran over me when he said "watching." Now I knew exactly where I'd seen him. In J.T.'s buildings Officer Jerry was well known, and by my estimation he was a rogue cop. Some months earlier, I'd been sitting in a stairwell interviewing a few prostitutes and pimps. I heard a commotion in the gallery. The stairwell door was partially open; looking out, I could see three police officers busting open an apartment door. Two of them, one black and one white, ran inside. The third, who was black, stayed outside guarding the door. He didn't seem to notice us.

A minute later the cops hauled out a man and a teenage boy. Neither of them resisted, and neither seemed very surprised. The teenager was handcuffed, and they forced him to the floor. The mother was screaming, as was the baby in her arms.

Then a fourth cop showed up, swaggering down the hall. It was Officer Jerry. He wore black pants, a black and blue fleece jacket, and a bulletproof vest. He started to beat and kick the father violently. "Where's the money, nigger?" he shouted. "Where's the cash?"

I was shocked. I glanced at the folks I'd been talking to in the stairwell. They looked as if they'd seen this before, but they also looked anxious, sitting in silence in the apparent hope that the cops wouldn't come for them next.

Finally the man relented. He, too, lay on the floor, bloodied. "In the oven," he said, "in the oven."

Officer Jerry went inside and returned with a large brown bag. "Don't fuck with us," he told the father. "You hear me?"

The father just sat there, dazed. The other cops took the hand-cuffs off the teenager and let him back into the apartment.

Just as Officer Jerry was leaving, one of the pimps sitting next to me accidentally dropped a beer bottle. Officer Jerry turned and looked down the gallery, straight at us. I jumped back, but he stomped into the stairwell. He cast his eye over the lot of us. "Get the fuck out of here!" he said. Then, noticing me, he smirked, as if I were no more significant than a flea.

Once he left, I asked one of the pimps, Timothy, about Officer Jerry. "He gets to come in the building whenever he wants and get a piece of the action," he said. Timothy told me that Sonny, the man that Officer Jerry had just beaten, stole cars for a living but had apparently neglected to pay his regular protection fee to Officer Jerry. "We always joke that whenever Officer Jerry runs out of money, he comes in here and beats up a nigger," Timothy said. "He got me once last year. Took two hundred bucks and then my girl had to suck his dick. Asshole."

In the coming months, I learned that Officer Jerry was a notorious presence in the building. I heard dozens of stories from tenants who said they'd suffered all forms of harassment, abuse, and shakedowns at the hands of Officer Jerry. It was hard to corroborate these stories, but based on what I'd seen with my own eyes, they weren't hard to believe. And to some degree, it probably didn't much matter whether all the reports of his abusive behavior were true. In the projects, the "bad cop" story was a myth that residents spread at will out of sheer frustration that they lived in a high-crime area where the police presence was minimal at best, unchecked at worst.

Now, sitting across the table from him at the Lounge, I started to feel extremely nervous. What if he somehow knew that I had recorded all these incidents in my notebooks?

He sat there sputtering with rage, shaking the table. I looked over at Reggie, hoping for some help.

"Jerry, leave him alone," Reggie said quietly, fiddling with his beer. "He's okay."

"Okay? Are you kidding me? You trust that motherfucking Ay-rab?!" Jerry tossed back his shot and grabbed the beer. I thought he might throw the bottle at me. He let out a nasty laugh. "Just tell him to stay out of my way."

"Listen, I'm only trying to get a better understanding of what you do," I said. "Maybe I could tell you a little bit about my research."

"Fuck you," Jerry said, staring me down. "You write any of that shit down, and I'll come after your ass. You got me? I don't want to talk to you, I don't want you talking to nobody else, and I don't want to see you around these motherfucking projects. I know who you are, motherfucker. Don't think I don't know what you're doing."

Reggie grabbed my arm and threw a twenty-dollar bill on the table. "Let's go," he said.

When we got to the car, Reggie started the ignition but didn't drive away. He began to speak gently but firmly, his tone almost parental. "Sudhir, I brought you here today because these guys wanted to know who you are and what you're up to. I didn't want to tell you that, because I knew you'd be nervous. They know you're watching, they know you've seen them in the building, they know you're going to be writing something. I told them that you were a good person. Jerry was too drunk—I'm sorry about that."

Reggie held his silence for a few minutes, looking out at the busy street.

"I think you have to make a decision, Sudhir," he said. "And I can't make it for you. I never really asked you what you'll be writing about. I thought you were just helping the club, but then Autry told me last week that you're writing about life in the projects. You and I have talked about a lot of things. But we never talked about whether you would write what I say. I hope not. I mean, if you are, I'd like you to tell me right now. But that's not really the problem, because I'm not afraid of what I do or what I am."

Up to this point, Reggie knew that I was interviewing families and others for my graduate research. A few months later, we wound up talking further about my dissertation, and he said it would be okay to include anything he'd told me, but we agreed to change his name so he couldn't be identified.

At this moment, however, what really concerned me was the re-action of his colleagues. "Reggie, are you telling me I need to worry if I write about cops?"

"Police don't talk a lot to people like you," he said. "Like Jerry. He doesn't want people watching what he does. I know you've seen him do some stupid shit. I know you've seen a *lot* of people do some stupid shit. But you need to decide: What good does it do to write about what he does? If you want to work around here, maybe you keep some of this out."

I left Reggie that evening not knowing what I should do. If I wanted to write about effective policing—like the good, creative work that Reggie did—I would feel compelled to write about abu-sive policing as well.

A week later I was talking to Autry about my dilemma. We were having a beer in the South Shore apartment where he lived with his wife and children. South Shore was a stately neighborhood with pockets of low-income apartments that someone like Autry could afford. He had moved there to keep his children away from street gangs.

Autry insisted that I not write about the police. His explanation was revealing. "You need to understand that there are two gangs in the projects," he said. "The police are also a gang, but they *really* have the power. I mean, these niggers run around with money and cars, but at any moment the cops can get them off the street. They know about you. They've been talking with me, and I've been telling them you're okay, but they want to know what you're looking for."

"Why didn't you tell me this before?" I asked.

"I didn't want to worry you, and you haven't done nothing wrong," he said. "But you need to do what I do. Never, never, *never* piss off the police."

When I pressed Autry on the subject, he wouldn't say anything more, other than flatly repeating his advice: "Don't write about them."

Two weeks later my car was broken into. It was parked across the street from the Boys & Girls Club. Curiously, however, neither the lock nor the window was broken; instead the lock had been expertly picked. My backpack and the glove compartment had both been thoroughly rummaged, with some pens, paper, a couple of candy bars, and my gym clothes strewn about. But nothing seemed to be missing. Although I sometimes kept a few notebooks in my backpack, on this occasion I hadn't.

I went inside to tell Autry. "Let's call Reggie," he said. "Don't touch anything."

We waited for Reggie inside the club, where a children's Christmas party was in progress. The mood was happy, especially since some local stores had donated crates of food for tenant families.

Reggie arrived wearing a Santa hat. He'd been at another Christmas party, passing out toys donated by police officers. When he saw my car, he dropped his head and then peered at Autry.

"Did you talk with him?" he asked Autry.

"I did, but he's pigheaded. He don't listen."

I was confused.

"Sudhir, is there any way you could let me know when you're going to come around here?" Reggie asked. "I mean, maybe you could page me and leave a message."

"What are you talking about? I come over here nearly every day! Can you guys please tell me what's going on?"

"Let's go for a walk," Reggie said, grabbing my arm.

It was freezing, and the wind was howling. We walked around the project buildings. The fresh snow made the high-rises look like gravestones sticking up from the ground.

"Sudhir, you're getting into something you shouldn't be messing with," Reggie said. "You've been reading about the gang busts, right?"

Yes, I told him. The newspapers had been reporting the recent arrests of some of the highest-level drug dealers in Chicago. These arrests were apparently intended to interrupt the trade between the Mexican-American gangs who imported cocaine and the black gangsters who sold crack.

Word on the street was that the FBI and other federal agencies were behind the arrests. Although I hadn't been in touch with J.T. lately—he was still busy settling into his expanded Black Kings duties—he had told me in the past that federal involvement frightened the gangs. "Once you see the feds, that's when you worry," he said. "If it's local, we never worry. As long as you don't do something stupid, you'll be okay." Although the recent arrests involved gang leaders more senior than J.T., and not even in his neighborhood, he was habitually concerned that federal officials would work their way down the ladder to him. He also reasoned that the feds would specifically target the Black Kings if possible, considering that the gang ran what was probably the city's smoothest drug operation.

Reggie now told me that the feds were indeed working Chicago—and hard. They were hoping to indict the drug gangs under the powerful Racketeer Influenced and Corrupt Organizations (RICO) Act, which was instituted in 1970 to combat the Mafia and other crime groups that dealt in money laundering, gambling, and union shakedowns. RICO had been so successful in disrupting Italian, Irish, and Jewish crime gangs that the feds were now using it to go after street gangs, claiming that they, too, were organized criminal enterprises.

Reggie explained that he, like most street cops, hated it when federal agents came to town. They were so eager for high-profile indictments, he said, that they'd use allegations of police improprieties to leverage local cops into turning over their gang intelligence. This in turn would disrupt the relationships that cops like Reggie had carefully built up in the community.

"What does all this mean for you?" I asked. "And for me?"

"For me it means I got to do everything by the book. For you it means you have to be very, very careful. I heard from Ms. Bailey that you're asking a lot of people about us. Now, that doesn't bother me, like I said before. But there are a lot of folks where I work who think you're trying to bust them, do you understand?"

"Bust them?"

"They think you're looking for dirt. Looking to find something to hold against them. I wouldn't worry about your car. Just trust me, it won't happen again."

After this talk with Reggie, I began to fear the police much more than I had ever feared J.T. and the gangs. As Autry had told me, it was the cops who had the real power. They controlled where and how openly the gang could operate, and, if so inclined, they could put just about anyone in jail. Still, as both Autry and J.T. had told me, the cops rarely arrested gang leaders, since they preferred to know who was in control rather than having to deal with an unpredictable leader or, even worse, a power vacuum. When I asked Reggie if this was really true, his response—he dropped his head and asked me not to press him on the issue—seemed to indicate that it was.

Not every cop in the projects was corrupt or abusive, but I had become nervous about getting on the cops' bad side. I had no desire to get beaten up or be regularly harassed. I'd grown up thinking of cops as people you trusted to help when things went bad, but that wasn't the way things worked here, even for me. Not that I'd endeared myself to the cops: I came into the projects by befriending a gang leader, after all, and I hung out with a lot of tenants who did illegal things for a living.

Looking back, I think it would have been better to learn more about the neighborhood from the cops' perspective. But this wouldn't have been easy. Most tenants probably would have stopped speaking with me if they thought I was even remotely tied to the police. One reason journalists often publish thin stories about the projects is that they typically rely on the police for information, and this reliance makes the tenants turn their backs.

As it was, the best I could do was try to learn a little bit from cops like Reggie. He could be just as creative in his approach to police work as some of the tenants were in their approach to survival. If this meant sharing information with gang members to ensure that their wars didn't kill innocents, so be it. Rather than arresting young gang members, Reggie and other cops used "scared straight" tactics to try to get them to stop dealing. I also watched many times as the police mediated disputes between hustlers; and even though they weren't always responsive to domestic-abuse calls, many cops did help Ms. Bailey scare perpetrators so they wouldn't come into the high-rise again.

It wasn't until months after my car was broken into that Reggie confirmed it had been the police who did it. Officer Jerry and a few of his friends were apparently concerned about the contents of my notebooks and wanted to find them. Bad Buck, a young man from Robert Taylor whom I'd befriended, had told the police that I kept my notes in my car. Reggie said that Buck had been caught holding a thousand dollars' worth of cocaine and had surrendered the information about my notes in exchange for not going to jail.

In early 1995 the newspapers began to report another story of major import for the residents of Robert Taylor, this one with even greater consequences than the federal drug busts. Members of Congress and the Clinton administration had begun serious discussions with mayors across the country to propose knocking down housing projects. Henry Cisneros, the secretary of housing and urban development, claimed that "high-rises just don't work." He and his staff spoke of demolishing these "islands of poverty," with the goal of pushing their inhabitants to live where "residents of different incomes interact with one another." Cisneros singled out Chicago's projects as "without question, the worst public housing in America today." The Robert Taylor Homes were said to be at the very top of the demolition list. They were to be replaced by an upscale townhouse development called Legends South, which would include just a few hundred units of public housing.

Most of the tenants I spoke with greeted this news with disbelief. Did the politicians really have the will or the power to relocate tens of thousands of poor black people? "The projects will be here forever," was the phrase I heard from one tenant after another. Only the most elderly tenants seemed to believe that demolition could be a reality. They had already seen the government use urban renewal—or, in their words, "Negro removal"—to move hundreds of thousands of black Chicagoans, replacing their homes and businesses with highways, sports stadiums, universities—and, of course, huge tracts of public housing.

From the outset urban renewal held the seeds of its own failure. White political leaders blocked the construction of housing for blacks in the more desirable white neighborhoods. And even though blighted low-rise buildings in the ghetto were replaced with high-rises like the Robert Taylor Homes, the quality of the housing stock wasn't much better. Things might have been different if housing authorities around the country were given the necessary funds to keep up maintenance on these new buildings. But the buildings that had once been the hope of urban renewal were already, a short forty years later, ready for demolition again.

Amid all this uncertainty, I finally heard from J.T. He called with the news that his promotion was official. He asked if I still wanted to join him in meetings with some citywide BK leaders.

"They're actually interested in talking with you," he said, surprise in his voice. "They want someone to hear their stories, about jail, about their lives. I thought they might not want to talk because of what's going on"—he meant the recent gang arrests—"but they were up for it."

I told J.T. that I'd been talking to my professors about winding down my field research and finishing the dissertation. I had completed all my classes and passed all my exams, and I was now focused on writing my study about the intricate ways in which the members of a poor community eked out a living. Bill Wilson had arranged for me to present my research at various academic conferences, in hopes of attracting a teaching position for me. My academic career probably started the day I met J.T., but the attention of established sociologists made me feel as though I had just now reached the starting gate. Katchen had completed her applications to law school, and both of us were expecting to leave Chicago soon.

There were other factors, too: Many of the tenants in Robert Taylor felt betrayed by me, cops were warning me not to hang out, and now the projects themselves were about to come down. All this combined to make it pretty clear that I wouldn't be spending time in the projects much longer.

J.T. reacted dismissively, saying I shouldn't even think about leaving now. "We've been together for the longest," he said. "If you really want to know what my organization is about, you got to watch what happens. We're on the move, we're only getting bigger, and you need to see this."

J.T. wouldn't take no for an answer. There was something childlike about his insistence, as if pleading with someone not to abandon him. He laughed and chatted on spiritedly about the future of the BKs, about his own ascension, about the "great book" I would someday write about his life.

I tried to take it all in, but the sentences started to bleed into one another. I simply sat there, phone to my ear, mumbling "Uh-huh" whenever J.T. took a breath. It was time to acknowledge, if only to myself, exactly what I'd been doing these past several years: I came, I saw, I hustled. Even if J.T. wouldn't allow me to move on just yet, that's what I was ready to do.

Not that this acknowledgment of my inner hustler gave me any peace. I was full of unease about my conduct in the projects. I had actively misled J.T. into thinking that I was writing his biography, mostly by never denying it. This might have been cute in the early days of our time together, but by now it was purely selfish not to tell him what my study was really about. I tended to retreat from conflict, however. This was a useful trait in obtaining information. But as my tenure in the projects was ending, I was noticing the darker side of avoidance.

With other tenants I played the role of objective social scientist, however inaccurate (and perhaps impossible) this academic conceit may be. I didn't necessarily feel that I was misrepresenting my intentions. I always told people, for instance, that I was writing up my findings into a dissertation. But it was obvious that there was a clear power dynamic and that they held the short end of the stick. I had the choice of ending my time in the projects; they did not. Long after I was finished studying poverty, they would most likely continue living as poor Americans.

EIGHT

The Stay-Together Gang

One July day in 1995, I drove to Calumet Heights, a neighborhood that lay just across the expressway from Chicago's South Side. In an otherwise run-down working-class area, Calumet Heights stood out for its many middle- and upper-class black families who took great pride in the appearance of their houses. The neighborhood was also home to several of the most powerful gang leaders in the Midwest, including Jerry Tillman and Brian Jackson of the Black Kings. In a practice common among gang leaders, Jerry and Brian had each bought a big suburban home for their moms, and they both spent considerable time there themselves.

Today they were throwing a BK pool party at Brian's house; Jerry was supplying the food and beer. Brian lived in a long, white, Prairie-style home built in the style of Frank Lloyd Wright. Parked on the lawn were a dozen expensive sports cars, which belonged to the BK senior leadership, and a lot of lesser sports cars parked along the curb, which belonged to the junior leadership. A bunch of young men stood around idly on the lawn, caps shading their eyes from the sun. These were BK foot soldiers, in charge of guarding their bosses' cars.

I parked my own rusting Cutlass at the curb and approached the house. I spotted Barry, one of J.T.'s foot soldiers, standing next to J.T.'s purple Malibu. He nodded me toward the house's rear entrance.

J.T. had been meeting regularly with Chicago's highest-ranking BK leaders for some time before he invited me to this party. I was excited. I had envisioned half-naked women sitting poolside and rubbing the bosses with sunscreen while everyone passed around marijuana joints and cold beer.

What I saw for real was far less glamorous. True to stereotype, there was an expensive stereo blasting rap music through a dozen speakers and some big crystal statues of wild animals, and a few people were indeed rolling joints. But overall the place looked as worn as an old fraternity house. The leather couches were badly stained, and so were the carpets. I found out later that the gangsters' mothers felt lonely in the suburbs and told their sons they preferred living in the ghetto, with their friends. Nor were there any half-naked women to be seen, or any women at all. It was a members-only party, and seemingly a pretty tight-knit affair. J.T. had told me that these gatherings were held every few weeks, more often if there were pressing matters to discuss. Although the events were mostly social, he said, the gang leaders inevitably wound up talking business as the evening wore on: Which wholesaler was offering the best and cheapest cocaine? Which neighborhood gangs were acting up and needed discipline?

I bumped into J.T. as he came out of the kitchen. We shook hands and hugged; he seemed to be in a good mood. Small groups of men were congregating in the kitchen, the dining room, and the living room; I could hear the roar of computer games in a back room. Everyone seemed relaxed and at ease.

J.T. brought me over to a group of men and introduced me as "the Professor," which prompted laughs all around. Most of the men were large, their potbellies perhaps the best evidence of a capacity for self-indulgence. They were all tattooed and wore showy gold and silver jewelry. As I would find out later, every one of them had been jailed on a felony at least once.

J.T. hadn't told me exactly how he'd explained my presence to his colleagues and superiors. I just had to trust him. No one seemed even remotely threatened—but then again I wasn't walking around with a tape recorder or asking intrusive questions. In fact, I didn't need to. The men would randomly come up to me and start talking about themselves and, especially, the history of the Black Kings. "In the 1960s, gangs were leading a black revolution," one of them said. "We're trying to do the same." Another took a similar tack, echoing what J.T. had told me many times: "You need to understand that the Black Kings are not a *gang;* we are a *community organization,* responding to people's needs."

One of the men put his arm around me warmly and escorted me into the dining room, where a poker game was being played. There must have been thirty thousand or forty thousand dollars in bills on the table. My guide introduced himself as Cliff. He was a senior BK, in his late forties, who acted as a sort of consigliere for the gang, providing advice to the up-and-coming leaders. "All right, folks, listen up!" he said, trying to gain the poker players' attention. They glanced up briefly. "This is our new director of communications," Cliff said. "The Professor is going to help us get our word out. Make sure you all talk with him before you leave."

I shuddered. J.T. was sitting on the couch with a beer in his hand. He just smiled and shrugged. Two thoughts ran through my mind. On the one hand, I was impressed that J.T. had the confidence to invite me and nominate me for such an exalted position (although part of me felt like I was on the receiving end of a surreal practical joke; perhaps they were just testing my mettle?). On the other hand, knowing that these men managed an organized criminal enterprise, I was scared that I was falling into a hole I could never dig myself out of. I had repeatedly tried to distance myself from the gang, or at least stake out my neutrality. But J.T.'s warning from years earlier rang just as true today: "Either you're with me or you're with someone else." In this world there was no such thing as neutral, as much as the precepts of my academic field might state otherwise.

attended several of these high-level BK gatherings. Although I didn't conduct any formal interviews, in just a few months I was able to learn a good bit about the gang leaders and their business by just hanging around. Over time they seemed to forget that I was even there, or maybe they just didn't care. They rarely spoke openly about drugs, other than to note the death of a supplier or a change in the price of powder cocaine. Most of their talk concerned the burdens of management: how to keep the shorties in line, how to best bribe tenant leaders and police officers, which local businesses were willing to launder their cash.

I did harbor a low-grade fear that I would someday be asked to represent the BKs in a press release or a media interview. But that fear wasn't enough to prevent me from attending as many parties and poker games as J.T. invited me to. I would joke on occasion with J.T.'s superiors that I really had no skills or services to offer them. They never formally appointed me as their director of communications—

or even made such an explicit offer, so I just assumed that no such role really existed.

As a member of the younger set of leaders who had only recently been promoted to these ranks, J.T. was generally a quiet presence. He didn't speak much with me either. But my presence seemed to provide him with some value. It signaled to the others that J.T. had leadership capacities and unique resources: namely, that he was using his link with a student from a prestigious university to help remake the gang's image in the wider world. To that end, the gang leaders continued to approach me to discuss the gang's history and its "community-building" efforts. I took most of this with a grain of salt, as I'd come to consider such claims not only blatantly self-serving but greatly exaggerated.

Watching J.T. operate in this rarefied club, I couldn't help but feel a sense of pride in him. By now I had spent about six years hanging out with J.T., and at some level I was pleased that he was winning recognition for his achievements. Such thoughts were usually accompanied by an equally powerful disquietude at the fact that I took so much pleasure in the rise of a drug-dealing gangster.

Now that he'd graduated into the gang's leadership, J.T. became even more worried about the basic insecurities of gang life—the constant threat of arrest and imprisonment, injury and death. This anxiety had begun to grow in the weeks after Price was wounded in the drive-by shooting. J.T. began asking me to review his life year by year so that I wouldn't be missing any details for his biography. By this point my dissertation had little to do with J.T., and I believe he knew that, even though I'd been hesitant to say so outright. Still, the arrests were making him nervous, and he wanted to be sure that I was faithfully recording the events of his life. He also became obsessed with saving money for his mother and his children in case something happened to him. He even began selling off some of his cars and expensive jewelry.

At the same time, he started to make more money because of his promotion. Not only were there additional BK sales crews whose earnings J.T. could tax, but, as if in an investment bank or law-firm partnership, he also began receiving a share of the overall BK revenues produced by drug sales, extortion, and taxation. By now he was probably earning at least two hundred thousand dollars a year in cash.

His promotion also carried additional risk. At the suburban meetings I attended, the leaders spoke anxiously about which gang leaders had been named in federal indictments and who was most likely to cooperate with the authorities. I also heard about a young gang member who'd been severely beaten because his bosses thought he had turned snitch.

Amid the beer drinking, gambling, and carousing at these parties, there was a strong undercurrent of paranoia. For me it was a bizarre experience, since the leaders began voicing their fears to me privately, as if I were a confessor of some sort, knowledgeable about their trade but powerless to harm them. Cold Man, a forty-five-year-old leader who ran the BKs' operation on the city's West Side, asked me to step outside for a cigarette so we could talk. He tended to take the long view. "We need to be careful in these times of war," he told me, alluding to the arrests and their potential to create turncoats within the gang. "Don't trust nobody, especially your friends. I love these niggers, they're my family, but now is not the time to go soft."

Pootchie, a smart thirty-year-old leader who'd recently been promoted along with J.T., one night asked me to sit with him in his car to talk. "I'm not going to do this forever," he said. "I'm here to make my money and get the fuck out."

"What will you do next?" I asked.

"I'm a dancer—tap, jazz, all of it. I'd like to get my own place and teach."

I couldn't help laughing. Pootchie looked sheepish. "Sorry!" I said. "I don't mean to laugh, but it's just surprising."

"Yeah, my father used to dance, and my mother was a singer. I dropped out of school—stupidest thing I ever did—but I got a business sense about me. I probably saved a few hundred grand. And I *ain't* getting arrested. No way. I got bigger things I'm into. Not like some of these jailhouse niggers. I ain't one of them. I'm an operator."

I learned that Pootchie's distinction between "jailhouse niggers" and "operators" was an essential one. These were the two kinds of leaders within the Black Kings. The first was devoted to building solidarity and staying together during difficult times, like the present threat of widespread arrests. These leaders were known as "jailhouse niggers," since they had learned from prison that you didn't survive unless you formed alliances and loyalties. These men tended to be the older leaders, in their late thirties or forties, and they tended to speak more of the BK "family" as opposed to the BK "business." The "operators," meanwhile, were a more entrepreneurial breed, like Pootchie and J.T. They were usually younger—J.T. was about thirty by now—and saw the gang primarily as a commercial enterprise. J.T. wanted to be a respected "community man," to be sure, but that was more of a practical gambit than an ideological one.

Riding back to the South Side one night with J.T. from a suburban poker game, I sat quietly in the dark. J.T. was in a somber mood. As we pulled up to my apartment building, he admitted that the federal indictments were driving everyone a bit mad. "No one trusts nobody," he said. "They'll shoot you for looking funny." J.T.

shook his head. "I never realized how easy life was when it was *just* the projects. If they think I'm talking with the cops, I'll be killed right away. Sometimes I think I should get my money and get out."

As he said this, I immediately thought, *I'd better get my data and get out!* But I didn't. I kept going back to the BK meetings. With the gang's most senior officers talking to me, I figured I'd better be careful about how I chose to exit the group. As paranoid as everyone was these days, now was not the time for sudden movements.

J.T.'s life had also become complicated by the possible demolition of the Robert Taylor Homes. He was smart enough to know that his success was due in considerable part to geography: The concentration of people around Robert Taylor and its great location, near traffic corridors and expressways, guaranteed a huge customer base. J.T. might have been a good businessman, but every drug dealer in Chicago knew that Robert Taylor was among the best sales locations in the city.

So if the projects were torn down, J.T. would lose his customer base as well as much of his gang membership, since most of his young members lived in Robert Taylor.

Accordingly, J.T. was far less sanguine about the demolition than some tenants were. He thought it was folly to think that poor families could alter the buildings' fate. Sometimes he'd just sit detachedly when we were together, muttering to himself, "Man, I need a plan. I need a plan. I *have* to think what I'm going to do. . . ."

He also had to worry about retaining his senior leaders, Price and T-Bone. They, too, were getting anxious, since their best shot at success—and their biggest incentive to stay in the gang—was the opportunity to become a leader. If Robert Taylor was torn down, then J.T.'s stock would probably fall, and so would theirs.

When I asked T-Bone how he felt about the future, he soberly described his vulnerability as a lieutenant to J.T. "I'm not protected, that's my main problem," he said. "I got nothing, so I have to be real careful. I mean, I save my money and give it to my mom. Like I told you, I want to get my degree and do something else with my life, start a business maybe. But with all the police coming around, I got to be careful. It's people like me who go to prison. The ones up on the mountain always strike a deal."

But if he left the gang suddenly, I asked him, wouldn't his bosses suspect he was collaborating with the police?

"Yeah," he said with a laugh. "If I leave the gang, these niggers will come after me and kill me. If I stay in the gang, the police will throw me in jail for thirty years. But that's the life. . . ."

As his voice trailed off, I wanted to cry. I liked T-Bone, so much so that sometimes I almost forgot he was a gang member. At the moment he seemed like a bookish kid, working hard and worrying about passing his classes.

Not long afterward T-Bone's girlfriend left a message instructing me to meet him at dusk in a parking lot near the expressway. I did as I was told. "You were always interested in how we do things," T-Bone said, "so here you go." He handed me a set of spiral-bound ledgers that detailed the gang's finances. He seemed remorseful—and anxious. He wondered aloud what his life would have been like if he'd "stayed legit." I could tell he was expecting a bad ending.

The pages of the ledgers were frayed, and some of the handwriting was hard to decipher, but the raw information was fascinating. For the past four years, T-Bone had been dutifully recording the gang's revenues (from drug sales, extortion, and other sources) and expenses (the cost of wholesale cocaine and weapons, police bribes, funeral expenses, and all the gang members' salaries).

It was dangerous for T-Bone to give me this information, a blatant violation of the gang's codes, for which he would be severely punished if caught. T-Bone knew of my interest in the gang's economic structure. He saw how delighted I was now, fondling the ledgers as if they were first editions of famous books.

I never shared the notebooks with anyone in law enforcement. I put them away for a few years until I met the economist Steven Levitt. We published several articles based on this rich data source, and our analysis of the gang's finances easily received the most notoriety of all the articles and books I have written. T-Bone probably had no idea that I would receive any critical acclaim, but he certainly knew that he was handing me something that few others—in the academy or in the world at large—had ever seen. Looking back, I think he probably wanted to help me, but I also believe he wanted to do something good before meeting whatever bad ending might have been coming his way. Given his love of books and education, it is not altogether inconceivable that T-Bone wanted this to be a charitable act of sorts, helping the world better understand the structure of gangland.

Perhaps the most surprising fact in T-Bone's ledgers was the incredibly low wage paid to the young members who did the dirtiest and most dangerous work: selling drugs on the street. According to T-Bone's records, they barely earned minimum wage. For all their braggadocio, to say nothing of the peer pressure to spend money on sharp clothes and cars, these young members stood little chance of ever making a solid payday unless they beat the odds and were promoted into the senior ranks. But even Price and T-Bone, it turned out, made only about thirty thousand dollars a year. Now I knew why some of the younger BK members supplemented their income by working legit jobs at McDonald's or a car wash.

So a gang leader like J.T. had a tough job: motivating young men to accept the risks of selling drugs despite the low wages and slim chance of promotion. It was one thing to motivate his troops in the Robert Taylor Homes, where BK lore ran deep and the size of the drug trade made the enterprise seem appealingly robust. It would be much harder to start up operations from scratch in a different neighborhood.

I got to witness this challenge firsthand one evening when I accompanied J.T., Price, and T-Bone to West Pullman, a predominantly black neighborhood on the far South Side. Although there were poor sections of West Pullman, it also had a solid working-class base, with little gang activity. That was where the three Black Kings were trying to set up a new BK franchise. J.T. had arranged a meeting with about two dozen young men, a ragtag group of high-school dropouts and some older teenagers, most of whom spent the majority of their time just hanging out. J.T. wanted to help them become "black businessmen," he told them.

They sat on wooden benches in the corner of a small neighborhood park. Most of them had boyish faces. Some looked innocent, some bored, and some eager, as if attending the first meeting of their Little League team. J.T. stood in front of them like their coach, extolling the benefits of "belonging to the Black Kings family, a nationwide family." He pointed to his latest car, a Mitsubishi 3000GT, as a sign of what you could get if you worked hard in the drug economy. He sounded a bit like a salesman.

A few of them asked about the particulars of the drug trade. Were they supposed to cook the crack themselves, or were they provided with the finished product? Could they extend credit to good customers, or was it strictly a cash business?

"My auntie said I should ask you if she could join also," one teenager said. "She says she has a lot of experience—"

J.T. cut him off. "Your auntie?! Nigger, are you kidding me? Ain't no women allowed in this thing."

"Well, she said that back in the day she was into selling dope," the teenager continued. "She said that you should call her, because she could help you understand how to run a business."

"All right, we'll talk about this later, my man," J.T. said, then turned to address the rest of the young men. "Listen, you all need to understand, we're taking you to a whole 'nother level. We're not talking about hanging out and getting girls. You'll get all the pussy you want, but this is about taking pride in who you are, about doing something for yourself and your people. Now, we figure you got nobody serving around here. So there's a real need—"

"Serving what?" the same teenager interrupted.

J.T. ignored him. "Like I said, you got no one responding to the demand, and we want to work with you-all. We're going to set up shop."

"Is there some kind of training?" asked a soft, sweet voice from the back. "And do we get paid to go? I got to be at White Castle on Mondays and Thursdays, and my mama says if I lose that job, she'll kick me out of the house."

"White Castle?!" J.T. looked over in disbelief at T-Bone, Price, and me. "Nigger, I'm talking about taking control of your *life*. What is White Castle doing for you? I don't get it—how far can that take you?"

"I'm trying to save up for a bike," the boy replied.

Hearing that, J.T. headed for his car, motioning for Price to finish up with the group.

"We'll be in touch with you-all," Price said assertively. "Right now, you need to understand that we got this place, you dig? If anyone else comes over and says they want you to work with them, you tell them you are Black Kings. Got it?"

As Price continued speaking to the teenagers, I walked over to J.T. and asked if this meeting was typical.

"This shit is frustrating," he said, grabbing a soda from the car. "There's a lot of places where the kids ain't really done nothing. They have no idea what it means to be a part of something."

"So why do you want to do this?"

"Don't have a choice," he said. "We don't have any other places left to take over." Most city neighborhoods, he explained, were already claimed by a gang leader. It was nearly impossible to annex a territory with an entrenched gang structure unless the leader died or went to jail. Even in those cases, there were usually local figures with enough charisma and leverage to step in. This meant that J.T. had to expand into working- and middle-class neighborhoods where the local "gang" was nothing more than a bunch of teenagers who hung out and got into trouble. If today's meeting was any indication, these gangs weren't the ideal candidates for Black Kings membership.

"I can't believe I'm doing this shit," J.T. said, walking around his car, kicking stones in the dirt. Between the dual threats of arrest and demolition, he seemed to be coming to grips with the possibility that his star might have peaked.

The Black Kings weren't the only ones anxious about the threat of demolition. All the tenants of Robert Taylor were trying to cope with the news. Although demolition wouldn't begin for at least two years, everyone was scrambling to learn which building might come down first and where on earth they were supposed to live.

Politicians, including President Clinton and Mayor Richard J. Daley of Chicago, promised that tenants would be relocated to middle-class neighborhoods with good schools, safe streets, and job opportunities. But reliable information was hard to come by. Nor would it be so easy to secure housing outside the black ghetto. The projects had been built forty years earlier in large part because white

Chicagoans didn't want black neighbors. Most Robert Taylor tenants thought the situation hadn't changed all that much.

The CHA began to hold public meetings where tenants could air their questions and concerns. The CHA officials begged for patience, promising that every family would have help when the time came for relocation. But there was legitimate reason for skepticism. One of the most inept and corrupt housing agencies in the country was now being asked to relocate 150,000 people living in roughly two hundred buildings slated for demolition throughout Chicago. And Robert Taylor was the largest housing project of all, the size of a small city. The CHA's challenge was being made even harder by Chicago's tightening real-estate market. As the city gentrified, there were fewer and fewer communities where low-income families could find decent, affordable housing.

Information, much of it contradictory, came in dribs and drabs. At one meeting the CHA stated that all Robert Taylor residents would be resettled in other housing projects—a frightening prospect for many, since that would mean crossing gang boundaries. At another meeting the agency said that some families would receive a housing voucher to help cover their rent in the private market. At yet another meeting it was declared that large families would be split up: aunts and uncles and grandparents who weren't on the lease would have to fend for themselves.

With so much confusion in the air, tenants came to rely on rumors. There was talk of a political conspiracy whereby powerful white politicians wanted to tear down Robert Taylor in order to spread its citizens around the city and dilute the black vote. There was even a rumor about me: word was going around that I worked for the CIA, gathering secret information to help expedite the demolition. I assumed that this theory arose out of my attempt to procure a Department of Justice grant for the Boys & Girls Club, but I couldn't say for sure.

Many tenants still clung to the idea that the demolition wouldn't happen at all, or at least not for a long time. But I couldn't find a single tenant who, regardless of his or her belief about the timing of the demolition, believed that the CHA would do a good job of relocation. Some people told me they were willing to bribe their building presidents for preferential treatment. Others were angry at the government for taking away their homes and wanted to stage protests to halt the demolition.

There was also a deep skepticism among tenants that their own elected leaders would work hard on their behalf. Ms. Bailey and other building presidents were being besieged by constituents desperate for advice.

One day I sat in Ms. Bailey's office as she waited for a senior CHA official to show up for a briefing. Several other tenant leaders were also waiting, in the outer room. Ms. Bailey made no effort to hide the fact that she, along with most of the other tenant leaders, had already agreed to support the demolition rather than try to save the buildings. "The CHA made things perfectly clear to us," she explained. "These buildings *are* coming down." She spoke to me as if I were a five-year-old, with no understanding whatsoever of city politics. "Of course, you got a few people who think they can stop this, but I keep telling them, 'Look out for your own family, and get out while you can.' I'm looking out for *my*self."

"What does that mean?" I asked.

"That means I got one shot to get what I can from the CHA for me and for my people. The CHA don't have no money, Sudhir! They made that clear to us. And you know they just want to get us out of here, so I'm going to get *something* out of this."

"Like what?"

"Well, I already told them I need a five-bedroom house in South Shore," she said with a rich laugh. Then she told me the building presidents' personal requests. "Ms. Daniels wants the CHA to give her son's construction company a contract to help tear down the buildings. Ms. Wilson made a list of appliances she wants in her new apartment. Ms. Denny will be starting a new business, and the CHA needs to hire her to help relocate families."

"And you think the CHA will actually agree to these demands?"

Ms. Bailey just sat and stared at me. Apparently my naïveté was showing once more.

I tried again. "You already got them to agree, didn't you?"

Again she was silent.

"Is that what this meeting is about?" I motioned toward the outer room where the other building presidents were waiting. "Is that why this guy from the CHA is coming?"

"Well, no," she said. "We already had *that* conversation. Today is about the families. Let me tell you how this process is going to go. I know it's early, but they're already tearing down the projects on the West Side, so there ain't no mystery anymore." The Henry Horner projects on the West Side were being razed to make way for a new sports arena, the United Center, which would host the Chicago Bulls, the Chicago Blackhawks, and, eventually, the 1996 Democratic National Convention. "We'll make our list, and they'll take care of our people."

"Your list?"

"I already told you the CHA has no money, Sudhir! What part of this don't you understand?" She grew very animated and then suddenly quieted down. "They can't help everyone. And you know what? They'll mess up like they messed up in the past. Not everyone is going to be taken care of."

Ms. Bailey said that she would likely be able to help only about one-fourth of the families move out safely. Her bigger job, she said, was to make sure that the remaining three-fourths grasped this reality. The CHA, she said, "plans to use most of their money to demolish the buildings, not help people move out."

So Ms. Bailey and the other building presidents made lists of the families who they felt should have priority in obtaining rent vouchers, assistance in finding a new apartment, or free furniture and appliances. This list, it turned out, didn't necessarily comprise the neediest families—but, rather, the building presidents' personal friends or tenants who had paid them small bribes.

I asked Ms. Bailey how much she was getting.

"Sudhir, I'll be honest with you," she said, smiling. "We'll be taken care of. But don't forget to put in your little book that the CHA also gets their share. We're all washing each other's hands around here."

It wasn't very pleasant to watch this entire scenario play out in two parallel worlds. In the media all you heard were politicians' promises to help CHA tenants forge a better life. On the ground, meanwhile, the lowest-ranking members of society got pushed even lower, thanks to a stingy and neglectful city agency and the constant hustling of the few people in a position to help. In the coming months, the place began to take on the feel of a refugee camp, with every person desperate to secure her own welfare, quite possibly at the expense of a neighbor.

Not everyone, however, was so selfish or fatalistic. For some tenants demolition represented a chance to start fresh with a better apartment in a safer neighborhood. It was particularly inspiring to watch such tenants work together toward this goal while their elected leaders mainly looked out for themselves.

One such optimist was Dorothy Battie, a forty-five-year-old

mother of six who had spent nearly her entire life in the projects. Dorothy lived in a building a few blocks away from J.T. She was a heavyset woman, deeply religious, who always had a positive demeanor despite having suffered through everything the projects had to offer. Her father and several nieces and nephews had been killed in various gang shootings. Dorothy had fought through her own drug addiction, then helped other addicts enter rehab. Some of her children were now in college, and one was a leader in a Black Kings gang.

Dorothy had never been an elected tenant leader, but she was a self-appointed godmother to countless families. She helped squatters find shelter, fed tenants who couldn't afford to eat, and provided day care for many children, some related by blood and others not. Spurred on now by the demolition, she began to act as a sort of relocation counselor for several families who were determined to live near one another in a new neighborhood. They thought that sticking together was their best, and maybe only, chance for survival. These families became informally known as "the Stay-Together Gang," and their undisputed ringleader was Dorothy.

I caught up with her one day in her living room as she was looking over a list of the families she most wanted to help.

"Let's see," she said, "I got Cherry, three kids. Candy, two kids. Marna, a son and a daughter. Princess, three kids. Carrie, two young girls. And there's probably a few more." All these young women were friends who shared baby-sitting, cars, and cooking. Now their mission, with Dorothy's help, was to find a place to live where they could keep their network intact.

"See, here's the problem," Dorothy explained. "I know what it's like out there in the private market. You end up in some apartment, with no one around, no one to help you. And you're scared. At least if a few people can move with each other, stay together, they can help each other. Lot of people out there don't like us because we come from the projects. They may not answer the door if we knock for help. So I want to make sure people don't get stuck in the cold."

It was important, she said, to start with the most stable family in the network. That was Cherry, who worked thirty hours a week as a fast-food cashier and also went to night school. Dorothy's plan called for Cherry to find an apartment in a good neighborhood and then bring the other families over.

While this plan seemed pretty straightforward, Dorothy told me that success was hardly guaranteed. "Things never go as planned," she said bluntly, "because we're dealing with poor people."

Dorothy's first obstacle was Ms. Reemes, a powerful tenant in her building, who was not elected to any office but had great influence with the CHA and police. Like Ms. Bailey, Ms. Reemes expected families to pay her a fee, anywhere from fifty to two hundred dollars, for smoothing the relocation process. Every family that Dorothy helped meant one less potential bribe for Ms. Reemes. Although the building hadn't even been singled out yet for demolition, Ms. Reemes was already accepting "deposits" from families who wanted a rent voucher or relocation services.

"She wanted *me* to give her a cut," Dorothy said, "and I told her I'm not even getting paid to help these people! So I told her to go to hell. That lady is so selfish."

As Dorothy told it, Ms. Reemes was so miffed by Dorothy's refusal to play the payoff game that she went on a harassment campaign. First, Dorothy said, Ms. Reemes put in a bad word about Dorothy with the CHA. Within a week Dorothy's two grown daughters, both of whom lived in the same building, received eviction notices for late payment of rent. This was particularly surprising, since one of her daughters had no income and was therefore excused from paying any rent at all. Dorothy successfully got the eviction notices rescinded. Then a CHA janitor cut off the electricity in Dorothy's apartment, but Dorothy paid a squatter to restore it. Ms. Reemes then tried to get the gangs to harass Dorothy, not realizing that Dorothy's own son was a senior gang leader. He paid Ms. Reemes a personal visit, and she backed down.

Through a classified ad in the *Chicago Sun-Times,* Dorothy found a two-bedroom apartment for Cherry's family in Woodlawn, a poor but stable neighborhood about two miles away, near Hyde Park and the university. Because Dorothy had a CHA connection who helped Cherry get a $500-a-month housing voucher, she had to pay only $150 a month out of pocket.

Soon after Cherry moved in with her children and an aunt who would provide day care, Dorothy found a large apartment nearby for Princess and her three children. The only problem was that Princess's brother and uncle heard about this and decided that they also wanted to move in. If they were found to be living there, Princess would lose her rent voucher on the grounds of illegal tenancy. Worse yet, her brother and uncle were drug dealers who wanted to use Princess's apartment as a new base of operations. "Princess has put up with those two fools for too long, and it's hurting her kids," Dorothy told me. "I wanted her to start over, and now her brother and uncle are going to mess everything up."

So Dorothy, with Princess in tow, went to confront the two men at a local bar where they hung out. Princess was worried, since both of them smoked crack and were prone to violence, but Dorothy feared no one. As Princess later described it, Dorothy stormed into the bar and loudly told the two men they'd have *her* to deal with if they moved in with Princess. The men threatened to beat up Dorothy and then stomped away. They retaliated by calling Princess's new landlord and, posing as CHA officials, warned the landlord that Princess was a gang member. The landlord promptly called Dorothy.

He didn't necessarily believe that Princess was in a gang, he said, but he wasn't willing to take the chance. So Princess lost her lease. Dorothy eventually found Princess another apartment, but it was smaller, more expensive, and a few miles away from Cherry.

And then Marna was thrown in jail for six months for stabbing her boyfriend. Dorothy moved Marna's children around from one apartment to another so that the social workers couldn't find them and send them to foster care. Soon after, Dorothy heard that Candy had promised J.T. that the Black Kings could stash guns and drugs in the new apartment that Dorothy was helping her rent. Since J.T. was paying Candy for this service, Dorothy had little leverage to persuade her to do otherwise. Within a year Candy would lose her lease (and her rent subsidy) when the landlord called the police, having seen so many people tromping in and out of her apartment.

The most astounding story concerning Dorothy—one that I could never independently verify—also had to do with the police. She told me that Ms. Reemes called in Officer Jerry, the rogue cop, who caught her in the lobby, dragged her into a vacant apartment, planted drugs on her, and threatened to arrest her for possession if she didn't stop competing with Ms. Reemes. When Dorothy refused, Officer Jerry arrested her, but she managed to enlist some other police officers, including Officer Reggie, to set her free. According to Dorothy, Officer Jerry returned two weeks later and told Dorothy that if she just paid Ms. Reemes a share of "her cut"—which, Dorothy insisted, didn't exist—then he would leave her alone.

In the end Dorothy's list included twelve families chosen for the Stay-Together Gang. Despite her perseverance, she was able to help only four of them move out together, to neighboring apartments in Woodlawn and South Shore. I would spend much of the next decade keeping track of the Robert Taylor Homes' former tenants to see how they adapted to life beyond the projects. As it turned out,

Dorothy's success rate was easily as good as that of the various social-services agencies contracted by the CHA, each of which was awarded hundreds of thousands of dollars to carry out the job. Dorothy herself would stay in Robert Taylor until it was demolished, and then she joined her daughter, Lee-Lee, in Englewood, a high-crime, predominantly black neighborhood a few miles away.

Dorothy's move to Lee-Lee's house was, unfortunately, a typical outcome for many tenants who left Robert Taylor and other CHA projects. While the goal of the demolition was to move families to safer, integrated communities, the CHA was so inept that nearly 90 percent of the relocated tenants wound up living in poor black areas that left them as badly off as being in the projects, or worse.

In place of the projects, the city began to build market-rate condominiums and town houses, three-story structures tucked cozily together instead of the sixteen-story high-rises separated by vast expanses. Robert Taylor tenants had been promised the right to return to the community once construction was done, but fewer than 10 percent of the units were set aside for public-housing families. It is little wonder that the prevailing wisdom in Chicago is that the Daley administration and the powerful real-estate interests, rather than creating new and improved low-income housing, in fact knocked down the projects to initiate a land grab. As of this writing, the new apartments are set to house mostly middle- and upperclass families.

A few months after T-Bone gave me the Black Kings' financial ledgers, Ms. Bailey invited me to a back-to-school party for the children in her building. J.T. had given her a thousand dollars to throw the party and to buy the kids some sneakers, clothes, and school supplies.

I hadn't been spending much time around J.T.'s building in the months leading up to the party. I was generally holed up in the library, working on my dissertation. My advisers and I had agreed that it should explore how families cope with poverty—specifically, how CHA tenants solved problems and kept the community together without much help from the government or charities.

When I arrived for the party, it felt like my first visits from years earlier. There were cars parked all around the basketball court, rap music blasting away, kids running everywhere, and squatters grilling burgers and hot dogs to earn a little money. J.T. and his senior officers were drinking beer and casting an eye over the entire scene. J.T., Ms. Mae, Ms. Bailey, and some of the other tenants greeted me with the same carefree attitude they had showed me when I first began coming around. As I watched Ms. Bailey and some of the other older women tend to the children, I couldn't help but feel kind of nostalgic. Everyone looked a bit older and more fatigued—just like me, I suppose.

I saw something out of the corner of my eye that stopped me cold: a small garden bursting with bright orange, red, and purple geraniums. In this vast stretch of concrete and patchy lawn, littered with broken bottles, used condoms, and empty crack vials, here was an oasis. I laughed to myself. Why hadn't I ever noticed it before?

I'd been so caught up with gangs, political chicanery, and the life of poverty that I had missed something so beautiful right there in front of me. What else had I missed because of my incessant drive to hustle?

I thought back to the last time I'd noticed any flowers in Robert Taylor. It had been well over a year earlier. The tenants were preparing for a visit from President Bill Clinton. They were incredibly excited, but also unnerved. His visit was meant to highlight the unprecedented levels of gang violence in Chicago public housing.

Clinton supported the use of police "sweeps," the warrantless searches that the Chicago Police Department was using to combat the gang and drug problems. While the ACLU and other groups decried the sweeps as a violation of constitutional rights, Clinton argued that the right to "freedom from fear" was more important. He wanted inner-city residents to believe, as he believed, that the scourge of street gangs required extraordinary measures, and his trip to Robert Taylor provided a firsthand opportunity to persuade them.

In the weeks before his visit, the project was turned upside down. The police conducted even more sweeps than usual, sometimes ransacking apartments indiscriminately. They also conducted random spot checks in the building lobbies, arresting a great many suspected drug dealers, including many young men who had nothing whatsoever to do with dealing drugs.

J.T. didn't go so far as to halt drug sales, but he was a bit more cautious, sometimes having his dealers take customers inside to an apartment to obtain the drugs rather than getting them on the street. He also stopped extorting from local stores, fearing that that might lead to arrest. And he stopped laundering money, stowing his cash in garbage bags until the neighborhood quieted down.

On the streets, city tow trucks hauled away abandoned vehicles— as well as a lot of vehicles that might have looked abandoned but were in fact just old and beat up. On top of all this disorder, the weather was unrelentingly hot and humid.

Still, there was hope in the air. Because of Bill Clinton's overwhelming popularity among African Americans, even the most cynical tenants—including the people whose cars had been towed— were excited about his visit. Tenant leaders led campaigns to spruce up their buildings' lobbies, hallways, and playgrounds. Tenant patrols went door-to-door asking people to tidy up their living rooms and clean their toilets; in one building, snakes and other strange pets were confiscated from certain households. And throughout the project, aged flower beds sprang to life.

In the early days of Robert Taylor, the buildings had competed against one another with flower gardens and other beautification projects. This dormant practice was now reborn in anticipation of the president's visit. He obviously couldn't visit all twenty-eight Robert Taylor buildings, and he might have time for just one. But this only heightened the intensity of the competition. A few tenant leaders called in favors with city officials to try to make sure their building was on the president's list. Some of them curried additional favor by turning in drug dealers to the police.

The 5011 building, located on the far south side of Robert Taylor, showed particular enthusiasm. This was fueled by the belief that a new construction project next door to 5011 was in fact the construction of a presidential podium. The tenant leader taxed the local gang twenty-five hundred dollars to fund a wide-scale restoration effort. The building's children were given new clothes and shoes; a mural of historic African-American figures was painted along the building's ground floor; a few particularly civic-minded tenants even wrote speeches, just in case the president called them up to the podium. And families planted rows and rows of flowers in a garden that had seen nothing but trash for years.

By the morning of June 17, 1994, the day of President Clinton's visit, the residents of 5011 were fully ready. But his entourage sped past quickly, without so much as a wave. He gave his speech in another part of Robert Taylor. A few of the tenants in 5011 moaned and groaned, but generally they were satisfied that the president had showed up at all. Parents broke out soda and beer, and their kids caught the spirit and launched a party. After the initial disappointment, no one seemed willing to utter a spiteful word. For a time at least, the community shared a deep spirit of satisfaction, of having pulled together. Over and over again, you could hear tenants remark that they hadn't seen such solidarity in decades.

Now, a year later, the flower bed outside J.T.'s building stood as a similar sign of hope—and, in light of the imminent demolition of the projects, a sign of proud obstinacy.

The back-to-school party was in full swing. Kids and grown-ups alike loaded their plates with food. A softball game started up, and a crowd of people gathered to watch. I milled about, saying hello to a lot of people I hadn't seen in a while.

Suddenly the sound of gunshots pierced the air, and everyone ran for cover. There were four or five shots, rapid fire, from what sounded like a pistol. Parents grabbed their kids and ducked behind cars or ran for the lobby. Above the blaring music, you could hear women screaming for their children. J.T. hollered for everyone to get down.

I found myself crouching behind a car parked near the building. Beside me were a few of J.T.'s foot soldiers, young men I barely knew. I asked where the shooting was coming from. They immediately pointed up toward the upper floors of the building.

"Niggers are probably high on dope," one of them whispered. "Or else you got an MC who snuck up in the building. It used to be an MC building before we took it over."

Some distance away I could see a thin, dark-skinned woman staggering toward us across the grassy expanse in front of the building. Her clothes were sloppy, and she was practically falling down, probably either drunk or high. As she came closer, you could hear her talking to herself, most of it gibberish. People started yelling at her to take cover. A few of J.T.'s men shouted nasty names and threw beer bottles at her. It was pretty common for drug dealers to treat drug users with disdain; they often justified their line of work by pointing out that they took money from the most useless members of the community.

Some more shots rang out from above, the bullets kicking up clouds of dirt a few feet from the woman.

"That ain't the MCs firing at us," said the foot soldier beside me. "That's just some nigger who is fucked up and looking to cause trouble."

Finally an older gentleman ran out, grabbed the staggering woman, and hustled her into the lobby. After about ten minutes with no more gunfire, most people felt comfortable enough to come out from their hiding places. Parents and children ran into the building, abandoning the party. The squatters and the hustlers, meanwhile, got back to their food and listened to the music. My heart kept racing for several minutes, but even I wasn't surprised by now that nobody even bothered to call the police.

I n the spring of 1996, I learned that I had received a junior fellowship at Harvard's Society of Fellows. I was ecstatic; it was a much-sought-after position, a three-year salaried research post. I went to tell J.T. the good news, and that I would soon be leaving town, although I still planned to maintain my ties to Chicago.

The smells of Ms. Mae's cooking—collard greens, cornbread, and smothered chicken—hit me as I walked in the door. "You still manage to get here right when the food is ready, don't you?" J.T. said with a laugh.

I apologized for missing the last few suburban Black Kings meetings.

"They still think you're the director of communications," he said, laughing again but looking at the TV instead of at me. "There's another meeting next Sunday if you want to come with me."

"Sure," I said, trying to sound enthusiastic. "That would be great." I explained why I'd been so busy lately. Until I learned of the Harvard fellowship, I had been applying for teaching jobs at universities all over the country, including Columbia University in New York.

J.T. interrupted my explanation. "You remember Curtis, that tall, dark boy you met?" He suddenly sat up and began to speak with great enthusiasm. "Curtis is from New Jersey, or at least he has work out there. Hey, what do you think about heading out there with me? I've been wanting to go and see how they do things. He and I have this bet. He says the women are hotter in *his* projects. Says I should come out and see."

I did remember Curtis, a nerdy-looking drug dealer who worked out of the housing projects in Newark. We had exchanged a few words at most when he came to visit J.T. about a year earlier.

"Somehow," I said to J.T., trying to sound appreciative, "I don't think that would be such a good—"

"Yeah, you're probably right. Probably not the best time for us to leave right now, especially with everything that's going on. You need to watch me do my thing, I know." He grew pensive. "I got a couple of big meetings next week, and you probably want to be around for that."

Before I could ask him about these meetings, he had another idea: "You know something? You remember how we talked about how gangs are different across the country?"

I had once told J.T. that gangs in New York and Boston were said to be much smaller than Chicago's gangs, rooted in local neighborhoods as opposed to being part of a citywide wheel. But no one, I told him, had managed to write an in-depth, multi-city study of street gangs.

"I could help you meet people all over the place!" he continued. He stood up to get a beer from the fridge. "We got people we know in L.A., in Las Vegas, St. Louis. Black Kings are nationwide! I mean, you and I could figure out how the whole thing works."

"So you'll be my research assistant!" I said with a laugh, not quite sure what he was proposing.

"No, no! You'll still be writing about *me*. The book will still be about *me*, but this will add a new dimension to it."

"Yes, it would add a lot, but I'd really have to check with my professors. I mean, I'm not sure what's going to happen once I move. . . ."

J.T.'s voice immediately took on a guarded tone. "No, I understand," he said. "I know you got a lot to think about. I'm just saying that I could help you. But yeah, you talk to your professors first. No big thing. . . ."

We sat there, not speaking, eyes on the TV. I kept hoping we'd be interrupted by Ms. Mae calling us for dinner, but we weren't. I didn't even have the energy to muster up a question about J.T.'s business or his life, as I'd always done previously whenever he sensed that my interests were shifting. Finally a college basketball game came on, and the blare of the crowd and the cheerleaders drowned out the silence between us.

With the demolition of Robert Taylor now formally scheduled to begin within a year, the drug economy in J.T.'s buildings was already faltering. Some of his best customers were tenants, and they were starting to move out. So were a lot of the BK foot soldiers who still lived at home with their moms. (J.T. offered to rent Ms. Mae a home in one of several neighborhoods, and she tried out a few, but she wound up coming back to a cousin's house a few hundred yards from Robert Taylor.) The whole place had also grown thick with police, called in to protect the streams of contractors, engineers, city planners, and other bureaucrats who were plotting the massive demolition.

With less demand for drugs, there was less work for J.T.'s rank-

and-file members. It was in his interest to place these young men in a new gang, since he never knew when he might need their help in the future. Given his standing in the BKs, it was certainly within J.T.'s power to reassign his foot soldiers to other BK factions throughout the city. But he was able to place only a handful at a time, and no more than a few dozen overall. Worse yet, this strategy tended to fail in the long term, since in most cases the host gang wouldn't fully accept the new member.

J.T.'s gang also had a lot of older members, in their thirties and even forties, who were unwilling to accept a transfer, since that typically meant a drop in seniority and, accordingly, income. Some of these men began to leave J.T.'s command altogether, trying to secure positions within other gangs around the city—occasionally, to J.T.'s deep displeasure, within a rival gang.

A few of J.T.'s men traveled as far as Iowa to try to set up shop. I never went along on any of these out-of-state recruiting trips, but judging from the frustration of the BK missionaries who returned to Chicago, this plan wasn't going to work out very well.

J.T. tried to hold things together, but the new economics of his situation conspired against him. He grew lonely, feeling as if he were being abandoned by his own BK family. His sense of paranoia grew even more acute. Whenever I saw him, he immediately began to speculate that the more senior BK defectors were revealing the gang's secrets to rival outfits: where the BKs stored guns and drugs, which cops were open to bribery, which local merchants were willing to launder money.

And then there were the arrests. The federal indictments that had begun to tear apart other gangs were now striking the Black Kings as well. Barry and Otis, two of J.T.'s younger members, had recently been arrested. I wondered how long J.T. would be able to stay free himself. One night, driving back from one of the suburban gang meetings, he mused that jail might actually be the best of his options, since anyone who escaped arrest for too long was suspected of being a snitch and placed himself in real danger on the streets.

Soon after this conversation, I heard that T-Bone had been arrested. He was eventually convicted of trafficking narcotics and sentenced to more than ten years in prison. His prompt transfer to an out-of-state prison fueled speculation that he was testifying against his peers to get a reduced sentence. I tried every avenue I could think of, but I had no luck reaching T-Bone. I eventually heard that he had died in prison, and he became celebrated in death for never having cooperated with the police to sell out other gang members.

For a time I thought that J.T. and I might remain close even as our worlds were growing apart. "Don't worry," I told him, "I'll be coming back all the time." But the deeper I got into my Harvard fellowship, the more time passed between my visits to Chicago, and the more time passed between visits, the more awkward J.T. and I found it to carry on our conversations. He seemed to have grown nostalgic for our early days together, even a bit clingy. I realized that he had come to rely on my presence; he liked the attention and the validation.

I, meanwhile, grew evasive and withdrawn—in large part out of guilt. Within just a few months at Harvard, I began making a name for myself in academia by talking about the inner workings of street gangs. While I hoped to contribute to the national discussion on poverty, I was not so foolish as to believe that my research would specifically benefit J.T. or the tenant families from whom I'd learned so much.

As demolition became a reality, and as J.T.'s gang continued to fall apart, so did our relationship. When I told him that I'd been offered a job teaching sociology at Columbia University upon completing my Harvard fellowship, he asked me what was wrong with teaching in Chicago. "What about high school?" he said. "Those people need education, too, don't they?"

The breakdown of the gang affected Ms. Bailey as well. When the gang didn't make money, Ms. Bailey didn't make much money either. And with demolition so near, she needed all the money she could get to help the tenants she wanted to help. She paid for day care so single mothers could go look for new apartments. She hired a car service to take tenants on their housing searches. She helped others settle their outstanding electricity bills so they'd be able to get service once they entered the private market.

But as the money ran out, some tenants began to turn on her. Even though the CHA was supposed to provide relocation services, it was Ms. Bailey who had stepped into the breach, for a fee, and so she was the one who now caught the blame. She was widely accused of pocketing the gang's money instead of using it for the tenants.

I had never seen Ms. Bailey cry until the moment she told me about these accusations. "I have lived here for almost my whole life, Sudhir," she said mournfully.

We were sitting in her office on a hot spring day. The old bustle was long gone. It used to be that we couldn't sit and talk for ten minutes before Ms. Bailey was interrupted by a needy tenant; now we had the room to ourselves for well over an hour.

"You've been told before that you work too closely with the gangs," I said. "Why does it bother you now?"

"Out there they don't have anybody," she said. "Out there they think they can make it on their own, but . . ." She tried and tried, but she wasn't able to finish her sentence.

I wanted to say something worthwhile but couldn't think of anything. "They'll . . . they'll be okay," I sputtered. "Hell, they lived through the projects."

"But you see, Sudhir, I know that and you know that, but *they* sometimes forget. It's like I told you many times: What scares *you* ain't what scares *them*. When they go to a new store or they have to stand at a bus stop in a place they never been to before, *that's* what scares them. I wanted to help them feel okay. And just when they need me, I can't be there for them."

"You can still do things—" I started to say. But I stopped. The pain on her face was evident, and nothing I could say would console her. I just sat quietly with her until we'd finished our coffee.

I saw Ms. Bailey a few more times, but she was never again the same. For health reasons she moved into her nephew's home in the middle of West Englewood, a poor black community about two miles from the projects. I visited her there. She had several ailments, she told me, but it was hard to sort out one from the other. "I stopped going to the doctor's," she said. "One more test, one more drug, one more thing I got to pay for. And for *what*? To live *here*?"

She waved her hands out at the miles and miles of poor tracts surrounding her nephew's house, tracts that held far too few of the people from her old high-rise home, the people who'd once given her life meaning.

Winter in Chicago comes fast, and it comes hard. The cold delivers a wallop, making you shudder longer than you'd expect. The first blasts of chilling wind off the lake feel like an enemy.

It was a late Sunday morning in November 1998, and I was waiting outside J.T.'s building one last time. About a half dozen Robert Taylor buildings had already been torn down, and his was due for demolition within a year. Nearby businesses had started to close, too. The whole place was starting to feel like a ghost town. I had changed as well. Gone were the tie-dyed shirts and the ponytail, replaced by the kind of clothes befitting an edgy young Ivy League professor. And also a leather briefcase.

I leaned against my car, stamping my feet to keep warm while waiting for J.T. I was just about to get back into the car and turn on the heater when I saw his Malibu charge down Federal Street.

J.T. had called the night before to request a meeting. In his characteristically ambiguous way, he wouldn't divulge any details. But he sounded excited. He did tell me that the federal indictments were probably over and that he wouldn't be arrested. I wanted to know how and why he had escaped arrest, but I didn't have the guts to ask. He'd always been secretive about his contacts in law enforcement. He also asked a few questions about what kind of research I'd be doing in New York. I mentioned some possible ideas, but they were vague at best.

We greeted each other with a handshake and a smile. I told him he looked like he'd put on a little weight. He agreed; between his work and the needs of his growing children, he said, there wasn't as much time to exercise. He pulled a small piece of paper from his pocket and handed it to me. There were several names and phone numbers printed in J.T.'s scratchy handwriting. Among the names was that of Curtis, the gang leader in Newark we'd talked about before.

"You should call these people," J.T. said. "I told Curtis that you wanted to see how things worked out there. He'll take care of you. But Billy Jo, that's the one who really knows what's happening in New York. Here, give him this."

J.T. had often talked about his friends who ran drug-dealing operations in New York. But what with the federal indictments, the demolition of Robert Taylor, and my own career moves, I had pretty much forgotten about them. Also, given how things had turned out with me and J.T.—it was pretty obvious by now that I wasn't going to write his biography—I was surprised that he'd go out of his way to put me in touch with his contacts back east.

He took out another sheet of paper, tightly folded over in fours, the creases a bit worn, as if he'd been carrying it in his pocket for a while. His hands were so cold that they shook as he unfolded it. He gave the paper to me and blew on his hands to warm them up.

"Go ahead, nigger, read it," he said. "Hurry up, it's cold!"

I began to read. It was addressed to Billy Jo: *Billy, Sudhir is coming out your way. Take care of the nigger. . . .* My eyes scanned down and caught a phrase in the middle of the page: *He's with me.*

I could feel myself breaking into a wide smile. J.T. reached into his car and pulled out two beers.

"I'm not sure I'm ready for another big research project just yet," I said.

"Oh, yeah?" he said, handing me one of the beers. "What else are you going to do? You can't fix nothing, you never worked a day in your life. The only thing you know how to do is hang out with niggers like us."

I nearly choked on my beer when he summarized my capacities so succinctly—and, for the most part, accurately.

J.T. leaned back on the car, looking up at the high-rises in front of us. "You think niggers will survive out there?" he asked. "You think they'll be all right when they leave here?"

"Not sure. Probably. I mean, everything changes. You just have to be ready, I guess."

"You hungry?" he asked.

"Starving."

"Let's go down to Seventy-ninth. There's a new soul-food place."

"Sounds good," I said, chugging the beer quickly. "Why don't you drive?"

"Oh, yeah," he said, jumping into the car, "and I got one for you! What would you do if you were me? I got this new bunch of guys that think they know everything. . . ."

He began telling me about his latest management dilemma with a gang he was running in Roseland, a neighborhood where a lot of the Robert Taylor families were relocating. As he spoke, I became lost in his voice. His steady and assured monologue comforted me; for a few moments anyway, I could feel as though little had changed, even though everything had. He turned on some rap music, opened up another beer, and kept on talking. The car screeched out of the parking lot, J.T. waved to a few women pushing strollers in the cold, and we sped down Federal Street.

Within a few years, J.T. grew tired of running a gang. He managed his cousin's dry-cleaning business, and he started up a barbershop, which failed. He had put away enough savings, in property and cash, to supplement his lower income. Once in a while, he did consulting work for Black Kings higher-ups who tried to revive their citywide hold on the drug economy. But this effort never came to fruition, and with the crack market severely depleted, Chicago's gangland remains fragmented, with some neighborhoods having little if any gang activity.

I still see J.T. now and then when I'm in Chicago. Although we've never discussed it explicitly, I don't sense that he begrudges my success as an academic, nor does he seem bitter about his own life. "Man, as long as I'm not behind bars and breathing," he told me, "every day is a good day." It would be hard to call us friends. And I sometimes wonder if we ever were.

But he was obviously a huge part of my life. For all the ways in which I had become a rogue sociologist, breaking conventions and flouting the rules, perhaps the most unconventional thing I ever did was embrace the idea that I could learn so much, absorb so many lessons, and gain so many experiences at the side of a man who was so far removed from my academic world. I can still hear J.T.'s voice when I'm on the streets far away from Chicago, somewhere in the unruly Paris suburbs or the ghettos of New York, hanging around and listening to people's stories.

AUTHOR'S NOTE

Many of the names and some of the identities in this book have been changed. I also disguised some locations and altered the titles of certain organizations. But all the people, places, and institutions are real; they are not composites, and they are not fictional.

Whenever possible, I based the material on written field notes. Some of the stories, however, have been reconstructed from memory. While memory isn't a perfect substitute for notes, I have tried my best to reproduce conversations and events as faithfully as possible.

ACKNOWLEDGMENTS

There is one basic truth in the South Asian immigrant experience: Do as your parents tell you. This notion was put to the test during my junior year of college, when I informed my father and mother that I wanted to study sociology. My mother seemed agnostic, but such decisions were made by my father, who said he preferred that I stay on the path toward a degree in bioengineering. I was not interested in science, and after several conversations we reached a compromise: I would study theoretical mathematics.

I knew that my father supported me, and I even understood his rationale. We were immigrants with no connections, no wealth, and all we had lay between our ears; a math degree would at least guarantee me a job.

A year later, when I told my father I wanted to apply to graduate programs in sociology, he continued to support me, giving advice that I now share with my own students. His counsel often took the form of parables and was laden with examples of people he had seen succeed (and fail). What he told me might take a full evening to relay, over wine and my mother's cooking, but the essence was always clear: write every day, visit your professors with well-formed questions, and always read everything that is recommended, not just what the professor requires.

He also taught me to shut up and listen to my advisers. In contemporary American institutions of higher learning, most people would find this instruction quaint; during a time in which the "student" has become the "customer," this sort of thinking is considered anathema. But my father was no fan of the American educational system, so he insisted that I spend my time listening. I owe my father more than he will ever know. In life, love, and work, his wisdom would prove exceedingly valuable.

Within a few weeks of my arrival at the University of Chicago, I was lucky enough to meet William Julius Wilson, the eminent scholar of urban poverty. He made an unforgettable impression on me: he was thoughtful, choosing his words carefully, and it was obvious that I'd learn a lot if I simply paid attention. My father's counsel echoed in my head: Listen to Bill, follow his advice, always work harder than you need to.

Throughout the course of my graduate studies, I ran into many obstacles, and Bill was always there to guide me. I brought him many typical grad-student dilemmas (*How should I prepare for my exams?*) and some that were less typical (*If I find out that the gang plans to carry out a murder, should I tell somebody?*). More than once I tested his patience; more than once he told me to stop going to my field site until things cooled off. I am one in a long line of students who have benefited from Bill Wilson's tutelage. For his patient direction, I remain grateful.

None of this is meant to discount the role that my mother has played in my life and career. She is the most caring and thoughtful person I have ever known; her voice always rang in my head when I needed to get around a roadblock. Thanks, Mom.

I can recall the initial conversations with my sister, Urmila, when I signed up to write this book. I was nervous, while she was overjoyed. She has always productively channeled her enthusiasm by keeping me honest and mindful of those who are less fortunate and who may never benefit from my writings.

At the University of Chicago and at Columbia, Professors Peter Bearman, Jean Comaroff, John Comaroff, Herbert J. Gans, Edward Laumann, Nicole Marwell, and Moishe Postone guided me through difficult waters. Katchen Locke, Sunil Garg, Larry Kamerman, Ethan Michaeli, Amanda Millner-Fairbanks, David Sussman, Benjamin Mintz, Matthew McGuire, and Baron Pineda were ever supportive, whether with humor, advice, or a glass of wine. Farah Griffin's writings inspired me to push on, Doug Guthrie encouraged me to pursue the venerable path of public sociology, and Eva Rosen read drafts diligently and is on her way to becoming an outstanding sociologist.

I never would have written this book if I hadn't met Steven Levitt, an economist who took an interest in my fieldwork. Over dinner one night at the Harvard Society of Fellows, Steven and I spent hours trying to connect the worlds of economics and sociology. To this day Steven remains a close collaborator and friend. I couldn't have attempted this act of hubris without his encouragement. Steven kindly introduced me to Suzanne Gluck, who helped shepherd me through the byzantine world of trade publishing. Suzanne is one of the wisest souls I have ever met. At Penguin, Ann Godoff has been a pleasure to work with, and I hope this is the first of many journeys under her stewardship.

In writing this book, I drew on the intellectual gifts and emotional sustenance of my close friend Nathaniel Deutsch. I pulled Nathaniel away from his precious daughter, Simona, on many occasions to rant, cry, or just throw up my hands. Nathaniel, I may never be able to return the favor, but I will certainly make sure Simi knows how kind you have been.

To Stephen Dubner, I owe an inexpressible debt. Stephen had the unenviable task of helping me put my thoughts on paper. It was not always easy for me to visit my past, and Stephen listened to my me-anderings patiently, offering the right amount of criticism and feed-back. I doubt that Stephen thinks of himself as a teacher, but he is one of the best.

I remain especially grateful to the tenants of the Robert Taylor Homes for letting me into both their apartments and their lives. Dorothy Battie has been a close friend, and Beauty Turner and the staff at the *Residents' Journal* newspaper have given of their time generously.

I still feel guilty about all those years that I let J.T. think I would write his biography. I hope that he at least reads these pages some-day. While a lot of it is my story, it plainly could never have happened without him. He let me into a new world with a level of trust I had no reason to expect; I can only hope that this book faithfully repre-sents his life and his work.

INDEX

He just wanted a decent book to read ...

Not too much to ask, is it? It was in 1935 when Allen Lane, Managing Director of Bodley Head Publishers, stood on a platform at Exeter railway station looking for something good to read on his journey back to London. His choice was limited to popular magazines and poor-quality paperbacks – the same choice faced every day by the vast majority of readers, few of whom could afford hardbacks. Lane's disappointment and subsequent anger at the range of books generally available led him to found a company – and change the world.

'We believed in the existence in this country of a vast reading public for intelligent books at a low price, and staked everything on it'
Sir Allen Lane, 1902–1970, founder of Penguin Books

The quality paperback had arrived – and not just in bookshops. Lane was adamant that his Penguins should appear in chain stores and tobacconists, and should cost no more than a packet of cigarettes.

Reading habits (and cigarette prices) have changed since 1935, but Penguin still believes in publishing the best books for everybody to enjoy. We still believe that good design costs no more than bad design, and we still believe that quality books published passionately and responsibly make the world a better place.

So wherever you see the little bird – whether it's on a piece of prize-winning literary fiction or a celebrity autobiography, political tour de force or historical masterpiece, a serial-killer thriller, reference book, world classic or a piece of pure escapism – you can bet that it represents the very best that the genre has to offer.

Whatever you like to read – trust Penguin.

read more
www.penguin.co.uk